flour + water

pasta

flour + water
pasta

THOMAS MCNAUGHTON

WITH PAOLO LUCCHESI

photography by Eric Wolfinger

TEN SPEED PRESS
Berkeley

CONTENTS

PREFACE: THE ORIGINS
David Steele and David White

I wrote the original one-page business plan for Flour + Water on the back of an envelope, over a decade before the restaurant actually became a reality. It started with a simple premise: In Italy, I saw how pasta was used as a delivery agent for seasonal ingredients; pizza took the same approach. Coming from the East Coast of the United States, where pasta sauces and menus stayed the same 365 days a year, this was an eye-opening experience for me. —David Steele

I grew up in Ireland, in a village of sixteen hundred people. It was your classic small town in the Irish countryside: It had a couple of churches, a town square, one dentist, two lawyers, two doctors, and ten pubs. When we had a full house, there were eight people at the dinner table: Mum and Dad and six of us siblings. Dining together was a part of our life, mostly because our father insisted that we come together at the table every day. My mother is a great cook, and our meals were always wholesome and delicious. There were always potatoes, and sometimes multiple potato dishes at once—everything that you'd expect from a rural Irish family. —David White

I grew up in New Jersey, coincidentally about fifteen miles from where Tom was raised. I put myself through college by working in restaurants. I started as a dishwasher at the age of sixteen and worked my way up to a prep cook. The higher up the ladder I got, the more quickly I realized that kitchen life is a very tough life. At the same time, I saw servers in the front of house working fewer hours and making more money. So I did the logical thing and moved out of the kitchen. I became a busboy, and by age eighteen I was managing an Italian restaurant in Wildwood, New Jersey.

I went to college not very far from my Jersey roots, at Temple University in Philadelphia. During that period, I waited tables at some of the best restaurants in the city. Most of those that know me have no idea, but I came inches from dropping out of college to go to culinary school. My dad talked me out of that plan. Instead, I graduated from college and went straight to Wall Street, still continuing to wait tables on the weekends. In all, I spent about eight years straight doing hard-core restaurant work.

I loved the restaurant industry but was shocked how most of the restaurants I worked at weren't run like real businesses. There was no awareness of food costs or labor costs, and most strikingly, there was no overarching strategy. Most restaurants I witnessed—including some very good ones—just planned on figuring it out as they went along. Eventually, with a little more seniority on Wall Street, I stopped waiting tables on the side. I vowed to return to the restaurant business and do it my way.

I spent my teenage years with the Jesuits at a boarding school, where they fed me big fat wedges of ham, the fat cap still unshaven, firm and bristly. Then I went to college in Dublin, intermittently working toward a liberal arts degree in history and Greek and Roman civilization. My rationale at the time, as a reluctant student, was that I might as well study something interesting that would lure me to a lecture here and there. By the time I graduated, I was itching to leave Ireland. Still naive and idealistic, I had the travel bug, bad. I wanted to see the world.

To travel, I would need employment. I figured that if I could wait tables, I would be able to work anywhere. And that's how I started in this business. Out of school, I got a job in a semi-decent restaurant in the heart of Dublin. It was named Gotham Cafe. As fate would have it, its specialty was pizza and pasta.

I ended up in the States kind of by accident. One day my older brother told me he was going to apply for one of the U.S. visas advertised in the paper. I asked him to put one in for me while he was at it. He did. I was chosen in the lottery, and he was not.

I had connections in New York, Boston, Chicago, and San Francisco. New York? I didn't want to go there. I was already burning the candle at both ends in Dublin. I needed to mellow out and figured New York would probably be a bad idea. Boston? Back then, I thought of Boston as a place with too much of a connection to Ireland; I wanted something different. And Chicago? I remember reading about a car that froze in a street at fourteen degrees below zero or something like that; no way was I enduring those extreme seasons.

California just seemed the coolest place. Everything I read about San Francisco was appealing, and it was the exact pace I was looking for. On top of that, a dear college friend made the offer of a couch upon which to surf. The decision was made.

When I arrived in California from New York, I had been working on Wall Street for nearly two decades. I was ready to finally pursue the restaurant idea. The concept of ubiquitous super-seasonality was something I had only witnessed in southern Europe. But in the Bay Area, I saw the influences of Chez Panisse and Zuni Café, basically doing the same thing that the Italians did. Chief among those places was LuLu, Reed Hearon's Provençal restaurant in SoMa. In my opinion, Reed Hearon is the most influential and underrated chef in San Francisco cuisine—not California cuisine as a whole, but San Francisco. He took the things that Alice Waters and Judy Rodgers were doing and made it his own.

Eating at LuLu changed my life. There was seasonality, a giant hearth, and a menu of wood-fired pizzas, truly great pastas, and the now-signature dish of mussels on a sizzling hot cast-iron plate. It was brilliant, and he was doing it twenty years before every single one of those components became trendy.

After rejections from dozens and dozens of restaurants around San Francisco, it became crystal clear to me how hard it is to get a job fresh off the boat. Restaurants were just not that into a guy without experience in this country, let alone this town. I finally ended up getting a job as a busboy in the bar at Postrio, Wolfgang Puck's famous Union Square spot. (I will never forget the guy who hired me, giving me my first job in the United States: Kim Beto.) It was 1997, when Postrio was at the tail end of its greatness but still a very good and professional restaurant. I was promoted to a barback a few months later, and then to the service bartender for the breakfast shift. It was great; I received wine deliveries and organized the cellar, and was exposed to a top-tier wine program. Behind the bar, I was rocking the blender and serving Ramos fizz cocktails to the blue hairs who trekked down from Nob Hill.

I bounced around for the next few years, working as a server at various places, always focused on opening my own restaurant eventually—until I wound up working front-of-house at Quince, an upscale Pacific Heights Italian restaurant.

It was there that I met a young kid named Thomas McNaughton.

Working at Quince had an intensity that I had never before experienced; it sometimes felt like what I imagine the military would be. Without a doubt I learned more there in one single year than I did in the prior five years I had been in San Francisco. If the dining room was intense, the Quince kitchen was a whole other beast. Removed from the gaze of the patrons, there was wildness to it, a stark contrast to the starched, unified choreography of the servers. Everyone who worked at Quince was there for the craft,

for the knowledge. We all worked hard, with our heads down, doing our time.

And there in the middle of it all, you had Tom working as a sous chef at the ripe old age of twenty-three. It was unbelievably impressive.

Every now and then, Tom and I would end up at the same bar after a dinner shift and tie one on, but our most significant bonding time took place right after we both left Quince. I was touring southern Europe, seeking inspiration for my upcoming restaurant, which would eventually become a place in North Beach named Nua. Tom was coincidentally also hopping around Europe at the same time, doing *stages* (short-term unpaid cooking stints) in Italy and Germany. We managed to connect in Seville and ended up spending five days eating and drinking our way through Andalucia.

I had heard of David White's restaurant before I met David White himself. His place, Nua, was a spectacularly good restaurant, but it was one that was completely underappreciated and lost in the tourist hellhole that was North Beach at the time.

At Nua, White embraced many of the same philosophies that I had in mind for my simmering restaurant idea: seasonality, a California expression of European sensibility, and a professional yet casual service style. There were some differences. Nua was more refined, more formal, and touched on a medley of Mediterranean influences, whereas my concept would center in Italy with pizza and pasta.

Nua got a great three-star review from Michael Bauer of the *San Francisco Chronicle*. It was solidly on the dining landscape, but I started hearing rumblings that White might want to sell.

My first restaurant was a meat grinder, man. It was so incredibly hard: from start to finish, two and a half years of having no life. I had never done it before, and I had to be and do everything: general manager, wine buyer, scheduling, payroll, hiring—basically every single thing except cook. The experience beat me down.

That said, it was certainly the defining experience of my career. There is a lot of growth born of adversity. If I knew then a fraction of what I know now, something terrible would have happened—the restaurant may have made it. In hindsight, that would have been the worst possible thing.

We opened to a deafening silence. Less than three months later, we got a three-star review in the *San Francisco Chronicle*. The hordes descended upon us, beat the crap out of us for a few months, and then disappeared as quickly as they came. The restaurant was in a massive hole, and I was drained. I had to close.

I met David Steele through a mutual friend of ours, a gentleman in the wine business named Ruben Morancy. Ruben knew that I was looking to sell Nua and basically get out of North Beach as soon as I could. He had a college friend who was looking to get in the game. At the time, Steele had this idea for a restaurant—Flour + Water—but needed an operations partner to build and run the restaurant.

I never really considered turning down the opportunity. Some of my friends thought I should take some time off after the Nua experience, but it wasn't even a choice to me. I certainly wasn't going to crawl under a rock and hide. I had nothing to lose. I just wanted to start fresh and get back in restaurant work.

So we had dinner one night, and the rest was history.

My theory at the time was to start the restaurant with a core of three primary partners: A business/strategy person like myself, an operations guy like David White, and a great chef. I suspected having these three people working together might create the ultimate synergistic partnership, with our competing perspectives forming a healthy tension.

White was the perfect partner. The guy has more knowledge than anyone else in the city in terms of getting shit done. He just gets things done, period. He has an amazing knowledge of food and wine, but he's the kind of guy who undersells his palate, so you only understand the depth of his knowledge by spending significant time with him.

Perhaps most importantly, especially in this business, he was not afraid of work. During the period when we were building Flour + Water, my mother came out to visit at one point. She and I had a late dinner somewhere in the Mission and then decided to stop by the construction site so I could show her my little project. It was well past midnight when we arrived at Flour + Water, but the lights were on. We walk inside and there is David White with a sledgehammer in hand. He was in the midst of knocking down a wall because the framer had put it up in the wrong spot, and the restaurant plumbing was going in the next day. I knew I had picked the right partner.

I immediately liked the idea of Flour + Water, and I liked where Steele was coming from. It was a restaurant concept for regular people. At the time—late 2008—the world was mired in a very dark time, economically. The market had crashed, and people were nervous and frugal. His feeling was that they wanted foods that were comforting, familiar, and not extravagant: pizza, pasta, humble salads, and long braises. We wanted to create really honest food with integrity and affordability. Everyone eats pasta and everyone eats pizza.

It was to be a simple and utilitarian restaurant, a mindset that was perfectly represented in the place setting that we still have to this day: plate, knife, fork, glass—and that's it. It bugs me when there are multiple kinds of forks, three different spoons, four sorts of knives. Our concept was about breaking bread in a welcoming, communal setting where it doesn't matter what you're wearing, or how much (or how little) money is in your pocket; it was proletarian.

David Steele was, and remains, the x factor. The most common partnership in the restaurant business features a talented chef in the kitchen and a charming, social, wine-savvy partner up front (I am none of those things, but you get the idea). It's the classic pairing. They do a restaurant, and it's all creativity and heart, but they miss critical reasoning and business acumen. They lack experience with numbers, and a way of looking outside the box at growth and development. David brought those different perspectives. While I was thinking about that night's lineup and opening the doors at 5:30 p.m., he was thinking about Year Two, Year Five, Year Ten—not necessarily from a financial perspective, but from an evolutionary and cultural perspective.

I did not believe in the idea that a restaurant, by its very nature, had to be soulless in order to have long-term financial sustainability. For the longest time, that seemed to be the assumed catch-22 in the restaurant world: be soulful or be profitable. I rejected that premise.

The second tradition in the restaurant industry that I rejected was that the working environment had to be militant. Coming up in the restaurant world, all I saw were oppressive working dynamics. I had been on those bottom rungs of the hierarchy—dishwasher, busboy—and I had seen the way that chefs and owners spoke to staff like worthless minions. I figured that the restaurant itself would be better if its workers genuinely loved coming to work and felt valued. To that end, the responsibility fell largely upon the primary partners to foster such an environment. With my work on Wall Street, I observed the best practices used by organizations to motivate their employees and promote a culture of positivity. I instituted bonuses for managers, and provided full health insurance coverage and retirement plans for all employees. I created the positions of director of wellness and music director, plus that of beekeeper to tend the rooftop beehives, all with the hope of promoting positive reinforcement instead of ruling by fear.

Approaching the restaurant industry from new angles—meaning angles from other industries, like finance, tech, theater, and real estate—has proven to be one of our greatest strengths from a business standpoint. Once Flour + Water eventually got up and running, we formed an advisory board of successful peers in various industries, including other local restaurant owners. We have quarterly meetings, and discuss a variety of relevant topics from health care to consulting. We share advice and brainstorm. It's a thing that is common in nearly every other industry, but for some reason, the food world hasn't quite adopted such a dynamic. It's been very worthwhile, both for us and for our esteemed board members.

So I guess my original goal was to have a restaurant business that would be an intersection between artisanship and general business principles—with a positive work environment. Those were the foundations for the "business plan" I wrote while still on Wall Street. The restaurant wasn't fully formed yet, conceptually or physically, but I did know it would be an Italian restaurant specializing in pizza and pasta. There is no food that people in America love more than pizza and pasta—myself included. Delicious simplicity is always current, and in San Francisco, there's a dining audience that can appreciate it—in fact, they demand it.

Steele had an idea, and the definite bones of the restaurant, but it needed flesh. We met every week for fourteen straight months, always talking concept, design, culture, strategy. Sometimes we would meet for dinner, sometimes we'd get coffee. Sometimes we'd drink a bottle of wine, sometime just water, but whatever we did, we always just met and talked and talked. Those meetings produced the Flour + Water business plan, which has become the template for everything we've done since.

We didn't have any aspirations to be well known and acclaimed. We wanted to fly under the radar, do it quietly. We even had the conversation of whether we wanted to get reviewed by Michael Bauer. We decided that we did not want to be reviewed. If he was to come in, that would be fine, of course. But it wasn't a goal—and that's less about Bauer, and more about what we were trying to do. We were trying to stay low-key and casual, a place that had nothing to prove other than it could be an enjoyable neighborhood spot.

People thought I was nuts for choosing the location that I did on the corner of Twentieth and Harrison Streets. This neighborhood, an untapped area of the Mission District, continues to evolve with Flour + Water and, later, with our next two restaurants on the same block, Central Kitchen and Salumeria.

When Flour + Water was still a pipe dream of mine, I was sitting at Café Gratitude on the southwest corner of Twentieth and Harrison and I looked across the street. There was a decrepit, rotten building on the southeast corner. Years ago it had been a crappy Ecuadorian restaurant and, even though the sign remained, it clearly hadn't been touched in ages. I was flirting with the Café Gratitude waitress at the time, and I remember trying to impress her. So, of course, I told her that I was going to build my restaurant right across the street. I never went out with her, but I did get my dream location.

We rolled out our business plan to potential investors, billing the restaurant as "an urban contemporary Italian/pizza restaurant and wine shop with a cuisine focusing on seasonal ingredients prepared in a simple and straightforward Italian style." There would be no bottles of wines over forty-nine dollars, dishes would be served family-style, lunch would be served daily. Of course, that all went out the window when Tom showed up.

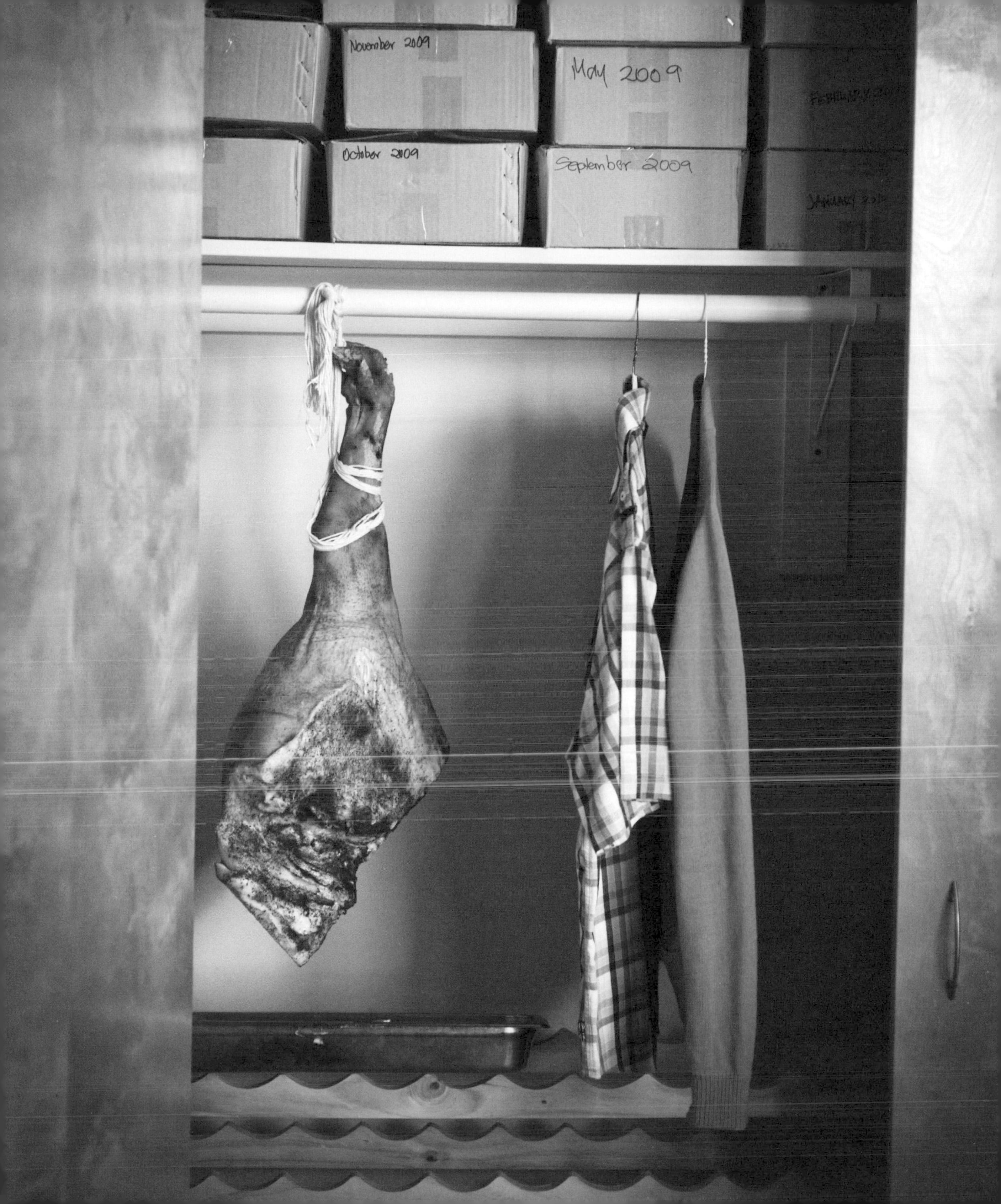
November 2009
May 2009
October 2009
September 2009

PREFACE: THE STORY CONTINUES

Thomas McNaughton

I live above the restaurant. It wasn't always that way. Thanks to David Steele and David White, the idea of Flour + Water was well in the works before I was ever involved. While they were composing their business plan, searching for a space somewhere in the Mission, and thinking about what kind of chef they might hire, I was on the other side of the world.

I was in Bologna, to be precise. At the time, I had spent several years cooking in upscale San Francisco restaurants, mostly French. I had come to a point where it was time to detach for a bit and explore the kitchens of Europe. I scrounged up the cash for a plane ticket to Paris and convinced a handful of Michelin-starred French chefs to let me work for them as a *stagiaire*—basically an unpaid kitchen intern. I learned a lot and remain grateful for the opportunities, but I still yearned for something different, something simpler, more elemental. I eventually found my way to Italy, and I found that missing variable in the country's farms, its lifestyle, and its pasta.

In particular, I fell in love with pasta during an extended stay in Bologna—we'll explore that experience a bit later—but as my bank account (or what was left of it) began to dry up, I started to think about saying goodbye to my Italian escapism and return to America to, you know, get a job again. Huddled at the local pay-by-the-minute Internet cafe, I began scanning Craigslist for new cooking gigs in the Bay Area.

I finally found a listing for a rustic Italian restaurant opening in San Francisco that was pretty vague about the details, except that they were looking for a chef. Possibly with the fog of a few early evening Aperol spritzes in me already, I emailed a quick response without knowing exactly to whom I was emailing. I didn't even sign the email.

It consisted of these three poetic sentences: "I'm in Bologna working in a pasta lab. Heard you're looking for a chef. I'd like to move back to the Bay Area and start a goat farm."

(It was more than slightly ridiculous, but it was honest: I really did want to be a goat farmer. I've always yearned for a farm and have always been obsessed with the origin of the amazing products used in great restaurants.)

A couple hours after sending off the email, I got this email response: "Is this Tom McNaughton? What in the hell are you talking about?"

It was signed "David White."

+

David White and I had previously worked together at Quince in San Francisco. Even though he worked up front on the service side and I was in the back behind the stoves, we always got along and even went out drinking a few times. I knew he was working on a new restaurant, too. In fact, when I read in the *San Francisco Chronicle*'s "Inside Scoop" column a year prior that White was opening a pizzeria named Flour + Water, I vividly remember thinking that he was a crazy person, and that the name was fairly hideous.

But the more he told me about the vision of the restaurant, the more I was intrigued and inspired. White had already partnered with David Steele, an "ideas guy" who came from the finance world. Together, they were looking for a chef for Flour + Water, a pizzeria and wine bar on the outskirts of San Francisco's Mission District. And so began the interview process over a series of nightly transatlantic phone calls.

I didn't have a cell phone, so nightly, I'd commandeer a phone booth on the cobblestone streets of Bologna. Armed with seventy-five euros worth of phone cards and a few forty-ounce Moretti beers, I'd get comfortable and the three of us would speak for hours. Pay cards would run out, calls would drop, but it worked. We talked about restaurants, we talked about life,

we mused on the philosophies we wanted to instill in a restaurant, and we analyzed their already-polished business plan. We got to know each other.

We were talking shop, so much so that I only half realized that they were interviewing me, too. About halfway through the final phone call, Steele interrupted one of my answers with an instant job offer, without even tasting my food. Not soon thereafter, I hopped on a plane and returned to America.

✛

There's a saying in the restaurant business that young chefs don't know what being a chef really is until they open their own restaurant, starting from the ground floor. I don't know who said that, but I quickly discovered that it is most certainly true.

I was only a few days removed from Italy when I first saw the blank white rectangle at the corner of Harrison and Twentieth that was the restaurant space. The building was a derelict two-story construction site that looked like it was going to keel over with the first gust of wind. I lost my breath; things just got real. Up until this point, I was still flirting with the

possibility that maybe I'd find a backseat role in the project, maybe as a consultant. Being thrown into the thick of the opening push quickly eliminated any hesitation and flung me into the fire.

Working in fancy, demanding kitchens is tough and I was a pretty confident cook, but building a restaurant—a *business*—from scratch is an entirely different animal. It forces involvement and tough decisions every step of the way. We were on a tight budget, so we had to get creative. We bought used plates from a local restaurant named Myth that just closed, and nothing got us more excited than buying our stove at an auction for five hundred bucks. When we won the stove, we were jumping around, full of adrenaline, like it was Vegas. The stove had the perfect dimensions for our kitchen, and it was obviously cheap; we quickly learned that it was also a piece of crap. The doors wouldn't close, the oven wouldn't calibrate. Sometimes you get what you pay for.

We spent hours doing our own construction work, aside from the guy who came from Italy to build the pizza oven piece by piece. David White in particular never seemed to leave the restaurant; in fact, I'm fairly certain he was literally spending nights at the construction site. He was a machine. The entire

build-out was done on a shoestring, and to this day, it's still the best business model we've done. We had a budget of six hundred thousand dollars and spent five hundred forty-five thousand dollars of that; finishing construction on time and fifty-five thousand dollars under budget is insane in the restaurant world—and down the line, having that cash in the bank proved to be critical.

On the food side, it was only a matter of weeks before we opened, and my vision for the menu was slowly coming into focus. The Davids' initial vision for Flour + Water was an incredibly rustic restaurant: warm olives, marinated beets, meatballs, and the like, with everything served family-style. It was a genre I loved, but the more I thought about it, the more I wanted to take it further. I came from a classic fine dining background, I fell in love with Italian regional cooking, and I was cooking with the bounty of Northern California. Fine dining techniques, Italian traditions, and local products. I thought the menu should combine all three of those components.

Less than four months after I left Italy, the doors of Flour + Water opened on May 15, 2009—and so did the floodgates.

+

Like most restaurant openings, the first few days at Flour + Water were complete mayhem. I would like to say that I was thrilled, nervous, or even terrified when the first customers started filing through the door. But the truth is, I was in the bathroom dry-heaving.

The plan had been to do a quiet, under-the-radar opening; we wanted to control opening day, not bite off more than we could chew. If one or two dozen people showed up, that would be perfect. The entire staff—both the kitchen and the front of house—could ease into the fire instead of getting tossed into it. About fifteen minutes before we were slated to open the doors, I popped my head out of the kitchen for some reason. There was a line forming.

Unbeknownst to me, word leaked out. We hadn't even served one dish *ever* and people were waiting already. Construction was still happening in pockets of the restaurant, as it would for much of the first several months of operation. Our hoods were broken, which in turn meant that the wood-burning pizza oven was blasting heat directly into the closet-sized kitchen, making it feel like one thousand degrees. Just in case there weren't enough cooks squeezed in there to begin with, we had metal workers trying to repair the broken hoods, welding with blowtorches as actual shards of metal rained down on our *mise en place*. It soon became so hot in there that the wine we stored on the top shelf in the kitchen started exploding. It was chaos.

If it wasn't so hellish, it would have been comedy. I felt like I was driving a car on the freeway with no brakes, and all I could do was try to harness it as much as possible.

For the first time in my career, I was in an executive chef role, and the wheels were falling off before the restaurant even opened. My cooks were disheartened that their prep work had metal shards in it, and we could all sense the approaching storm. I called the entire staff together. Today, we have over 140 employees between all of our restaurants, but on the opening day at Flour + Water, there were only nine of us. We were a group of people who barely knew each other and had been thrown into this intense, crazy situation.

We all walked outside and huddled up in a corner down the block. I gave an impromptu speech of sorts, highlighting the fact that restaurant work is, by nature, chaotic. This was cooking; it's a career of crazy conditions and unreasonable pressure. Then, I made everyone scream individually. Each person took a turn yelling as loud as he or she could, for as long as he or she could. We released the steam, found our composure, bound ourselves together, and got to work on the project we had building for months.

We did 136 covers that first night. To this day, we've never gone below 136. From our vantage point, it might have been tumultuous, but from the guests' point of view, we did pretty well.

During those first few months, the beautiful chaos seemed to continue unabated, at 100 miles per hour. Part of that was because I didn't want any prep cooks when we opened up. I had this idealistic goal that every ingredient we cooked would go straight from the farm to the chefs' hands. I quickly learned that not everything worked as well as the ideal. My cooks were soldiers, to be sure. We were all working fifteen-hour days until 4 a.m., happy but exhausted. More than once, I woke up to the morning dishwasher poking me because I fell asleep in the dining room.

We didn't have any space to butcher whole animals, let alone store them, but we did anyway. We would break down pigs on the communal table at the end of service. Oftentimes, this ritual took place while the last guests were finishing up their meals. We would invite the straggling diners to have an after-dinner drink at the bar; I like to think that most of the diners rather enjoyed the spectacle of the butchery.

We had one tiny little walk-in refrigerator. Whenever someone had to get something in the walk-in, they had to maneuver around a pig or boar, or its parts. One night, when trying to change a keg, our bartender moved a pig, and four jugs of chicken stock spilled on her.

We even opened the restaurant with the idea that we would cure our own salumi. Prior to opening, we had three hundred pounds of meat hanging at Bi-Rite, a grocery store a few blocks away. We honestly thought it would last for months and months, which would, in turn, give us plenty of time to make subsequent batches. Our pancetta lasted about a week. The rest disappeared in the following fortnight. Just about every table ordered a salumi plate. So that cache of cured meat didn't last long. It would be an entire year before we got the salumi program up to speed.

The point of it all for me—making the salumi, having cooks do their own prep work, only butchering whole animals—was to instill values and traditions into the restaurant . . . even without having the practical means to do so. We would quickly find ways to adjust. At the time, the ambitions were probably a little lofty and more than a little bit unrealistic, but over time we eventually grew into them. Now, several years later, those values are a driving force behind the restaurant.

But nowhere was that evolution more evident than with our pasta production. Our opening-day menu was evenly balanced between antipasti, pizza, pasta, and entrees. There were five pasta dishes on the menu. Only two of them were stuffed, both of those very basic shapes: mezzalune (half-moons) and tortelli (envelope-like pockets; basically the rectangular version of mezzalune). For comparison, the total number of pastas offered at the restaurant today—between the à la carte and pasta-tasting menus—is nearly four times that original menu. All pastas are still made in-house.

Originally, we produced the night's pasta on a paltry three-by-five-foot table wedged into the garde manger station in the kitchen, which, by the way, was still sweltering from those aforementioned hood malfunctions. We simply had no room for the pasta production, and we couldn't keep up with the demand. By our second week, our little forty-nine-seat restaurant was doing 225 covers a night consistently. Even though we'd stay open until midnight, we would start running out of pasta by 9:30 p.m.

Things had to change. Not only was the arrangement unsustainable from a production standpoint, but as our reputation for pasta grew, running out early became more and more of an issue. Plus, I had designs to expand our pasta operation far beyond the basics. I wanted to explore the complexity of pasta and use it to showcase the bounty of Northern California ingredients. In short, I wanted more.

Behind the restaurant was a little structure, used for dry storage since we had zero room for anything in the restaurant itself; basically, it was a plywood shed propped up over dirt. The original long-term plan was that we would build an entirely new building extension in that back area, with first-floor storage and a second-floor events space and art gallery. I had different ideas. With our pasta corner of the kitchen increasingly untenable for production, we needed a dedicated space to work on pasta, which was naturally evolving into the kitchen's greatest strength.

The premise for the room came straight from Italy. When I was in Bologna, I spent the majority of my days in a pasta *laboratorio*. Despite the science connotation, the pasta lab is anything but futuristic; it is a collection of mostly older ladies, huddled around a wooden table, making pasta by hand in the same fashion that pasta has been made for generations. The lab is the epitome of craftsmanship and artisanship—and it all revolved around a center table.

I wanted to re-create that place as best I could, or at least create my version of it. Remember how the original build-out for Flour + Water came in fifty-five thousand dollars under budget? We put that money back into the restaurant, reinvesting it in different arenas. I convinced the Davids to convert the empty space into a pasta-making room. It had plenty of natural light, further brightened by white tiles lining the room and blond wood tabletops. We added a walk-in refrigerator, sinks, a bathroom and eventually even a bulky pasta extruder.

But the pièce de résistance was the massive twelve-by-five-foot butcher block in the center of the room. Not only would the room function as a prep kitchen for the restaurant, but during the evenings, we could use it as a private dining room, seating up to fourteen people around the butcher's block, thus giving us a return on the initial investment. Suddenly, we were able to roll out sheets of pasta dough that were twenty-four feet long instead of three feet. Multiple cooks—instead of just one—could huddle around the table and make the night's pasta.

With the maturation of the pasta program, we found our wheelhouse. The room was a game changer, and it was the first major step toward establishing a major pasta culture in the restaurant. We still served pizza and a medley of other dishes, but from that point, Flour + Water truly became a pasta restaurant.

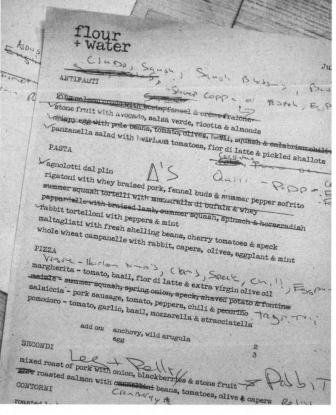

INTRODUCTION:
From Bologna to San Francisco

Pasta is woven into the cultural fabric of Italy—it pretty much *is* culture in Italy—but it holds a particularly high place in the hierarchy in Bologna. It was there that I fell in love with pasta—and where I *really* learned to make pasta.

The dominance of pasta in Bologna is evident within minutes of walking around the city. Just like taquerias inhabit every corner of the Mission in San Francisco, and the neon signs of pizza-by-the-slice joints light up Manhattan neighborhoods, so does fresh pasta rule the windows of Bologna markets. Sold by weight or by the bundle, fresh pasta is inescapable there. It comes in a rainbow of dough colors, and in all sizes, though you can be assured every shop proudly displays the requisite pasta signature of Bologna: nickel-sized tortellini. You might even see old ladies in the window, rolling out fresh pasta for tourist passersby.

But as someone once told me, Italy is "under the table." In other words, to really, truly understand the essence of anything in Italy, you have to look a little harder, immerse yourself, and start to peel back the layers. Look past the Disneyland-like gloss of touristy restaurants in the city center with the overpriced microwaved tagliatelle Bolognese. Instead, seek out the under-the-radar olive grove in the countryside that has quietly been making oil in the same way for decades, or the hobbyist miller who taught himself how to produce the best flour in the area. Or see it in the the pair of young brothers at Zavoli Farms who are single-handedly maintaining tradition by raising indigenous heritage breed pigs in the easternmost, sun-kissed hills of Emilia-Romagna while pushing forward by experimenting with new techniques for making salumi.

As it happens, my "under the table" moment in Bologna actually took place above its streets. Having found myself in Italy looking for a change of pace from the fine dining kitchens of San Francisco, France, and Germany, I met a gregarious Bolognese native named Marcello via John Pauley, a chef I met while working at La Folie in San Francisco. Marcello had an available room in Bologna. Once he found out I was a cook looking to learn about Italian cuisine, he wasted no time in referring me to a place that would change the course of my career: Bruno e Franco la Salumeria.

The salumeria itself is glorious, its shelves stocked with jars of vibrant green olives, giant wheels of pungent cheese, and myriad cured pork products, all procured from the best in the region. Across the street is a little second-story room overlooking the salumeria. The street-level entrance is completely unmarked save for a hidden little buzzer. You wouldn't find it if you weren't looking for it; it cryptically reads "*Laboratorio*."

Up a narrow flight of stairs lies the salumeria's pasta "laboratory"—a small workshop consisting of a few tables and little else. It's where all the fresh pasta sold in the salumeria is made. In old-school Bologna, the *laboratorio* and the salumeria have a symbiotic relationship; one exclusively makes the product and the other exclusively sells it. Compared to the splendor of the salumeria, the pasta lab room is incredibly bare bones, and despite the name, there's nothing scientific or laboratory-like about the place. It is more like a glimpse into the past.

Inside, there are a dozen Italian ladies of all ages dressed in pastel pink chef coats, making fresh pasta in the same way they did the day before, and the day before that, and the day before that. They only make a handful of pasta types: Bologna's sacred tortellini are the most prolific output of the room. Rounding out the day's work are batches of tagliatelle, passatelli, paglia e fieno (straw and hay), Roman-style gnocchi, and finally, depending on the day, maybe a few orders of ready-to-bake cannelloni. The entire day's production will sell out downstairs in the salumeria, and it will be restocked the next day.

Spanning several generations, the women themselves are the tableau of Bologna, and of Italy. Some of them come from an older generation, the generation that grew up in the war-ravaged years of the 1940s and 1950s, when food was scarce. They speak softly with an air of authority, often drifting off into dialect, basically acting like the Italian *nonna* you always imagined, telling winding anecdotes and politely answering your dumb question in that old, Italian matter-of-fact way that makes the question seem even dumber. Other ladies are younger. Some came from other careers; some have known nothing but pasta making. Some are natives of Bologna; some moved here from elsewhere in Italy. The ones from the south, for example, spark arguments about which region's cuisine is better. Whatever their origins, they all tell bawdy jokes, they gossip about town, they smoke in the bathroom during breaks. Many are mothers, since a job making pasta is amenable to family life. Their workday starts at dawn, allowing them to leave in time to pick up the children from school.

They are all wonderful and charismatic characters in a marvelous play.

Varying personalities aside, the women are all united through their work at the pasta *laboratorio*, where they work as a single, perfectly functioning unit. One rocks back and forth as she rolls out sheet after sheet of fresh handmade pasta dough with her *mattarello*, a long wooden Bolognese rolling pin. The women use *matarelli* made especially for the *laboratorio* by a blind woodworker down the block; mechanical pasta machines are frowned upon, to say the least. Another woman is mixing gnocchi dough by hand in the corner, while a third, working at the window, wields a weathered knife to precisely slice pasta dough into the uniform shreds of tagliatelle.

The rest of the ladies hover around a table near the entrance, methodically forming the day's worth of tortellini to be sold downstairs. While they twist the circular shapes, their constant chatter fills the room. The pasta lab is a time capsule—a fully functioning preservation of Bolognese culture and tradition. It is true craftsmanship.

There are no assigned jobs, but each woman floats from one table to the next. Maybe the youngest one—or the one who came to work late that day—will get stuck making the cannelloni; forming the filled pasta is the messy, labor-intensive job that no one else wants to do. The voices of the ladies barely overshadow the rhythmic, dull sounds of the rolling pin slowly doing its dance, stretching the pasta dough over the wooden table, forming their *sfoglia*—the sheet of fresh pasta dough. When the dough is completely flattened into a massive, imprecise four-foot-wide sheet, it is slid over to another table, where the tortellini are formed by other ladies.

Every hour or so, the teenage kid from the downstairs salumeria arrives to take a few trays of pasta down to the salumeria, looking at me and gently sighing how glad he is that he didn't have to be the only guy upstairs in the lab anymore. He confesses, in his broken English, that he felt uncomfortable when the ladies would discuss, as he put it, "feminine topics." He smiles and takes the trays of pasta downstairs to the display case.

I found myself in the pasta lab by chance, and I stayed for months. The ladies became family, though I'm pretty sure they made fun of my Italian language skills (or lack thereof). After working as a fine dining soldier for years, I felt myself yearning for a change, for something more soulful, more personal. I found it in the unlikeliest of laboratories, along with a new pasta passion.

PART ONE

THE DOUGH

HOW TO MAKE PASTA DOUGH

Pasta dough consists of very few ingredients. Mixed in are a spoonful of olive oil and a pinch of salt. The two key ingredients, though, are flour and water. Sometimes the water is conveyed via eggs and sometimes the moisture component is just straight water. Before we can understand how to make pasta, and all that entails, it's useful to understand its basic components.

FLOUR

In the restaurant, we make all kinds of pasta dough. We create flavored dough by adding various spices, and we experiment with regional specialty recipes. But for the most part, pasta dough can be divided into two overarching families: pasta made with zero zero flour and eggs and pasta made with durum semolina flour and water.

Each grain of wheat contains three main components: the outer protective layer called the bran, the tiny embryo germ, and the endosperm—the largest part of the grain. Plants, like animals, evolve natural defense and fertilization mechanisms. Wheat is no exception. If you were to swallow a whole wheat berry, it would impossible for your digestive system to break down the grain's outer protective layers. Crushing the whole grain by milling renders wheat digestible. Refined flour is made when the bran and the germ are sifted away, leaving only the soft endosperm. Wheat is broadly classified as either hard or soft. Durum wheat, a type of hard wheat, thrives in the dry heat of southern Italian fields. It's a type of wheat that is rich in gluten and other proteins, and it has long been a staple crop of the southern regions. Durum wheat—and its resulting semolina flour—is the core ingredient in both fresh hand-rolled semolina pasta (like our orecchiette and cavatelli) and extruded pasta (familiar mass-produced dried shapes like spaghetti, rigatoni, and so on).

The characteristics of durum wheat directly correlate to the final characteristics of the pasta. Semolina-based pasta—most of the dried pasta you're used to buying—is noticeably more textured and much denser than its soft wheat counterparts. It has a ton of bounce and resistance to the bite. In the restaurant, we only combine semolina flour with water.

The other type of flour we use in the restaurant to make pasta is zero zero. It's not a type of wheat but the degree of "fineness" of the milled flour. Zero zero is the most finely ground flour, almost like powder. Refined flours like zero zero consist of only the endosperm and are very nearly always made with soft wheat. Soft wheat contains far less gluten but more starch than its hard counterparts. Varieties of soft wheat grow well in northern Italy, and, as you might guess from the name, it is easier to mill into the ultra-fine zero zero grind.

Zero zero flour is traditionally more expensive as well, another big reason why it flourished in the wealthier northern half of Italy as opposed to the historically poorer south. It thrived especially in the particularly rich (and pasta-obsessed) region of Emilia-Romagna.

EGGS

Whenever I tell any Italian that the name of my pasta-centric restaurant is Flour + Water, I always get the exact same confused, matter-of-fact response: "Flour and water? But there are eggs in pasta. What about the eggs?"

Indeed, eggs are key at the restaurant, probably even more so than the flour or water, since we use them in the majority of our pasta dough. The general public doesn't connect how crucial eggs are to pasta, but in my opinion, they are just as important as the type of flour.

Eggs are fascinating ingredients on their own, but even more so when discussing pasta. Yes, eggs are delicious to eat in a dozen different ways: poached, fried, boiled, scrambled, sous vide, and so on. But the thing that sets eggs apart from nearly every other ingredient is that they are also versatile cooking tools. Eggs are used to set flan, brown pastries, and even give texture to cocktails. Eggs have the same versatility in pasta. The first thing you'll notice in egg pasta dough is that the yolks provide a nice, attractive yellow color—though some chefs have been rumored to "cheat" and add saffron to the dough to make it more orange—a fake tan, if you will.

Generally speaking, an egg consists of a yolk and a white. If you've ever seen a little red blood line in the egg, that means it's a fertilized egg. Eggs that have been fertilized by the rooster will always be stronger (better) in color and flavor, especially since it means they're usually coming from a small farm. More importantly, the yolks contribute richness to the noodle. They make pasta soft and delicate, as well as pliable. You'll notice that our ravioli dough includes egg whites as well; we incorporate whites because they make the dough more elastic and durable due to their protein content—key for stuffed pastas. In the following chapter, we will discuss how each component of the egg affects the final outcome of the particular doughs.

We get our flour from Italy, but we get our eggs from two places: a 4-H youth program north of San Francisco and a small producer located about 30 minutes east of the city in the Berkeley Hills. At both sources, the eggs are organic and cage-free. The hens are fed with grain and allowed to roam freely at the farm. Happy chickens with the correct diet make good eggs, which in turn make good pasta.

How to buy good eggs? The easy answer is to buy them from farmers' markets as often as you can. At the supermarket, avoid eggs from chickens that were given antibiotics or proteins. Get the freshest eggs you can. Eggs have a long shelf life, especially in supermarkets, but as with most agricultural products, fresher is better. When eggs are freshly laid, a very small air pocket is formed between the egg white and the shell. Since eggs are porous, that air pocket grows over time, gradually dehydrating the egg in its shell. The older an egg, the bigger the air pocket. When fresh eggs are cracked, the yolk comes out as a beautiful intact sphere, not a watery glob. To test how old an egg is, put it in a glass of water. A fresh egg will sink to the bottom and stay there. An old egg will float. In the store, if you give an egg a gentle shake, an older egg will slosh around in its shell—you can hear it. Fresh ones will be denser and heavier in the shell.

I prefer to buy large eggs, not extra-large. For the longest time, we were buying extra-large eggs in the restaurant, thinking that we were getting a better value. Then we eventually realized that the yolks (which we were mainly after) are just about the same size in large and extra-large eggs; the extra-large ones only have bigger whites.

The first time I saw the farm eggs used to make pasta in Bologna, I was shocked. Not only were the yolks perfectly round and robust, but they were an incredibly vibrant, deep orange hue. I had never seen that color before in egg yolks. I soon learned that in Bologna, eggs yolks are, quite logically, called "rossi"—literally, the "reds" of the eggs.

Once I asked the folks in Bologna *how* they get the yolks so red and flavorful. Their answer was simple: they feed the chickens their favorite bright orange food—carrots.

Nowadays, I have a dozen chickens on the roof of the restaurant, and we're taking that lesson of the carrot-fueled eggs and expanding upon it. Raising chickens is an extension of the idea that we are better as cooks if we fully understand how ingredients are cultivated. That, in turn, allows us to cultivate ingredients on our own in the way that is optimal for our purposes, be it a housemade salumi flavored as we like it or a garden of rare fresh herbs on the rooftop, procured for a fraction of the wholesale price. We experiment with the feed we give our chickens to better understand the effect of diet on eggs. Our current sweet spot for chicken feed involves a mix of turmeric, carrots, organic livestock feed pellets, and leftover kitchen foodstuffs, like salmon trimmings, that are high in omega-3 fatty acids.

WHAT EXACTLY HAPPENS WHEN FLOUR IS COMBINED WITH WATER?

The process starts as soon as flour is mixed with moisture, whether pure water or via eggs (which contain mostly water). On a molecular level, the initial hydration gives mobility—lubrication—to the previously inert, coiled flour proteins. The proteins absorb the water and begin to stretch out and bloom, almost like a dried jasmine flower that unfurls in a cup of a hot tea. As the proteins flourish, they unravel on top of their neighboring proteins that are doing the same thing. Bonds are serendipitously formed. The result is a web-like network of gluten, a phenomenon that is largely exclusive to wheat—and one that makes pasta and bread possible.

That network of gluten doesn't form instantaneously upon hydration. When the flour is introduced to the water or eggs, the mixture is very dry, so much so that it can be challenging to incorporate all the flour into the initial dough mass.

Extensive kneading followed by a resting phase is necessary to properly and fully hydrate the dough. It seems counterintuitive at first, but the dough feels more hydrated and more pliable after it's been kneaded and allowed to rest for 30 minutes. The dough needs time to fully hydrate. What's actually happening is that the water that originally sparked the molecular movement and formed the network of gluten is no longer needed. Once the water has done its job, it gets released and lubricates the rest of the dough, thereby becoming more apparent to us.

There are four basic genres of pasta dough that we make at the restaurant. We've also included a fifth—*mattarello* dough (page 160)—because it's traditionally significant, if not very common in America.

+ Egg dough: A yolk-based dough made with zero zero flour for hand-cut noodles like tagliatelle, farfalle, garganelli, and others.

+ Ravioli "rav" dough: A whole egg–based dough made with zero zero flour, used for all stuffed pasta, like tortellini, mezzalune, raviolini, and more.

+ Hand-rolled semolina dough: A dough made with semolina flour and water, common in southern Italy in shapes like orecchiette and cavatelli.

+ Extruded semolina dough: A dough made with semolina flour and water and pressed through an extrusion machine into shapes like spaghetti, bucatini, rigatoni, and others.

There are a few other regional specialty doughs (corzetti stampati, stradette, bigoli), but those are all more like riffs on the above frameworks.

Egg Dough

With the exception of the dough for extruded pasta, which gets mixed in the extruding machine (page 16), the process for making pasta dough is basically the same for all of our pasta doughs: Mix, knead, rest. The final mixing step—rolling the pasta—is where the divergences lie. Like most things, making fresh pasta gets easier with practice.

The only difference between our two egg-based doughs is that our standard egg dough includes yolks only, whereas ravioli dough—we call it rav dough, for short—includes whole eggs. There are several reasons why we have two types of egg dough.

First and foremost is flavor. Yolks have a very high fat content, thereby enriching the flavor and creating that rich, almost unctuous taste associated with fresh egg pasta that is used for unstuffed shapes big and small. So the name of the game is reaching the happy place where you can get the most egg yolks (flavor) into the dough without tipping the scale in the wrong direction. Egg yolks contain about 50 percent water, and the rest is largely fat and proteins. Adding too much fat causes the webbed structure of gluten to go from nicely elastic (good for rolling and shaping) to soft and far too pliable. Our egg dough, which is the result of trial and error, contains the most fat possible while still functioning as a pasta should.

On the other hand, an egg white—the albumen—consists of about 90 percent water and 10 percent protein. Egg whites are largely neutral, basically a flavorless and colorless filler. As they dilute taste, we don't use them for the standard egg dough.

Their utility lies in the other kind of egg dough—rav dough, which we use for all stuffed pasta. When making stuffed pasta, the dough should have extra elasticity and durability so it can hold its shape through the stretching, filling, and twisting that stuffed pasta requires. Those qualities come through the use of whole eggs—or more precisely, the inclusion of egg whites. When egg whites are added to zero zero flour, two things happen. Immediately the flour absorbs the water, as usual (see previous section). However, once the water from the egg whites is absorbed into the flour, the egg whites' proteins are left behind and those proteins become very concentrated. Instead of those egg proteins having to mobilize nine times their weight in water, all the water has disappeared and it's suddenly much easier for the proteins to find each other and hook up to create new protein structures. These extra protein structures maintain the rav dough's integrity while you form the shapes and cook the final dish.

When it comes to making fresh pasta, whenever possible, do everything on a smooth wood surface. The entire process—from mixing to shaping—is easier on a porous wood surface, which results in a dough with much more texture than one that is made on a smooth surface such as metal or marble. This texture directly affects how sauces will cling to the surface of the finished pasta.

To be as accurate as possible, we recommend following the weight measurements when making dough. We've included both volume and weight in the recipes throughout the book, but here, specific weight measurements are particularly important.

Also, have a spray bottle of water nearby. Spritzing with water is a handy trick when making dough. Using a spray bottle allows you to introduce as little moisture as possible to the biggest work surface possible, thereby binding together the dry dough into one mass without greatly affecting the overall hydration level of the dough. This is a necessary step for all the dough recipes in this book. Our pasta dough recipes keep the hydration as low as possible to allow us to be able to use zero additional flour when later rolling out the dough. When first mixing the dough it will seem like the recipe is far too dry. A few spritzes will bind the dry dough and allow it to become one mass.

Equipment
Large fork + Bench scraper + Spray bottle

Rav Dough

Makes 556 grams/19.6 ounces of dough

360 grams 00 flour (2 well-packed cups, unsifted)
5 grams kosher salt (1 teaspoon)
100 grams whole eggs (½ cup/about 2 large eggs)
90 grams egg yolks (⅓ cup/5 to 6 yolks)
6 grams extra-virgin olive oil (1½ teaspoons)

Standard Egg Dough

Makes 644 grams/22.7 ounces of dough

360 grams 00 flour (2 well-packed cups, unsifted)
1¼ teaspoons (2 big pinches) kosher salt
300 grams egg yolks (1¼ cups/18 to 20 yolks)
1½ teaspoons extra-virgin olive

Step One: Mixing

To start, place the flour on a dry, clean work surface, forming a mound about 8 to 10 inches in diameter at its base. Sprinkle the salt in the middle of the mound. Using the bottom of a measuring cup, create a well 4 to 5 inches wide, with at least a half inch of flour on the bottom of the well.

Slowly and carefully add the wet ingredients (eggs and olive oil) into the well, treating the flour as a bowl. Using a fork, gently beat the eggs without touching the flour walls or scraping through the bottom to the work surface.

Then, still stirring, begin to slowly incorporate the flour "walls" into the egg mixture, gradually working your way toward the outer edges of the flour, but disturbing the base as little as possible. If the eggs breach the sides too soon, quickly scoop them back in and reform the wall. Once the dough starts to take on a thickened, paste-like quality (slurry), slowly incorporate the flour on the bottom into the mixture.

When the slurry starts to move as a solid mass, remove as much as possible from the fork. Slide a bench scraper or spatula under the mass of dough and flip it and turn it onto itself to clear any wet dough from the work surface.

At this point, with your hands, start folding and forming the dough into a single mass. The goal is to incorporate all the flour into the mass, and using a spray bottle to liberally spritz the dough with water is essential. It is a very dry dough, and it cannot be overstated how important it is to generously and constantly spritz to help "glue" any loose flour to the dry dough ball.

When the dough forms a stiff, solid mass, scrape away any dried clumps of flour from the work surface, which, if incorporated in the dough, will create dry spots in the final product.

Step Two: Kneading

Kneading is an essential step in the dough-making process: it realigns the protein structure of the dough so that it develops properly during the resting stage that follows.

Kneading is simple: Drive the heel of your dominant hand into the dough. Push down and release, and then use your other hand to pick up and rotate the dough on itself 45 degrees. Drive the heel of your hand back in the dough, rotate, and repeat for 10 to 15 minutes. This is how Italian grandmas get their fat wrists.

Pasta is easy to underknead but virtually impossible to overknead (unlike bread, where each type has its sweet spot or ideal kneading time). That said, even though the dough cannot be overkneaded, it can spend too much time on the worktable—and, as a direct result, start to dehydrate and be more difficult to form into its final shape. For best results, I think a 10 to 15 minute range is a solid guideline. When the dough is ready, it will stop changing appearance and texture. The dough will be firm but bouncy to the touch and have a smooth, silky surface, almost like Play-Doh. Tightly wrap the dough in plastic wrap.

Step Three: **Resting**

At this stage, the flour particles continue to absorb moisture, which further develops the gluten structure that allows pasta dough to stand up to rolling and shaping.

If you plan to use the dough immediately, let it rest at room temperature, wrapped in plastic, for at least 30 minutes prior to rolling it out (the next step). If resting for more than 6 hours, put the dough in the refrigerator. It's best to use fresh dough within 24 hours. Under proper refrigeration, the dough will hold for 2 days, but I try to avoid letting it rest that long, simply because the eggs yolks will oxidize and discolor the dough. It won't affect the flavor or the texture, but the dough will develop a slightly off color and a grayish-greenish hue.

The Final Step: **Rolling Out the Dough**

Rolling is the last phase of the mixing process. Rolling out pasta by machine—whether it's a hand-crank model or an electric one—should be a delicate, almost Zen-like art. You can only roll out dough that has rested for at least 30 minutes at room temperature. If it has rested for longer in the fridge, give the dough enough time to come back to room temperature. The fat content of pasta dough is so high that it will solidify when cold, so it needs to come back to room temperature to be easier to roll.

The process for rolling sheets of pasta dough is the same whether you have a hand-cranked machine or an electric one, like we have in the restaurant.

To start, slice off a section of the ball of dough, immediately rewrapping the unused portion in plastic wrap. Place the piece of dough on the work surface and, with a rolling pin, flatten it enough that it will fit into the widest setting of the pasta machine. You do not want to stress the dough or the machine.

It's crucial to remember that whenever the pasta dough is not in plastic wrap or under a damp towel, you're in a race against time. The minute you expose the pasta to air, it starts to dehydrate. This creates a dry outer skin that you do not want to incorporate into the finished dough; the goal is to create a dough of uniform consistency.

Our dough is purposely very dry. We do not add any raw flour in the rolling process. Extra flour added at this point sticks to the dough and, when cooked, that splotch turns into a gooey mass, a slick barrier to sauce. It dulls the seasoning and flavors of both the dough and the finished dish.

Begin rolling the dough through the machine, starting with the widest setting. Guide it quickly through the slot once. Then decrease the thickness setting by one and repeat. Decrease the thickness setting by one more and roll the dough through quickly one more time. Once the dough has gone through three times, once on each of the first three settings, it should have doubled in length.

Lay the dough on a flat surface. The dough's hydration level at this point is so low that you'll probably see some streaks; that's normal, which is the reason for the next crucial step: laminating the dough.

Using a rolling pin as a makeshift ruler, measure the width of your pasta machine's slot, minus the thickness of two fingers. This measurement represents the ideal width of the pasta sheet, with about a finger's length on each side, so there's plenty of room in the machine. Take that rolling pin measurement to the end of the pasta sheet and make a gentle indentation in the dough representing the measurement's length. Make that mark the crease and fold the pasta over. Repeat for the rest of the pasta sheet, keeping that same initial measurement. For best results, you want a minimum of four layers. Secure the layers of the pasta together with the rolling pin, rolling it flat enough that it can fit in the machine. Put the dough back in the machine, but with a 90 degree turn of the sheet. In other words, what *was* the "bottom" edge of the pasta is now going through the machine first.

This time around, it's important to roll out the dough two to three times on each setting at a steady, smooth pace. We've created this gluten network—a web of elasticity—so if you roll it too fast, it will snap back to its earlier thickness, thereby lengthening the time you're going through each number.

The more slowly you crank the pasta dough, the more compression time the dough has; it's important to stay consistent in the speed in order to keep a consistent thickness. You should be able to see and feel the resistance as the dough passes through the rollers. On the first time at each level, the dough will compress. It's time to move onto the next level when the dough slips through without any trouble. The first few thickness settings (the biggest widths) usually require three passes; once you're into thinner territory, there's less pasta dough compressing, so it goes more quickly and two passes get the job done.

When handling the sheet of dough—especially as it gets longer—always keep it taut and flat. Never grab or flop or twist the pasta. The sheet should rest on the inside edges of your index fingers with your fingers erect and pointed out.

The hands don't grab or stretch the dough; instead, they act as paddles, guiding the sheet of dough through the machine. Handling the dough with your fingers pointed straight out alleviates any pressure on the dough, which stretches and warps it.

Use the right hand to feed the machine and use the left hand to crank. Once the pasta dough is halfway through, switch hands, pulling out with the left hand. If you have trouble doing it alone as the dough gets longer and thinner, find a friend to help juggle the dough, or roll out a smaller, more wieldy batch.

Once you roll out the dough, immediately form it into shapes.

HOW THICK SHOULD YOU ROLL THE DOUGH?

All machine settings correspond to different thickness, so there's no uniform end point. Experience and touch come into play; once you do it a few times, you'll get a good sense of what you like, and what thickness works best.

That said, thickness relates to the shape you are making. For the most part, doughs will be rolled out to $1/16$ inch, or slightly thicker or thinner.

Just slightly thinner than $1/16$ inch (but not so thin as $1/32$ inch) is the proper thickness for all stuffed pastas and tajarin (page 110). A good rule of thumb is that the finished dough should be slightly translucent. If you can see the outline of your fingers behind it, or the grain of the wood table through the pasta, you're in good shape. For most (but not all) hand-cranked machines at home, it's the second-to-last setting.

The $1/16$-inch measurement is used for tagliatelle, tagliarini, paglia e fieno, garganelli, and cappellacci dei briganti. For most (but not all) hand-cranked machines at home, it's the third-to-last setting.

The fattest pasta we make is just slightly *over* $1/16$ inch. Shapes formed of this thickness are usually flat: pappardelle, chitarre, stradette, corzetti stampati, maltagliati, lasagnette, cannoli, farfalle, and pizzoccheri. For most (but not all) hand-cranked machines at home, it's the fourth-to-last setting.

THE IMPORTANCE OF LETTING DOUGH REST

It took me a couple weeks, and maybe a little sweet-talking, but the Bologna ladies finally allowed me to roll out the dough on my own. To this point in my job (ok, internship) at the pasta *laboratorio*, I had been relegated to the corner, plopping out ground meat into tortellini after tortellini. I had held my own in some of the toughest kitchens in San Francisco and France, but this was something different, something more intimidating. The pecking order was very clear, and I was firmly established on the bottom. So the fact that they were about to let me roll out a sheet of dough was a benchmark occasion. I felt like they gave me the keys to a Ferrari.

Hands shaking and head down, I chose one of the giant rolling pins—the *mattarellos*—from the bin in the corner of the room. I quickly grabbed a ball of dough and approached the table. I could feel all their eyes on me as I plopped the yellow ball on the wooden table and began rolling. I rolled hard. A lot. But after every thrust extending the dough, the dough snapped back to its original shape. I rolled harder and faster and more frantically. I went on for five more minutes, but the

dough simply wouldn't extend. For weeks I had watched the ladies roll out a three-by-four-foot rectangle of dough in less than 10 minutes. Five minutes turned into 10 minutes. Sweat formed on my brow, partly out of exhaustion, partly out of frustration, and partly out of embarrassment. Clearly these women had superhuman strength or something.

Finally, one of the ladies took pity on me and told me to stop. I did, and looked up at them. They all had little grins, stifling giggles. I soon learned that I had erroneously grabbed one of the dough balls that was just made. The dough didn't have time to rest. That was my lesson in one of the key parts of pasta making.

Resting is the point in the process when the elasticity of pasta dough forms, thanks to the formation of gluten strands, and the wheat fully absorbs the liquids. In the pasta lab, they only roll dough that has rested 18–24 hours. My rule of thumb is that dough should rest for at least 30 minutes in plastic wrap at ambient temperature. After 30 minutes, either roll it out immediately or put it in the fridge.

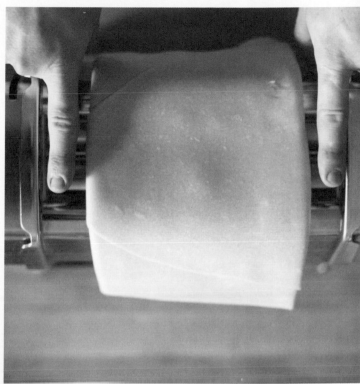

Hand-Rolled Semolina Dough

Semolina dough is the purest definition of flour and water.
Whereas most pasta in northern Italy consists of eggs and flour in some combination, in the southern regions, pasta is most often made solely with semolina flour and water. The reason for this is practical: eggs were historically too expensive for southerners—and durum wheat thrived. Also known as durum pasta, semolina-based pasta is the dried version that is most common in stores today.

Semolina is a dense, coarse, and "hard" flour, a stark contrast to the softer zero zero. As a hard flour, it has a higher protein content, and thus supports more gluten structure, so far less kneading is required when making a semolina-based dough. Semolina dough is also very different from its zero zero counterparts in that it is much denser, requiring more cooking time. We use hand-rolled semolina dough for shapes like trofie (page 52), pici (page 140), orecchiette (page 56), and strozzapreti (page 128). The nice part about making these shapes is that no pasta machine is required. All the shapes are made by hand.

Equipment
Large fork + Spray bottle

Makes 514 grams/18 ounces of dough

180 grams semolina flour (1 cup)
180 grams 00 flour (1 cup)
178 grams salted warm water (¾ cup made with 10 grams/
1 tablespoon kosher salt)

Combine the flours. Place the flour mixture on a dry, clean work surface, forming a mound about 8 to 10 inches in diameter at its base. Using the bottom of a measuring cup, create a well 4 to 5 inches wide, with at least a half inch of flour on the bottom of the well. Using a fork to stir the middle of the well, slowly pour in the water, trying to keep the integrity of the walls during this first step. Combine the flour and water into one mass and knead until fully incorporated. The dough will be dry. If necessary, using a spray bottle, spritz with water several times to "glue" the loose flour to the mass.

Once you've formed a ball, knead the dough: drive the heel of your dominant hand into the dough. Push down and release, and then use your other hand to pick up and rotate the dough on itself 45 degrees. Drive the heel of your hand back in the dough, rotate, and repeat for 8 to 10 minutes.

Wrap the dough tightly with plastic wrap. Let rest for at least 30 minutes at room temperature before using. If you're not using it after 30 minutes, put it in the refrigerator.

The dough ball is now ready to be shaped for use in a particular recipe, such as orecchiette, which are rolled by hand.

Extruded Pasta Dough

Pasta extrusion is the technique that helped catapult pasta's development several times over the course of history.

Pasta had already been around for a few centuries when a rudimentary version of the extrusion press was invented in the late sixteenth century, a development that allowed pasta to be made (and sold) more easily, quickly, and in larger quantities. The mechanization and commercialization of dried pasta took another leap forward during the Industrial Revolution that swept the Western world during the late nineteenth century, when extruding machines took on their modern form, and a host of other pasta machines also came into the picture: kneading machines, rolling machines, pasta-drying machines.

When flour and water are combined in an extruding machine, the water hydrates the flour as they churn in the body of the extruder. When the two ingredients are fully integrated in the mixer, the newly formed dough is ready to be pushed through the die at the bottom, which determines its final shape. The dough is squeezed through the small holes of the die, emerging as spaghetti, rigatoni, macaroni, and so on, depending on which die is used. When the pasta goes through the die, the immense pressure and heat of the extrusion immediately hydrates the dough and instantly bonds the molecules. The structure of the dough is transformed, from a flour and water mixture that was crumbly, loose, and sandy into firm noodles that are ready to be dried.

Also of note about extruded pasta is the effect that the process has on the pasta's texture. The rougher the pasta's surface, the more sauce is going to adhere to the pasta—and that's a very good thing. Extruded pastas typically have very rough surfaces, due to the pressure and stretching of the extrusion technique, especially when brass dies (as opposed to plastic ones) are used.

I doubt any home cooks have access to a commercial pasta extruder. Ours weighs several hundred pounds and takes up a large corner of our Dough Room. However, you can now buy home versions, either as a free-standing tabletop machine or as an attachment for a stand mixer, that work pretty well. Of course, dried extruded noodles are also sold in nearly every market in America.

The golden ratio for extruded pasta is three parts semolina flour to one part warm water. The smallest batch we make at the restaurant is six thousand grams of flour, which nets about forty orders. The amount you use will be dependent on how much you want—and how much your extruder can hold.

Extruded pasta will stay fresh for up to four days in the refrigerator, uncovered. This is how we store the extruded pasta in the restaurant.

If you want to fully dry the pasta, place it on a parchment-lined baking sheet or perforated basket and completely dehydrate the pasta at room temperature. Fluff the pasta after 12 hours; it should be completely dry after 48 hours. Store in a brown paper bag in a dry space; it will keep for several weeks.

Equipment
Stand mixer + Wooden spoon
Pasta machine + sharp knife

With a Home Extruder
Makes 482 grams/17 ounces of dough

360 grams semolina flour (2 cups)
120 grams warm water (½ cup plus 1 tablespoon)

Sprinkle a baking sheet with semolina flour and set aside.

Put the flour in the bowl of a stand mixer fitted with the paddle attachment. With the mixer on high speed, very slowly drizzle water into the bowl. When half the water is incorporated, stop the machine and mix the flour with a wooden spoon or your hands to make sure the water is evenly distributed. Continue mixing and drizzling until all the water is incorporated into the dough.

The dough is ready to be extruded when it feels like wet sand—crumbly and almost flaky, barely holding together. If you squeeze a handful in your fist, it should stick together, slightly pulling on your skin.

Extrude the pasta following the manufacturer's directions for your machine or attachment. With a sharp knife, cut the noodles to the desired length as they emerge from the extruder and lay them on the prepared baking sheet to dry.

HOW TO COOK THE PASTA

Cooking pasta well takes *slightly* more care than the usual boiling and draining. In fact, you won't find any bowl-shaped colanders at Flour + Water. Reserved pasta water is an essential ingredient in pan sauces—our keys to cooking pasta.

WATER

In his book dedicated to pasta, James Beard declared that predicting how long pasta will take to cook in boiling water is "the one inexplicable art in pasta making." Between the water, the volume, the heat, the pasta, and the environment, there are just too many variables to make blanket statements about cooking time. When dealing with store-bought dried pastas, the directions on the box are a good starting point, but in truth, the only real way to cook pasta properly in water is to taste the pasta continuously as it cooks.

In the restaurant, we cook most pasta about 80 percent of the way in the water, and the final 20 percent in the adjacent sauté pan. When done properly, the water acts not only as a cooking vehicle but also as a seasoning agent and a crucial ingredient in the finishing sauce.

We serve our pasta al dente, but al dente does not mean undercooked. The goal is to cook it to the point where it has as much texture as possible while still finishing clean on your palate. Properly cooked pasta shouldn't stick to your teeth.

While it might sound painfully obvious, the first thing to do is to make sure you start with enough water. If the noodles are too crowded in the pot, they'll stick to each other and won't cook evenly. For most portions in this book, four quarts of water in a six-quart stock pot should create enough space in the pot.

First, bring the water to a boil. Then toss in the other additions—salt and semolina flour, which are just as important as the water. If the water is not boiling, the salt will not dissolve well, so you cannot test the water for saltiness; it should taste just slightly less salty than sea water. We will use the same cooking water to help build our sauces in the next step.

The purpose of the semolina is to create a starchy water, a component in the emulsified sauce that will be used to finish the dish. Starch stabilizes the sauce. Starch and water are the basis for a sauce's structure. In the kitchen of Flour + Water, we have pasta water boiling throughout the night, and it doesn't take long for the pasta water to start to pick up the residual starch released from the noodles that are going in and out of

the boiling water on a regular basis. During service, our cooks use splashes of the starchy water in the finishing sauces on pasta dishes. Obviously, home cooks do not have the luxury of a vat of constantly boiling starchy water to help bind sauces. So, when testing recipes for this book, we figured that a heaping handful of semolina mimics that starchy restaurant kitchen pasta water, thereby creating a perfect foundation for the sauce.

When the pasta is dropped into the water, keep the pasta moving. Stir the noodles so the noodles don't stick to other noodles or the bottom of the pot. As noted earlier, the general rule is to cook the pasta 80 percent of the way in the water, and the final 20 percent in the pan. It's an admittedly rough rule in a medium that usually relies on ultra-specific measurements and timing. We've included the cooking times for pasta in individual recipes. Consider them a guideline. Variables like the freshness of the pasta and the thickness of the pasta will inevitably alter the cooking times. Thus, experience and personal preference come into play, as you develop the ability to detect when a pasta is about 80 percent done. But the point that cannot be emphasized enough when cooking pasta is this: *constantly taste the pasta.*

Our equation for the perfect pot of pasta water: For 4 quarts of water, add ¼ cup of kosher salt and a handful of semolina flour. Once the seasoned water is ready and boiling, it should develop a bubbling white foam on the surface.

COOKING À LA MINUTE: PAN SAUCES

The recipes in this book are nearly identical to the ones we use in the restaurant. The final cooking step is very quick, usually less than five minutes. Most of the time-intensive work comes in the prep work: making the pasta, making the braised meat for the sauce, slicing the vegetables, and so on. Nearly all the dishes can be prepped ahead of time and then cooked or "assembled" or both when ready to eat. (Not to mention, you can swap out dried pasta in many of the recipes.)

Our pasta dishes in the restaurant—and this book—are nearly always finished with a version of a pan sauce, made à la minute. Now, usually when I say the words "emulsified butter sauce," home cooks freak out and get intimidated. Please don't. The sauce is simply butter that has been melted to coat and accentuate the accompanying ingredients.

The entire philosophy of pan sauces is simple: the starting point of any sauce is thinner and wetter than the finished product. As the sauce reduces to the perfect consistency, it's also cooking the pasta.

The trick, however, is timing. The sauce is reducing while the pasta is cooking, so the goal is to bring both components to perfection at the same time. It's a balancing act.

A pan sauce has achieved the proper sauce-like consistency when it is thick enough to coat the back of a spoon. At that moment, the bubbles in the pan will be getting larger and the bubbling will slow down as the sugars and starches begin to thicken to the perfect level. If you run a spoon along the bottom of the pan, the sauce should have enough structure that it holds for a moment, but enough fluidity that it eventually oozes back into the spoon's line. (If the sauce gets too dry before the pasta is completely cooked, a splash or two of starchy pasta water can be used to "reset" the sauce.)

The reality of the science is that once pasta is cooked in water, it doesn't absorb any more flavor from the finishing pan sauce. Because pasta is water-soluble, it absorbs only the water from the sauce, not any aroma or oils. Instead, the pasta is *adsorbing* the flavors, meaning the flavor only sticks to the surface of the pasta. That simple tidbit of information blew my mind when Harold McGee, the San Francisco–based author of *On Food and Cooking* (one of my all-time favorite books), explained it. For years, I had been teaching cooks that finishing pastas in pan sauces helped noodles absorb flavor, but as it turns out, that false impression comes from the amount of sauce that adheres to the surface of the pasta.

BUTTER

There's no other way to put this: The recipes in this book use a generous amount of butter.

That's the way it is in the restaurant, too, especially during the colder months. I'm not quite sure if the reason traces back to the strong northern Italian influences, or my traditional French culinary training. We usually go through about twenty pounds of butter a night—nearly all of it for the finishing sauces for our pasta dishes.

Obviously you should try to buy the best possible butter at the market, and always opt for unsalted butter, simply because the balance of flavors and seasoning should be in the cook's control. I prefer butter with 86 percent fat content. This is the standard percentage for table butter; any butter with a higher fat content will be difficult to emulsify into the finished sauce.

We recently began making our own butter at both Flour + Water and our sister restaurant, Central Kitchen. Making butter is a fairly straightforward process, and it's a great example of the value of making ingredients in-house.

HOW TO USE
THESE RECIPES

The word *dipende* pops up a lot in Italy.

It technically means "depends," but for some reason, Italians use the word to answer everything as a sort of non answer, a declaration that shades of gray persist. How many eggs do you put in that recipe? "Dipende." How do we get to so-and-so address? "Dipende." How's the food at that restaurant? "Eh, dipende." How much does that bottle of wine cost? "Ah, dipende."

Maybe it's just because they don't want to answer the dumb question that the American (me) asked, but it's my hope that the recipes in this book can take on the same mindset of dipende. The pasta dishes that follow are some of the many versions we use at the restaurant, but in most cases the recipes are just base models that can—and should—be tweaked once you learn the technique.

Even though we've used all of these recipes in the restaurant, in many ways, this book represents the opposite of how we like to cook in the restaurant. We change our restaurant menu on a daily, and sometimes hourly, basis. We buy stuff and then formulate dishes out of those seasonal ingredients. It sounds cheesy, but if I'm in the test kitchen trying to write a menu, I usually can't do it. But, if I step into the walk-in fridge or wander around the farmers' market, the juices start flowing. So much of cooking depends on seeing, feeling, and tasting

an ingredient—taking in its size, its heartiness, its color, its acidity. I know that the restaurant probably runs less efficiently because of that attitude—it would be much easier to give my team a menu and say we're cooking these exact same dishes for the next month or year—but that inspired philosophy of fluid cooking runs rampant in the Bay Area. And because of it, there's much more soul and creativity embedded into our culinary landscape.

The recipes in this book are the framework according to which we cook. I encourage you to swap ingredients based on what produce is available; that's what we do in the restaurant on a daily basis. If you don't like bell peppers, use Padrón peppers. If you can't find quail, use chicken. If you're not going to go shoot a wild boar, your dinner party will probably survive with a pork shoulder instead. Many of the longer meat braises can stand on their own without pasta as well.

We write the pasta section of our menu with the goal of balancing different ingredients and different shapes—stuffed, long noodles, short noodles—and that's how we thought about the recipes in the book as well. Some of the pasta shapes are tricky and will take some practice; others are simple. Just about all of the pasta shapes—or at least similar versions—can be bought at good grocery stores. Many are available in dried form.

Does it matter which pasta shape goes with which pasta sauce? It's a question I've been asked many times. And my answer is yes, pasta shapes absolutely do matter.

It's all about the texture of a pasta dish when you eat it. Texture is just as important a component in cooking as flavor; it's how an eater perceives the flavor. As many of the recipes in this book attest, I don't always adhere to the gospel of pasta tradition wherein nearly every pasta shape has only one lawful sauce companion. That said, the traditions do have merit.

The thing I love about Italian cuisine is how much it is driven by tradition. Most regions or even towns have paired pasta shapes and its designated sauce. When using a distinct regional shape, we will pay homage to it and use tradition as a guide, but with our own ingredients from Northern California. That in itself is an Italian food sensibility: use the ingredients that grow around you, and treat them simply.

When it comes to the sauces that accompany pasta, the general thought is this: Stuffed pastas are adorned with a simple sauce because it's the pasta shape and the pasta filling that should sing—they are the stars of the dish. On the other hand, unstuffed, unadorned noodles—like spaghetti—are often accompanied by more complex sauces and garnishes. If it's complicated on the inside, it's simple on the outside, and vice versa.

The recipes in this book are the compositions that we do in the restaurant, from the ingredients to the techniques to the shapes. There are reasons for them all—but not rules. If you must substitute pasta shapes (or use dry pasta), try to get as close as you can to the original recommendation. Keep long noodle dishes with long noodles, for example. The shape is

a tool for flavor, be it the filling or the sauce.

One of the most common questions when cooking pasta is one of the most basic ones: How much pasta to boil?

The recipes in this book are designed for four people as a starter or intermediate course, or for two people as a main dish. In the restaurant—and in this book—we follow the general guidelines when it comes to pasta portions:

+ Fresh noodles (long and short): 3-4 ounces per person

+ Dried noodles (long and short): 2-3 ounces per person

+ Large stuffed pasta shapes (tortelloni):
  8-10 pieces per person

+ Medium stuffed pastas (tortelli, mezzalune et al.):
  12-14 pieces per person

+ Small stuffed pasta shapes (tortellini, agnolotti dal plin):
  18-20 pieces per person

Little things affect the end result of any dish, and hopefully experience will breed intuition. Even if two people precisely follow the same recipe, there will usually be variance. My advice? When finishing a pasta dish with a pan sauce, always keep two things on hand: a little extra liquid (like the starchy pasta water or a stock) and a little extra fat (like butter or olive oil). These two tools can help balance the sauce if it's too thick or thin to ensure a proper consistency.

At the restaurant, we make just about everything from scratch. I don't expect all home cooks to follow the same process of making a pork jus from leftover pork bones, but just in case, we've included recipes for most of the stocks and such here.

HOW TO STORE FRESH PASTA

Once pasta shapes are formed, always place them, equally spaced, on a baking sheet sprinkled with semolina flour. Stuffed pasta should be placed in the refrigerator, where it should always be left uncovered. Covering the pasta will trap moisture from the filling, in turn hydrating the dough to the point that it will become sticky and hard to manage. Stuffed pasta can always be frozen on the semolina-lined baking sheet.

After a few hours the pasta will be frozen, and at that point you can collect it in a freezer-safe plastic bag for easier storage.

Unstuffed pasta can be left out at room temperature indefinitely. Dry the pasta on an unlined baking sheet for 48 hours, fluffing it after 24 hours. Store in a brown paper bag at room temperature in a dry place. Semolina-based doughs will last longer than egg-based doughs.

I meet with my team every night after service to go over the next day's menu. The menu development at nighttime is a necessity; it enables us to cook how we like to cook. I never want my restaurant to have a static menu. I want to explore, and I want to learn. I'm OK with failure through experimentation if value comes out of the mistakes. So, in the wee hours of the night, my chefs and I examine the list of what our purveyors tell us will be delivered the next day, and we formulate a menu based on what we like to cook and what we think our guests will like to eat. Oftentimes, we'll call our fish guy and see what he's expecting to catch. Maybe we'll tweak a few dishes from the night before, or maybe we'll dip into the greatest hits . . . or maybe we'll look at what we've got and float a few completely new ideas. It all depends.

We hope that you enjoy these recipes and that you embrace the joy of making pasta at home. And if you're absolutely stumped, send us an email at book@flourandwater.com.

GUIDELINES FOR FOLDING PASTA

Shaping pasta easily becomes second nature, but here are some helpful tips to get you going.
+ Seal the dough firmly but gently. Don't squeeze the pasta too much; don't mash it. Once adhered, the dough will stick just fine. The goal is to form shapes with uniform thickness, which will allow for even cooking.
+ Don't be afraid to twist and turn the pasta shapes. Many of the shapes are complex and require some dramatic twists. You obviously don't want to tear the dough, but the pasta should be pliable enough to stretch and twist with ease.
+ When dealing with stuffed pastas, be sure to push all of the air out of the filling.

PART TWO

THE RECIPES

SUMMER

DURING THE FIRST FEW MONTHS OF FLOUR + WATER, I moved into the apartment unit directly above the restaurant. Actually, calling it an apartment unit at that point would have been a little generous. There was no running water, so I joined the gym across the street for showering purposes; for bathrooms, I used the restaurant downstairs. It was exactly how the glamorous life of a chef is portrayed on television.

One morning I woke up in a literal haze. The building was engulfed in smoke, thanks to a small stockpot fire in the kitchen downstairs. Damage was minimal, but the entire restaurant smelled terrible, so we had to close for ten days. During the hiatus, we took the opportunity to redesign the kitchen to accommodate our steadily increasing pasta focus and the numbers of covers we were doing. Only two years into the restaurant's life, we gutted the kitchen, bought an extruder, and installed a second pasta cooker— which might not sound like such a big deal, but doubling the output from that station changed everything.

Pre-fire, we were making four different shapes. Post-fire, we put a minimum of seven daily-changing pasta dishes on the regular menu, with another five on a newly created pasta tasting menu. Add in the three private dining rooms, and we found ourselves producing up to twenty different shapes of pasta a night. If the inception of the Dough Room planted the seeds for our new emphasis on pasta production, then the redesigned kitchen brought it to maturity.

It was summer, 2011.

+

Summer best reflects the ingredient-driven philosophy of Flour + Water pasta. During the summer, Bay Area markets overflow with produce, and the bounty of local farms translates directly to the dining room. When trying to explain how we approach cooking, I describe the restaurant as specializing in regional Italian food, without turning our back on regional California ingredients. It's not an attitude that we invented by any means, but I like to think that we have our voice in the conversation.

That Italian—and yes, Californian—sensibility boils down to learning what grows around you, and then letting it speak on the plate. It is a mindset that gives our menu constant motion and fluidity. Pasta is the canvas—and in summer, we simply happen to have a lot of colors at our disposal.

Eggplant Mezzalune with Cherry Tomatoes

Growing up in New Jersey, I was subjected to bastardized versions of Italian food throughout my childhood, much of which involved massive amounts of coagulated cheese and cloyingly sweet tomato sauce. One of the pillars of East Coast Italian-American cuisine is, of course, eggplant Parmesan—fried slices of breaded eggplant, buried in an avalanche of red sauce and melted cheese.

Many of our dishes at Flour + Water have roots in familiar flavor combinations, and this is my Northern California take on those eggplant Parmesan flavors—tomatoes, eggplant, melted cheese—with a key twist of smokiness from the treccione scamorza, a smoked mozzarella cheese. (If you can't find treccione scamorza, use another smoky soft cheese, like smoked mozzarella; in a pinch, any good mozzarella will suffice as well.)

Eggplant always lends itself beautifully to smoky flavors, and it's a common flavor pairing in southern Italy, where smoked soft cheeses are abundant. If you ask a southerner—like Angela Moncada, one of the ladies in the pasta *laboratorio* whose family came from Sicily to Bologna—about the best home-cooked southern dishes, *melanzane alla parmigiana* is invariably at the top of the list. What's *not* so common in southern Italy are stuffed pastas. But here, we incorporate those southern flavors in a stuffed pasta shape named mezzalune (half moons).

Mezzalune are probably the most basic stuffed pasta shape in this book—just one fold of a circle—and a great way to get your feet wet in the stuffed pasta realm.

Serves 4

Equipment
Blender + Baking sheets + Pasta machine
Rolling pin + 2½-inch ring mold or cookie cutter
Piping bag (optional) + Spray bottle

Store-bought option
Any fresh, cheese-stuffed pasta

Eggplant Filling
2 large globe eggplants, halved lengthwise (700 grams)
Olive oil
Kosher salt
¾ cup treccione scamorza cheese, finely diced (131 grams)
¼ cup grated Parmigiano-Reggiano cheese
Grated zest and juice of 1 lemon
Freshly ground black pepper

Tomato Sauce
3 tablespoons extra-virgin olive oil
1 medium clove garlic, very thinly sliced
1 cup cherry tomatoes, stemmed (150 grams)
Freshly squeezed lemon juice (optional)

Mezzalune
1 recipe Rav Dough (page 7)
1½ tablespoons Aleppo pepper

Marinated Cherry Tomatoes
1 cup cherry tomatoes, halved (200 grams)
Sea salt
Cracked black pepper
1 tablespoon extra-virgin olive oil

To Finish
2 tablespoons extra-virgin olive oil
Kosher salt
1¼ cups loosely packed whole fresh basil leaves
Freshly grated Parmigiano-Reggiano cheese, for finishing

Preheat the oven to 325°F.

To make the filling, with a knife, score a shallow crosshatch pattern in the flesh of the eggplant to allow steam to penetrate while cooking. Lightly season the eggplant flesh with olive oil and a pinch of salt. Place the eggplant halves, face down, on a baking sheet. Roast in the oven until the flesh is soft and fully tender when pierced with a knife, about 25 minutes. Scoop out the flesh and add to the jar of a blender. Puree until smooth.

Quickly transfer the eggplant puree to a mixing bowl while still hot, and, with a wooden spoon, stir in the treccione scamorza and Parmigiano-Reggiano. Mix until the cheeses are melted and well incorporated. Add the lemon zest and juice and season with salt and pepper. Refrigerate the filling until ready to use. The filling can be refrigerated up to 3 days.

To make the sauce, add the olive oil and garlic to a cold sauté pan and cook over medium-high heat until the garlic starts to brown, 2 to 3 minutes. Add the whole cherry tomatoes and cook until they start to blister and their skin just starts to break. Don't overcook—you want a fresh tomato sauce, not a concentrate. Transfer the tomato mixture to the jar of a blender and puree until smooth. Season to taste; if your tomatoes aren't very acidic, add a squeeze of lemon juice. Set aside.

Dust 2 baking sheets with semolina flour and set aside.

To make the pasta, follow the instructions for the Rav Dough (page 7), incorporating the Aleppo pepper with the dry ingredients.

Using a pasta machine, roll out the dough until the sheet is just translucent (see page 10). Cut a 2-foot section of the dough sheet and cover the rest of the dough with plastic wrap.

Using a 2½-inch-diameter ring mold or round cookie cutter, cut out rounds of dough.

Using a piping bag or a spoon, place a teaspoon of filling in the middle of a dough round, leaving ¼ inch of dough bare around the edge. Fold the circle in half to create a half-moon shape. Use a spritz of water from a spray bottle to help seal it if necessary. Start the seal at the top crest of the half-moon (12 o'clock): gently but firmly seal the dough, removing the air pocket by moving your fingers down the edges on both sides simultaneously, caressing the filling to create a tight, airless pillow.

Put the mezzalune on a flat surface and crimp the edges with a fork. Working quickly, place the mezzalune, slightly apart, on the prepared baking sheet. Don't let the mezzalune touch each other or they may stick together. Repeat until you run out of dough or filling. You should get about 45 to 50 pieces. Let them sit uncovered while you make the marinated tomatoes. The tomatoes should be made no more than 30 minutes before using them or they will start to break down.

To prepare the marinated tomatoes, season the tomatoes generously with salt, pepper, and the olive oil. Allow to marinate for 20 minutes before plating.

To finish, bring a large pot of seasoned water to a boil (see page 18). Add the 2 tablespoons olive oil and ½ cup pasta water to a cold 12-inch sauté pan. Place the pan over high heat and bring to a simmer.

Drop the filled mezzalune in the large pot of boiling water.

Once the pasta is cooked 80 percent through, until almost al dente, 2 to 3 minutes, transfer to the sauté pan using a hand-held strainer and stir to incorporate. Reserve the pasta water. Add the tomato sauce to the pan and season with salt. Bring the sauce back up to a simmer and cook until the sauce coats the back of a spoon and the pasta is tender, 2 to 3 minutes. Remove from the heat.

To serve, divide the pasta and sauce between four plates. Garnish each serving with fresh basil, marinated cherry tomatoes, and freshly grated Parmigiano-Reggiano.

Burrata Triangoli with Preserved Lemon, Summer Squash, and Mint

Any ingredient that can't be had in abundance becomes a hot commodity in today's day and age. In the Bay Area, squash blossoms are that delicate ingredient.

The window for squash blossoms usually begins inching open in late May or early June, heralding the late spring's slow drift into early summer. It stays open for a few months, but there's a catch: they must be fresh. If you pick one off the vine, slice it, and eat it, you get sensations of fruitiness and pollen that disappear once they've been sitting and wilting for a few days. The freshest ones are those you buy at the farmers' market.

The blossoms come in, and we want to use them on everything. We put them atop pizzas and fold them into pastas and salads.

For a stuffed pasta, burrata triangoli are a very straightforward affair. The filling is a whipped, uncooked mixture of seasoned burrata, and forming the triangular shape requires just one basic fold-and-seal flick of the wrist. You can buy preserved lemons at specialty markets or Middle Eastern markets, but it's incredibly easy to make them yourself—see page 42, for our recipe. Or you can substitute a teaspoon of grated lemon zest; it won't have quite the same nuances, but it will work.

Serves 4

Equipment
Baking sheets + Pasta machine + Rolling pin
Piping bag (optional) + Fluted wheel cutter
Straight wheel cutter (optional) + Spray bottle

Store-bought option
Any fresh, cheese-stuffed pasta

Burrata Filling
1 cup burrata (215 grams) diced
2 tablespoons freshly grated Parmigiano-Reggiano cheese
1 tablespoon minced fresh mint
2 teaspoons kosher salt
Grated zest of 1 lemon
Freshly ground black pepper

Triangoli
1 recipe Rav Dough (page 7)

To Finish
8 or 9 squash blossoms
1 tablespoon preserved Meyer lemon peel, finely minced
¾ cup unsalted butter (142 grams)
½ cup diced mixed yellow and green summer squash (62 grams)
¼ cup fresh mint cut in a chiffonade
1 tablespoon minced fresh Italian parsley
Juice of 1 lemon
⅓ cup shelled pistachios, toasted, cooled, and finely chopped (40 grams)
Freshly grated Parmigiano-Reggiano cheese, for finishing

To make the filling, take the burrata out of its liquid and chop it into small dice. In a large mixing bowl, combine the burrata with the rest of the filling ingredients and mix well. Set aside.

Dust 2 baking sheets with semolina flour and set aside.

To make the pasta, using a pasta machine, roll out the dough until the sheet is just translucent (see page 10). Cut a 2-foot section of the dough sheet and cover the rest of the dough with plastic wrap.

Cut the sheet of dough into 3-inch squares with a straight wheel cutter, or a knife and a ruler. Using a piping bag or spoon, place a heaping teaspoon of the filling in the middle of each square, leaving ¼ inch of dough bare around the edge.

Fold the filled square so the opposite corners meet, pressing to create a triangle. Use a quick spritz of water from a spray bottle to help seal it, if necessary. Gently but firmly seal the top corner and remove the air pocket by moving your fingers down the sides from the point down simultaneously, caressing the filling to make a tight, airless pillow. With a fluted cutter, trim the pasta along the two edges, leaving about ¼ inch of pasta around the filling.

Working quickly, place the triangoli on the prepared baking sheets, spaced apart. Don't let the triangoli touch each other or they may stick together. Repeat until you run out of dough or filling. You should get 30 to 40 pieces.

To finish, bring a large pot of seasoned water to a boil (see page 18).

Clean the squash blossoms by pinching just above the base and twisting to separate the delicate leaves from the core. Tear each squash blossom leaf lengthwise by hand into 4 or 5 smaller pieces; set aside.

Rinse the diced preserved Meyer lemon peel well under cold running water. Drain and set aside on a paper towel.

Drop the pasta in the boiling water.

Add the butter to a cold 12-inch sauté pan and place over high heat. When melted, add ½ cup of the seasoned pasta water, the preserved lemons, and the yellow and green squash. Bring to a simmer over high heat, stirring constantly. Once the pasta is cooked 80 percent through, until almost al dente, 2 to 3 minutes, transfer to the saucepan with a handheld strainer and stir to incorporate. Reserve the pasta water. Continue to simmer to reduce the sauce and create an emulsion until the sauce coats the back of a spoon. When the pasta is tender, 2 to 3 minutes, add the squash blossoms, mint, parsley, and lemon juice. Toss to combine.

To serve, divide the pasta and sauce between four plates. Garnish with the chopped pistachios and freshly grated Parmigiano-Reggiano.

Preserved Lemons

Meyer lemons belong near the top of the list of ingredients essential to California cuisine. Maybe it's because they are ubiquitous in Northern California, but mostly I think it's just because they're delicious. Sweeter and less acidic than standard varieties of lemon, fresh Meyers are at their finest in winter, like most citrus. We use fresh Meyer lemons constantly in the restaurant during the cold months, but preserving them in a simple brine allows us to use them throughout the rest of the year.

Preserving Meyer lemons has become an annual rite of winter in the restaurant. By summer, those lemons—usually a couple hundred pounds worth—are ready to be used. The timing is perfect. That's when the Northern California shopping cart overflows with summer produce—squashes, eggplants, tomatoes—that finds its perfect complement in the salty, tart explosion of flavor of a preserved Meyer lemon.

The act of preserving lemons follows the exact same principle as curing meats: take one ingredient, add salt and aromatics—and give it time. It's a perfect example of the Old World technique of simple transformation, letting time take hold, and making the whole that much more incredible than the original ingredients.

Salt and sugar are all you really need to cure lemons, but I also like to incorporate aromatics and spices—like coriander or fennel seeds—to the mix. Playing with the spices from batch to batch keeps things interesting; it's a way to express your personal tastes. This basic method works with any citrus— lemon, limes, oranges, grapefruits, and so on.

Let the lemons cure for at least ninety days before using them. Once preserved, the lemons will last indefinitely, but I think they're best at the six-month mark. When ready to use, they will be quite salty. Only the rind, full of floral notes, is used. The flesh is scooped out and discarded. I also recommend rinsing off the finished rind before using to mellow out the flavor; in the restaurant, we pour hot water on the rinds and let them soak for thirty seconds.

Use preserved lemons the same way that you might use lemon zest—as an addition to sauces, roasts, vinaigrettes, and pasta fillings.

`Makes 12 preserved lemons`

9 cups kosher salt (1.53 kilograms)
3 cups sugar (610 grams)
1 tablespoon red pepper flakes
1½ teaspoons fennel seeds
1½ teaspoons coriander seeds
1½ teaspoons whole black peppercorns
3 bay leaves, crumbled
1½ pieces star anise, broken into small pieces
12 large Meyer lemons (about 3 pounds/1.36 kilograms)

To make the curing mixture, combine the salt, sugar, red pepper flakes, fennel seeds, coriander seeds, peppercorns, bay leaves, and star anise in a large mixing bowl. Set aside.

To prepare the lemons, hold one lemon, stem side down, on a cutting board. With a sharp knife, halve the lemon from the top, cutting almost to the bottom but stopping about ½ inch from the base. Rotate the lemon 90 degrees and slice again, stopping about ½ inch from the base. You are basically quartering the lemon but leaving the bottom intact so the lemon stays together. Repeat with the remaining lemons.

Pour ¼ inch of the curing mixture into a clean and dry 1-gallon glass jar. Hold one quartered lemon over the bowl of curing mixture, base side down. Spread the quartered sections open and pack the cavity with as much curing mixture as possible. Place the lemon, cut side up, in the jar. Repeat with more lemons—you'll get about 4 lemons per layer—until you get an even layer on the bottom of the jar. As each layer is completed, generously cover the lemons with curing mixture, then press down firmly with your fist to pack the lemons as tightly as possible. You are trying to squeeze as much juice out of the lemons as possible. Repeat the layering process until the jar is filled. When the jar is almost full of lemons, add curing mixture to reach the top of the jar, punching down on the mixture to get it as tight as you can. Seal the jar.

Reserve the remaining salt mixture, which should be about 2 cups, depending on the size of your lemons.

Store the lemon jar in a cool, dark place at room temperature. After 48 hours, the dry curing mixture in the jar should begin to change into a wet brine; around this time, the liquid level will drop below the top layer of lemons. When that happens, fill the jar to the top with the remaining salt mixture. Seal the jar again and let it rest in a cool, dark place for a minimum of 90 days, until ready to use.

Tomato Farfalle with Chicken Polpettine, Roasted Peppers, and Basil

When considering new dishes for the restaurant, we're always thinking about how a particular pasta "eats." It's a process of trial and error. We might have nailed the flavor of a dish, but how does the dish itself *behave*? Is it easy to eat? It's not a question unique to pasta dishes either; chefs need to ask the same questions for all dishes, whether it's a composed ratatouille or a simple sandwich. If it's difficult to eat, then what's the point?

I love the way farfalle eat. Short noodles move differently, and there is a reason why farfalle (Italian for "butterflies") are made commercially on a grand scale. In the pasta shape canon, they are outliers. Since they're made with egg dough (one of the few "short" shapes in this book made with egg dough), they have that rich, deep, eggy flavor. However, the small crimp in the middle—the bow tie's knot—gives the shape the dense texture of a semolina-based noodle like orecchiette or campanelle.

We have farfalle variations on the menu throughout the year. Maybe it's because of the familiar name, but farfalle are a perennial crowd-pleaser. They're almost always paired with some sort of meaty ragu (braised duck, slow-cooked pork, quail) and a leafy green of some sort. In the summer, I like to keep the formula simple: chicken meatballs, summer peppers roasted to a smoky sweetness, and a big handful of whole basil leaves.

Serves 4

Equipment
Pasta machine + Rolling pin + Straight wheel cutter (optional) Fluted wheel cutter + Baking sheets + Spray bottle

Store-bought option
Dried Farfalle or any short pasta

Farfalle
1 recipe Standard Egg Dough (page 7)
1.5 ounces tomato powder *available mail order
    or at specialty grocery stores (optional)

Chicken Polpettine
2 slices sourdough bread, crusts removed (75 grams)
1 cup whole milk (237 milliliters)
8 ounces minced or ground chicken, preferably dark meat
⅓ cup chopped prosciutto (50 grams)
1 tablespoon chopped fresh Italian parsley
1 tablespoon chopped fresh thyme
1 tablespoon chopped fresh savory
3 cloves garlic, finely chopped
1 large egg
½ cup grated pecorino cheese
Kosher salt
Freshly ground black pepper
¾ cup extra-virgin olive oil (140 grams)
1 cup diced yellow onion (136 grams)
½ cup diced carrots (68 grams)
½ cup white wine (118 milliliters)
Sachet: 1 tablespoon whole black peppercorns, 1 tablespoon fresh
    thyme leaves, 1 bay leaf, wrapped in cheesecloth and tied
    with kitchen string
3 cups chicken stock (710 milliliters; page 169)

Roasted Peppers
3 to 5 summer peppers (such as Jimmy Nardellos; 145 grams)
1½ tablespoons pure olive oil
2 teaspoons kosher salt

To Finish
Kosher salt
4 tablespoons unsalted butter (57 grams)
¼ teaspoon sherry vinegar
1 cup loosely packed whole fresh basil leaves
Freshly grated Parmigiano-Reggiano cheese, for finishing

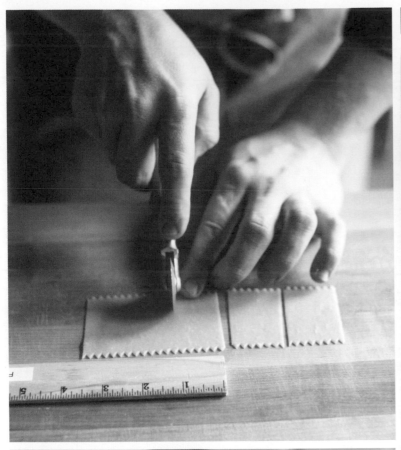

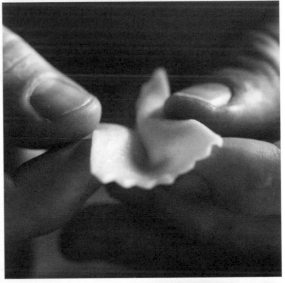

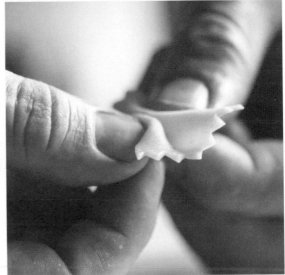

To make the pasta, follow the instructions for the Egg Dough (page 7), incorporating the tomato powder with the dry ingredients.

Dust 2 baking sheets with semolina flour and set aside.

Using a pasta machine, roll out the dough as instructed until the sheet is just translucent (see page 10). Cut a 2-foot section of the dough sheet and cover the rest of the dough with plastic wrap.

Using a straight wheel cutter or a knife and a ruler, cut the pasta into 1½-inch-wide strips. With a fluted cutter, cut across the strips every 2 inches, creating rectangles.

To make the polpettine, put the bread in a small mixing bowl, cover with the milk, and leave to soak for 30 minutes. In a large mixing bowl, combine the chicken, prosciutto, parsley, thyme, savory, and 1 teaspoon of the garlic. Squeeze the milk out of the bread and add the bread to the meat mixture. Stir the egg into the mixture to bind it. Add the grated pecorino. Season with salt and freshly ground black pepper. Polpettine can be made 3 days ahead and stored in the refrigerator.

To shape the polpettine by hand, gently form a heaping tablespoon or so of the meat mixture into a small ball. Transfer to a baking sheet lined with parchment.

Once the polpettine are rolled and ready, heat the oil on high heat in a 4-quart pot or Dutch oven. In two batches (unless you can fit them all in the pan at once without touching each other), sear the polpettine for about 5 minutes, or until well browned, occasionally turning to allow for even coloring. With a slotted spoon, remove the polpettine to a plate and set aside. Repeat with the second batch.

When all of the polpettine are browned and out of the pot, add the onions and carrots and sauté, still on high heat, until the vegetables are softened, about 8 minutes. Add the remaining garlic and cook for another 2 to 3 minutes, being careful not to burn it. Quickly add the white wine and herb sachet. Cook the wine down until it's almost evaporated.

Add the chicken stock and bring it to a simmer. Add the polpettine. Reduce the heat to low and gently simmer the polpettine for roughly 25 minutes. Remove the pot from the heat and let the polpettine cool in their braising liquid. Remove the sachet. Set aside.

Preheat the oven to 375°F.

To prepare the peppers, toss the peppers with the olive oil and kosher salt. Arrange the peppers evenly spaced on a baking sheet and roast until the skins are completely wrinkled and the peppers are charred, about 20 to 25 minutes. When done, put them in a bowl, cover with plastic wrap, and let them steam for another 20 to 30 minutes to loosen the skins. When fully cool, peel off the skin, remove the seeds, and julienne the flesh.

To finish, bring a large pot of seasoned water to a boil (see page 18).

In a 12-inch sauté pan, bring the polpettine and braising liquid back up to a simmer over medium heat. Add the julienned peppers. Season to taste with salt.

Drop the farfalle in the boiling seasoned water. At the same time, add the butter and the sherry vinegar to the sauté pan, stirring to create an emulsion

Once the pasta is cooked 80 percent through, until almost al dente, 2 to 3 minutes, add it to the sauté pan and increase the heat to high. Reserve the pasta water. Stir constantly, incorporating the pasta in the sauce. Continue to cook until the sauce coats the back of a spoon and the pasta is tender, about 2 more minutes. Remove from the heat and fold in the basil.

To serve, divide the pasta, polpettine, and sauce between four plates. Finish with freshly grated Parmigiano-Reggiano.

Spaghetti with Albacore Confit, Pole Beans, and Chile

So many of the recipes at Flour + Water are influenced by Emilia-Romagna and the rest of the northern half of Italy, but in the summer, I find myself looking more often to the south for inspiration. It's the time of year when olive oil reigns supreme, resulting in light, pungent dishes ripe with fresh garlic and red pepper flakes.

Here in Northern California, everyone talks about tomatoes and stone fruits as the true heralds of summer—and rightly so. But for me, it feels like summer when albacore tuna arrives. Albacore tuna is an environmentally sustainable fish, and when tuna comes to Bay Area waters, usually in June, it goes straight on the menu.

As with pigs, we only buy whole fish. So when our fish guy snags us a 30-pound, three-foot albacore tuna from the icy Pacific Ocean waters, we utilize every part of that fish over the course of several days. On day one, we'll butcher the tuna immediately and serve the center-cut chop that same night as a crudo appetizer. The precise slices of raw fish will be accompanied on the plate by halved Sungold cherry tomatoes, a drizzle of extra-virgin olive oil, pole beans, and red pepper flakes. We even roast the bones in our wood oven to create a rich, smoky fish stock. The next night, the cheeks and tail meat will get poached in olive oil into a *conserva* and then combined with the same ingredients—cherry tomatoes, pole beans, and chile—and served either as an appetizer or in a simple pasta dish.

When making the dish at home, high-quality canned tuna in olive oil is a good substitute for an easy weeknight dish. Use a 6-ounce can.

Serves 4

Equipment
Blender

Store-bought option
Dried Spaghetti

Tuna Confit
1 6-ounce fillet of albacore tuna (198 grams)
    (or 6 ounces canned tuna)
1½ teaspoons fennel seeds, toasted
1½ teaspoons cracked black pepper
Kosher salt
4 cups pure olive oil, or enough to submerge the tuna
    (960 milliliters)

To Finish
1½ cups cherry tomatoes, preferably Sungold (165 grams)
1½ cups summer pole beans (green haricots verts,
    yellow haricots, yellow wax beans, or all three; 115 grams)
3 tablespoons pure olive oil
½ cup red onion, diced (75 grams)
Kosher salt
3 cloves garlic, thinly sliced
½ teaspoon red pepper flakes
⅓ cup white wine (75 milliliters)
8 ounces homemade dried spaghetti (see Extruded Dough, page 16)
    or store-bought dried spaghetti (227 grams)
¼ cup reserved tuna cooking oil
    or oil from canned tuna
2 cups fresh baby spinach (55 grams)

To prepare the tuna, generously season the tuna fillet with the toasted fennel seeds, cracked black pepper, and kosher salt. Allow to rest, refrigerated, for at least 1 hour but no longer than 12 hours. When you're ready to cook, allow the tuna to come to room temperature, which should take about 30 minutes.

Preheat the oven to 250°F.

To poach the tuna, combine the olive oil and tuna in a deep ovenproof saucepan. The tuna should be submerged. Cook for 30 minutes, and then check to see if it's fully cooked through. It should flake apart when touched with a fork. Remove the tuna from the oil and set aside on a plate, but reserve the oil.

Blend the cherry tomatoes to a smooth puree in a blender. You should get about ¾ cup of puree; set aside.

Have an ice bath ready, and blanch the pole beans by cooking in salted boiling water until tender, 3 to 4 minutes. Remove from the water and immediately shock in the ice bath. When cool, remove from the ice bath, draining off any water, and pat dry with paper towels. Cut the pole beans into 2-inch segments and reserve in a bowl.

Heat a 12-inch sauté pan over medium heat. Add the olive oil. When it's shimmering, add the onions with a pinch of salt and sweat until translucent but not browned, 4 to 5 minutes.

To finish, bring a large pot of seasoned water to a boil (see page 18).

Add the garlic and red pepper flakes to the sauté pan with the onions and continue to cook until the garlic is translucent, 2 to 3 more minutes. Add the white wine and continue to cook until the liquid is reduced by half, about 1 minute. Add the tomato puree and bring to a simmer. Add the pole beans and return to a simmer. Flake the albacore and add to the pan, gently tossing to warm the tuna.

Add the pasta to the boiling water.

Meanwhile, add ½ cup of the pasta cooking water to the sauté pan and return to a simmer. Once the pasta is cooked 90 percent through, until almost al dente, add it to the sauté pan and gently toss to combine. Reserve the pasta water. Increase the heat to high to finish cooking the spaghetti, about 90 seconds. Add the ¼ cup tuna cooking oil and swirl the pan to create a sauce, constantly moving the pasta in the pan so it cooks evenly. If you need to add more pasta water to thin the sauce while the pasta finishes cooking, do so in small spoonfuls.

When the pasta is tender, remove the pan from the heat, fold in the baby spinach, and toss to wilt, about 30 seconds. Taste for seasoning and adjust with salt, as needed.

To serve, divide the pasta and sauce between four plates.

Trofie with Heirloom Tomatoes

There's a beautiful simplicity in a quick, barely cooked tomato sauce at the height of tomato season. I experience the same moment of revelation when I taste a perfect margherita pizza, or an expertly cut piece of sashimi.

But, as many chefs will tell you, simplicity is often the hardest thing to achieve. This summer sauce is a celebration of tomatoes, so it's important to keep the flavors clean and clear, just ever-so-slightly touched by the heat of the stove. The garlic should be there, but it is subtly and gently cooked—neither browned nor raw. The tomatoes themselves should barely be cooked throughout the process. First, they should only hit the boiling water for a few *seconds* to enable them to be peeled; later, in the pan, they'll kiss the oil in a quiet fry that highlights their natural acidity. You don't want the tomatoes or the juices to reduce into a thicker, concentrated sauce.

To accompany the tomatoes, tear up any soft summer herbs—basil, tarragon, chives, chervil, mint. You can't add too much of one leaf or the other.

A similar nonuniformity makes trofie special. They are small twists of semolina dough, with a quirkiness and imprecision emblematic of handmade pasta—each one will be a little different. In their native Liguria, trofie are most often paired with pesto. Here, their delicacy lets the light tomato sauce shine without overwhelming it. If you opt to buy dried pasta instead of making your own, gemelli is trofie's long-lost twin.

There are a few schools of thought for shaping the thin and wispy spiral trofie shapes. One way is to twist the dough between two palms to create the trademark spiral. I prefer curling the dough around a little metal spindle for a tad more consistency and ease of production. The spindle should be a straight piece of thin, round metal wire. A snippet from a metal clothes hanger works very well. About 8 inches long is preferable.

That said, most long, thin dried noodles—spaghetti, angel hair, and the like—will work just fine.

The sauce is a fresh, quick one for a warm weeknight at home. Extra-virgin olive oil, fresh tomatoes, and herbs—it's a dish that is the epitome of Italy . . . and California.

Serves 4

Equipment
8-inch piece of thin metal wire + Baking sheets

Store-bought option
Dried trofie, genelli, angel hair, or spaghettini

Trofie
1 recipe Hand-Rolled Semolina Dough (page 14)

To Finish
2 pounds heirloom tomatoes (907 grams)
Sea salt
¼ cup plus 3 tablespoons extra-virgin olive oil (105 grams)
½ cup minced shallots (60 grams)
8 cloves garlic, thinly sliced
1½ cups chopped summer herbs (any combination of soft herbs such as basil, tarragon, chervil, chives, and/or mint)
Freshly ground black pepper, for finishing
Red pepper flakes, for finishing (optional)
Freshly grated Parmigiano-Reggiano, for finishing

Dust 2 baking sheets with semolina flour and set aside.

To make the pasta, cut off a baseball-sized portion from the mass of dough. Place it on a flat wood surface and wrap the rest of the dough in plastic wrap.

Roll the chunk of dough between your hand and the board until you achieve a long, thick rope about 8 inches long by ½ inch wide. Using a knife or bench scraper, cut the dough crosswise into ⅛-inch-thick pieces (bean size). This may seem small, but it's okay.

If using your hands to roll the twist, for each trofie, roll the piece of dough gently between your palms to form a spiral shape that is about 1 inch long. Put the shaped pasta onto the prepared baking sheet, slightly apart. Don't let the trofie touch or they might stick together.

If using the wire to form the twist (my preferred method), for each trofie, gently roll the piece of dough with your fingers into a string about 2½ inches long. Lay the dough string at a 45-degree angle to the edge of your work surface. Lay the metal wire parallel to the edge of your work surface, putting its tip crosswise on the tip of the string that is close to your belly, folding the tip slightly around the rod. Using gentle and consistent pressure, push the wire straight away from you, rolling the dough along with the wire, keeping some space between the spirals. The dough will spiral around the wire. Use a light and smooth pressure; too much pressure will cause the dough to stick to the wire.

To release the dough from the wire, sprinkle it lightly with semolina if needed, and hold the trofie with your fingers while gently removing the wire. The finished shape should be about 1 inch long. Put each trofie onto the prepared baking sheet. Repeat with the remaining dough.

Have ready a bowl of ice water.

To finish, bring a large pot of salted water to a boil. With a knife, remove the stems of the tomatoes and score an X at the blossom end (cutting through the skin only, not the flesh). On a baking sheet, separate all the tomatoes by size into three groups (they don't have to be exact).

Blanch each group of tomatoes separately—about 10 seconds per group should do the trick, depending on their size. With a slotted spoon, quickly transfer them to the ice bath and then transfer them from the water to a baking sheet lined with a towel to cool. Once cooled, the skin should peel right off.

 seeds as possible and add the tomatoes to a mixing bowl. Season with sea salt. Allow to sit while you prepare the other ingredients.

Bring a large pot of seasoned water to a boil (see page 18).

Combine ¼ cup of the olive oil, the shallots, and the garlic in a cold 12-inch sauté pan over medium heat; bring the mixture to a gentle simmer, then decrease the heat to low. Sweat until translucent. You don't want the garlic to brown. This dish is all about the tomatoes; you don't want muddled, dark flavors.

Once the garlic and the shallots are tender, add the tomatoes, reserving the excess tomato liquid.

At the same time, drop the pasta in the boiling water.

Increase the pan heat to medium-high and almost fry the tomatoes in the olive oil. You want to tame the acidity of the tomatoes but avoid a concentrated tomato flavor. Once the pasta is cooked 80 percent through, until almost al dente, 2 to 3 minutes, add it to the pan. Return the pan mixture to a simmer and add the herbs and season with salt. Toss to combine. If the sauce is too dry, add in a scoop of the reserved tomato liquid at the very end of cooking. Remove from the heat.

To serve, divide the pasta and sauce between four plates. Garnish with freshly ground pepper, red pepper flakes, if using, the remaining 3 tablespoons of olive oil, and a generous amount of freshly grated Parmigiano-Reggiano.

Orecchiette with Rabbit Sausage and Padrón Peppers

Fresh orecchiette (translated as "little ears") is a thing to behold, a taste that most people have never experienced. If any fresh pasta speaks to the importance of texture, especially when compared to lesser storebought versions, it's orecchiette. The value of this pasta is found in its stretch marks, the hallmark of any hand-made orecchiette. Stretch marks perform the invaluable role of gripping the sauce, a prized quality that becomes most apparent in handmade pastas that have been made on porous wood.

Orecchiette are made with semolina dough, which is made only with flour and water—no eggs. It's a super-rustic style that hails from southern Italy, and compared to its eggy counterparts, the dough itself is very dense. In fact, it's so dense that orecchiette--and similar shapes made with this semolina dough, like cavatelli--are cooked differently, and longer, than other pastas. With these pasta dishes, we only cook the pasta halfway in the water; the other half of the cooking is done in the pan, while steadily adding stock, like one might cook a risotto.

Since the pasta is so hearty, it can stand up to big flavors, especially the spicy ones that are common in southern Italy.

No special equipment, not even a pasta machine, is needed to form orecchiette from scratch, which makes them especially good to make at home with a group of friends. All you need is a blunt-tipped knife and some practice.

Serves 4

Equipment
Butter knife + Baking sheets

Store-bought option
Dried orecchiette

Orecchiette
1 recipe Hand-Rolled Semolina Dough (see page 14)

To Finish
1 tablespoon pure olive oil
½ pound rabbit or other savory sausage, uncased and formed into 1-inch balls (227 grams)
½ cup diced red onions (66 grams)
¼ cup finely diced carrot, about ½ small carrot
4 cloves garlic, sliced
¼ cup white wine (60 milliliters)
1 cup chicken stock (240 milliliters; see page 169)
2 teaspoons extra-virgin olive oil
1 cup sliced Padrón peppers (69 grams)
1 tablespoon unsalted butter
2 teaspoons sherry vinegar
Freshly grated Parmigiano-Reggiano, for finishing

Dust 2 baking sheets with semolina flour and set aside.

To make the pasta, cut off a small, 2 inches by 5 inches, chunk from the semolina dough and cover the rest of the dough with plastic wrap. With your hands, roll the piece of dough into a rope about 1 foot long and ½ inch wide (similar to a thick pen's width).

Cut off a ½-inch piece of dough from the rope. Using a butter knife, push down very firmly on the far edge of the dough with the sharp edge of the blade, and with your other hand on the flat part of the blade held over the pasta, drag in toward your body. Basically, you're rolling the blade over the pasta.

When the dough has almost wrapped around the knife tip, insert your finger into the "dome" of the pasta. Make sure to scrape the whole piece of dough through, even as it starts to encapsulate your index finger. It should fold onto the tip of your finger. Keep it there.

Invert the dough over your other hand's thumb, creating an inverse dome. The orecchiette should be uniform in thickness. Stretch marks are good, because it creates a wrinkly surface that's great for catching sauce. Lift the orecchiette off your thumb with the fingertips of your other hand. Arrange the orecchiette on the prepared baking sheet. Repeat until you've run out of dough. You should have 80 to 90 pieces.

Leave the pasta uncovered to air dry at room temperature until ready to cook. You can keep them unrefrigerated for up to a day, but wrap the tray in plastic.

Bring large pot of seasoned water to a boil (see page 18).

In a 12-inch sauté pan on high heat, heat the 1 tablespoon olive oil. When hot, add the sausage. Cook, stirring occasionally, until evenly browned, about 1 minute. Add the onions and carrots. Cook until the onions are slightly translucent, about 2 minutes. Add the garlic, continuously stirring to make sure it doesn't burn. Once translucent, after about 90 seconds, add the wine. Cook the wine until the pan is almost dry, 4 to 5 minutes. Add the chicken stock, bring to a simmer, and decrease the heat to low.

Drop the fresh orecchiette into the boiling water. Once the pasta is cooked 80 percent through, until almost al dente, about 2 minutes, transfer to the sauté pan. Reserve the pasta water. Stir to incorporate the pasta and increase the heat to high.

Add the 2 teaspoons extra-virgin olive oil to the simmering pan sauce and fold in the Padrón peppers.

Let the pasta finish cooking in the meat sauce. When the pasta is tender, add the butter to the pan and stir quickly to emulsify. Add the sherry vinegar and season with salt to taste. Remove from the heat.

To serve, divide the pasta and sauce between four plates. Finish with freshly grated Parmigiano-Reggiano.

BIGOLI, THE *TORCHIO*, AND ULTRA-REGIONALISM IN ITALY

Bigoli is a pasta that hails from Venice, high in the northern reaches of Italy. Unlike many of its egg-and-flour counterparts in the area, bigoli dough has milk and butter as its key ingredients. Also, it's made with a *torchio*, a dramatic and unique pasta-making tool from the Veneto.

Perched on the edge of a table, ready for action, the *torchio* looks like some sort of medieval torture instrument. The mound of fresh dough is wedged into its chamber. The handle is cranked and turned, forcibly descending onto the dough, which is pushed through the brass die at the bottom and slowly extruded as long strands of pasta. Bigoli noodles stretch out through the bottom and are trimmed into lengths with a knife. The end result is a long, dense noodle similar in appearance to spaghetti.

In fact, the *torchio* taught me one of my best lessons in Italian ultra-regionalism. An American friend wanted me to bring him back a *torchio* from one of my trips to Rome, so I was frantically running to all the restaurant supply stores in the city to find one.

In every single Roman shop, the exchange was the same:
Me: "Hey, I really need a *torchio*. Do you have one?"
Shopkeeper: "*Scusi?*"
Me: "*Torchio?*"
Shopkeeper, finally taking pity on me, switching to English: "What is *torchio*? Is that something American?"
Me: "No, it's a pasta extruder."
Shopkeeper [staring blankly]
Me: "It's from the Veneto. For making pasta."
Shopkeeper [staring blankly]: "We are in Rome. Why would we have something from Venice?"

The lesson? Italy is wildly regional when it comes to cuisine, so much so that dishes and names are entirely unfamiliar from city to city. That's part of the reason I like to give traditional dishes a Bay Area twist—I think of Northern California as simply another region of Italy.

But if you find a *torchio*, know that it is an awesome tool and using it to make bigoli is very easy—and much cheaper than buying an extruder. If you can get your hands on one, either in the Veneto or online, I highly recommend it.

Makes 757 grams of dough

Equipment
Torchio + Baking sheets

Bigoli
270 grams 00 flour (1½ cups)
270 grams semolina flour (1½ cups)
3 tablespoons whole milk
3 large eggs (150 grams)
2 tablespoons unsalted butter
1¼ teaspoons kosher salt

To make the pasta, follow the instructions for mixing standard egg dough (page 7), using these ingredients. When the dough is a unified mass, let it rest for 15 minutes before starting to knead. This will allow the dough to hydrate. After 15 minutes, knead it for the standard 10–15 minutes (see page 7). Then let it rest *again* for the normal time, a minimum of 30 minutes, before putting it in the *torchio*.

Line a baking sheet with parchment paper and dust the parchment with semolina flour. Set the prepared baking sheet under the *torchio*. Dust another baking sheet with semolina flour and set aside.

To make the bigoli, open the top hatch of the *torchio*. Mold a small piece of dough into a small cylinder, about the same size as the cavity of the *torchio*. Close the hatch and turn the crank (don't worry if you hear hissing—it's just pressure releasing from the *torchio*). Once the extruded noodles are about 12 inches long, cut the bigoli by scraping the die with a knife or pastry scraper. Place the bigoli on the flour-dusted baking sheet (it's fine if they touch). Repeat until all the dough is used.

Bigoli with Fresh Shelling Beans, Tomato, and Pancetta

I'm making the call: This is my favorite pasta at Flour + Water. I think it's because it's just such a comforting dish. While hopping around Italy, I always joked that when people in Bologna have a bad day, they go home and eat tortellini in brodo to heal the pain; I think I'd get over crappy Yelp reviews and a stressful night on the line with a big bowl of bigoli with beans, tomato, and pancetta.

Even though it sounds simple, there's so much nuanced flavor and texture going on in the bowl. You can substitute dried beans, but fresh shelling beans are a particularly nice fit, simmered just enough that they're creamy but they still hold their shape. It's like the Italian version of pork and beans.

Then there's the bigoli—an extruded spaghetti-like pasta from the Veneto region that is traditionally made in a special hand-cranked machine called a *torchio* (see page 60 for more on the *torchio*). At first glance, the noodles may bear a resemblance to thick spaghetti, but upon closer inspection, they have a completely unique surface. It's rough and stretched, almost like pasta dreadlocks. You'll never see or eat a pasta that has more grip to the sauce.

You can easily substitute any long-strand semolina noodle—spaghetti, bucatini, linguine, and so on—for the bigoli, but if you can make or find it, do it.

Serves 4

Equipment
Torchio + Baking sheets

Store-bought option
Dried bucatini

Shelling Beans
1 cup fresh shelling beans (185 grams)
Sachet: 1 tablespoon whole black peppercorns,
    ½ bunch fresh thyme, and 2 cloves garlic, smashed,
    wrapped in cheesecloth and tied with kitchen string.
¼ yellow onion
¼ carrot
½ stalk celery
Kosher salt

To Finish
5¼ ounces guanciale, diced (150 grams)
1 medium red onion, diced (115 grams)
2 tablespoons minced garlic
1 cup San Marzano tomato puree (225 grams/8 ounces)
1 cup cooked shelling beans (185 grams)
½ teaspoon red pepper flakes
8 ounces bigoli (page 60) or dried spaghetti (230 grams)
1½ cups reserved bean cooking liquid (340 grams),
    with more set aside
1 cup dried bread crumbs (65 grams; page 65)
2 teaspoons fresh thyme, chopped
Freshly grated Parmigiano-Reggiano, for finishing

To make the beans, in a medium pot, combine the beans with the sachet, the onion, carrot, and celery. Add enough water to cover the beans by 1 inch, season with 2 large pinches of salt, and simmer over medium heat until the beans are cooked and have a creamy texture, about 30 minutes. Remove from the heat and cool to room temperature in the cooking liquid. Reserve the liquid; the bean liquor will be our cooking liquid for the pasta.

To finish, bring a large pot of seasoned water to a boil (see page 18).

In a 12-inch sauté pan on high heat, heat the guanciale. You want to render the fat for the pasta, and also crisp it up. Cook for 2 minutes, then decrease the heat to medium.

Continuously stir with a wooden spoon on medium heat until the guanciale is reduced to about half its size and has rendered out a fair amount of fat, another 4 minutes.

Reserve 3 tablespoons of the rendered fat and discard the rest. Stir in the onions and return the heat to high. Cook until the onion is translucent, 2 to 3 minutes. Add the garlic and cook for

1 minute. Add the tomato puree, drained shelling beans, and red pepper flakes. Once the mixture starts to simmer, decrease the heat to medium and cook for another 5 minutes. This isn't a slow-cooked red sauce; it's a flash tomato sauce, so we just want to marry the ingredients. Remove from the heat.

Drop the pasta in the boiling water. Cook the pasta about 70 percent through. For this dish, you want to cook the pasta more in the pan because the heartier your sauce is, the more time it needs together to marry the flavors.

Drain the pasta and transfer to the sauce; increase the heat to high. After about a minute, add the 1½ cups bean liquor. As it's reducing and concentrating, taste the pasta to see when it's ready. If it's getting too dry, feel free to add a splash of leftover bean cooking liquid or pasta water to balance the sauce. When ready, remove from the heat.

To serve, divide the pasta and sauce between four plates. Sprinkle the pasta with bread crumbs, thyme, and Parmigiano-Reggiano.

HOW WE MAKE OUR BREAD CRUMBS

Preheat the oven to 350°F.

Rip the bread into rough cubes. In a large bowl, toss to coat with olive oil and a pinch of salt. Bake until golden brown. Season with salt. Place in a large bowl and crush until reduced to fine crumbs, or place in the bowl of a food processor and process until fine.

Black Pepper Tagliatelle with Mussels, Lardo, and Corn

I'm allergic to shellfish, but since I never had fresh seafood growing up—aside from frozen shrimp (don't ask)—I didn't encounter this little problem until culinary school. My unfortunate affliction really hit home at one of my first real restaurant jobs. At Gary Danko, in San Francisco, I was tasked with breaking down about eighty lobsters a day. So there I was, a twenty-year-old scissoring endless crustaceans with an increasingly red face and swollen hands that resembled chorizo sausages. It made an already arduous task about a million times worse. By the time the lobsters were done, I looked like I had walked through a forest of poison oak.

Still, I always tasted the shellfish, both in the kitchen and as a diner—and I still do. (For the longest time, I had it in my head that if I taste and taste and taste shellfish, eventually I'll build some immunity. Well, I'm starting to suspect that it's having the opposite effect. I swear my shellfish allergy is worsening.)

As a chef, I think it's important to appreciate what all flavors can contribute to a dish. For example, I don't particularly care for ultra-bitter radicchio, but I try to understand how it can be used, and I often do use radicchio in the restaurant. Truth be told, I really appreciate the briny, salty, and clean flavors that shellfish bring to a dish. Those flavors find a nice home in a simple dish like black pepper tagliatelle paired with some sort of cured pork (I particularly like lardo here, but pancetta or bacon will also work).

Serves 4

Equipment
Pasta machine + Rolling pin + Baking sheets

Store-bought option
Dried tagliatelle or fettuccine

Black Pepper Tagliatelle
1 recipe Standard Egg Dough (page 7)
4 tablespoons freshly ground black pepper

Mussels
40 mussels (500 grams)
6 tablespoons kosher salt (64 grams)
3 tablespoons pure olive oil
1 small yellow onion, cut into small dice (65 grams)
½ cup diced fennel (65 grams)
3 or 4 whole sprigs of thyme
5 cloves garlic, sliced
½ cup white wine (120 milliliters)

To Finish
4 ounces lardo, cut into ½-inch cubes (115 grams)
4 cloves garlic, minced
1 cup corn kernels (140 grams)
3 tablespoons extra-virgin olive oil or lemon-infused olive oil
Grated zest and juice of 1 lemon
2 tablespoons chopped fresh Italian parsley
2 tablespoons chopped fennel fronds
Whole fennel fronds, for garnish

Dust 2 baking sheets with semolina flour and set aside.

To make the pasta, follow the instructions for standard egg dough (see page 7), incorporating the black pepper with the dry ingredients.

Using a pasta machine, roll out the dough to the $\frac{1}{16}$-inch-thick setting (see page 10). With a knife, cut the dough into 12-inch strips. Make two stacks of strips, four strips per stack, thoroughly dusting between layers with semolina flour. Allow the dough to dry for 30 to 45 minutes, or until the dough has a slightly dry, leathery texture. It should still be pliable. Fold each stack like a letter, forming three even layers.

Cut the folded dough into ¼-inch strips, shake off the excess semolina, and form into small nests on the prepared baking sheets.

To prepare the mussels, put them in a large bowl, sprinkle with 2 tablespoons of the salt, and set under cold running water for 1 hour. Every 20 minutes, empty the bowl, sprinkle with another 2 tablespoons salt, and set under running water. Repeat until the mussels are completely rinsed and free of dirt. To test if they're clean, rub them under water and shake to see if they release any dirt. Set aside.

Heat the olive oil in a sauté pan over high heat. Add the onion and fennel and cook until slightly softened, about 3 minutes. Add the thyme and the garlic and cook for another minute, stirring constantly. Add the mussels, stir to incorporate, and quickly add the wine. Cover and cook on high heat until all of the mussels have fully opened, about 2 minutes. Remove them from the pan and set aside in a bowl to cool.

Remove the mussel liquid to another bowl, and the onions and fennel to a separate bowl, and reserve; the pan juice will be your cooking liquid for the pasta later. You should have about 1½ cups. When cool enough to be handled, open the mussels and reserve the meat, discarding the shells.

Bring a large pot of seasoned water to a boil (see page 18).

To finish, in a 12-inch sauté pan on high heat, heat the lardo. You want to render the fat for the pasta, and also crisp it up. Cook for 2 minutes, then add the reserved onions and fennel. Cook until the vegetables are translucent, 2 to 3 minutes. Add the garlic, cook for 1 minute, and then add the reserved mussel liquor. Let simmer for 1 minute, then add the corn.

Drop the pasta in the boiling water. Once the pasta is cooked 80 percent through, until almost al dente, 2 to 3 minutes, add it to the sauté pan. Add 1 cup of the pasta water and, still on high heat, stir everything together. Add the olive oil, lemon zest, and lemon juice. Stir, and then fold in the chopped parsley and chopped fennel fronds. Remove pan from the heat and fold the mussels back in.

To serve, divide the pasta and sauce between four plates. Drizzle with olive oil and garnish with whole fennel fronds.

Corzetti Stampati with a Pesto Due

I never collected baseball cards or stamps as a kid, but I've got a pretty good collection of vintage pasta equipment these days. Whenever I'm in Bologna, I always make the rounds to my favorite kitchen supply shops for some irresponsible spending and impulse buying. When I visit other Italian cities, I seek out regional tools that I've never seen before, just like I always order the regional specialties in restaurants.

In Liguria, the corzetti stamp is that tool. The simple yet often ornate two-piece wooden stamps might actually be the most stylized of all the pasta-making tools. One half of the stamp cuts the dough into flat discs, and the other brands them. This two-piece set is carved out of local wood and almost resembles a wooden door handle that sits atop a pedestal. Once upon a time, family crests were carved into the molds; nowadays pretty much any design is fair game.

The dough for corzetti stampati is singular as well. It incorporates white wine, thereby giving it a completely unique consistency when cooked: more doughy, more chewy, more elastic. To make true corzetti stampati, you'll need an authentic wooden stamp—you can find them easily on the Internet—but home cooks can easily just cut 2-inch circles using a cookie or biscuit cutter, or even a cup. You'll lose the unique ridges on the finished pasta coins, but the unique chewiness of the dough will still shine.

Corzetti stampati have been on the menu since day one at Flour + Water. I still remember that dish: I served the pasta with braised squid and fava beans. Here we serve them with dueling pesto sauces typical of the region.

Serves 4

Equipment
Pasta machine + Rolling pin
Corzetti stamp or 2- to 2½-inch ring mold or cookie cutter
Mortar and pestle or food processor + Baking pan

Store-bought option
Dried corzetti, or any dried noodle you like

Corzetti Stampati
1 large egg
½ cup white wine (118 milliliters)
1½ cups (360 grams) 00 flour

Walnut Pesto
½ cup whole shelled walnuts
Kosher salt
Grated zest of ½ lemon
¼ cup extra-virgin olive oil (60 milliliters)

To Finish
3 ounces pole beans, cut on the diagonal into 1-inch segments (90 grams)
1 tablespoon pure olive oil
½ clove garlic, sliced
12 fresh basil leaves
½ cup Pesto (page 77)
½ cup Walnut Pesto
Freshly shaved Parmigiano-Reggiano, for finishing

Dust 2 baking sheets with semolina flour and set aside.

To make the pasta, in a bowl, mix the egg and the white wine. Mix with the flour following the instructions for mixing standard egg dough (see page 7). Using a pasta machine, roll out the dough to slightly over ¹⁄₁₆ of an inch (see page 10).

If you have a corzetti stamp, cut out dough rounds using the bottom of the stamp. Put the pasta disk between the two parts of the stamp and apply pressure to create the pattern. If you don't have a corzetti stamp, cut out dough rounds with a 2- to 2½-inch ring mold or cookie cutter. Set the corzetti stampati aside on the prepared baking sheet. You should have about 35 corzetti stampati.

Preheat the oven to 350°F.

To make the walnut pesto, toast the walnuts in an ovenproof sauté pan in the oven until completely toasted and fragrant, about 12 minutes, tossing them every 3 minutes. It's a good idea to always set a timer when toasting nuts, because they're easy to forget. A baking sheet also works fine, but the sauté pan gives you more surface contact with the hot pan—and makes them easier to toss.

You can use a food processor for this next step, but I prefer to use a mortar and pestle because it gives you more control over the grind. Place the nuts in a mortar and pestle, season with a pinch of salt, and begin lightly crushing them. You want to pound the nuts until they are coarsely ground but still very chunky. The nuts are ready when they're about the same size as the nuts in chunky peanut butter. It's important to keep this pesto chunky because it will add a much-needed layer of texture to the final dish. If using a food processor, make sure to only pulse the nuts so you don't turn them into walnut butter; keep it crunchy.

Add the lemon zest and olive oil and stir with a spoon to combine. Adjust salt to taste and set aside.

Have ready a bowl of ice water.

To finish, blanch the pole beans by cooking in salted boiling water until tender, 3 to 4 minutes. Remove from the water and immediately shock in the ice bath. When cool, remove from the ice water, drain, and set aside in a bowl.

Bring a large pot of seasoned water to a boil (see page 18).

Drop the corzetti in the boiling water and cook until about 90 percent cooked through, until almost al dente, about 2 minutes.

Right after you drop the pasta in the water, combine the olive oil and the garlic in a cold sauté pan. Turn the heat to high and cook until the garlic slivers just begin to soften, 1 to 2 minutes. You don't want to brown the garlic at all.

Add the pole beans and ¼ cup of the pasta water to the sauté pan and bring to a simmer. Fold in the fresh basil leaves and stir well to wilt them.

At this point, the pasta should be ready. Transfer the pasta to the sauté pan and continue cooking until the water gently coats the pasta but has not completely evaporated.

To serve, spread an equal amount of the pasta and sauce in an even layer on four flat plates. For each serving, spoon the two pestos over the top. Finish with freshly shaved Parmigiano-Reggiano.

Pesto

To me, pesto is the ultimate summer dish—partly because of its micro-seasonality. Even though you can get supermarket basil all year in the Bay Area, perfectly vibrant fresh basil is only available for a few select weeks of the dog days of summer.

One of our farmers, Martin Bournhonesque, grows Genovese basil for us; it's slightly more floral and subtly sweet than the more common variety. Martin's farm has no name, and chefs have to navigate a waiting list to get on his distribution radar, but when he comes in with his basil on one random summer morning, it's well worth it.

The other big appeal of pesto is its lightness. Bright, green, and vegetal, it is a stark contrast to the meat-centric and butter-basted dishes of Emilia-Romagna that tend to dominate the restaurant in the colder months. Genoa, Liguria's seaside capital and the birthplace of pesto, is only a few hours' drive from Bologna, but it trumpets a completely different cuisine. With apologies to focaccia and minestrone, pesto is probably Liguria's biggest contribution to the food world. We make different types of pesto depending on how it will be used in the dish. If we want a chunkier pesto, we grind it in a mortar and pestle, the old-fashioned way. Other pesto dishes require a smoother puree and more concentrated flavor, in which case the blender is the preferred route.

Most pesto in Liguria—and, for the most part, in America—is raw. And the basic structure of any pesto is the same: raw leaves (basil, arugula, nasturtium, ramp, radish, and so on), nuts (pine nuts, walnuts, hazelnuts), garlic, cheese, salt, and olive oil. That said, pesto is highly regulated in Liguria, from the exact geographic origins of the basil (Liguria), the pecorino (Sardinia), and the nuts (Tuscany), all the way down to recipe specifics, like the number of leaves in the sauce (thirty).

I like my pesto with a bright green color, a more concentrated flavor, and an oily, sauce-like consistency, so we do things a bit differently than the gospel method. Our standard recipe requires blanching the basil leaves very quickly. That's not the only detour. Usually, the cheese in pesto is a tangy sheep's milk pecorino; I opt for Parmigiano-Reggiano, which has enough nuttiness that allows us to skip another traditional component, the pine nuts.

Makes about ½ cup

Equipment
Blender

---

2 cups loosely packed fresh basil leaves
½ cup extra-virgin olive oil (118 milliliters)
¼ clove garlic, sliced
½ teaspoon kosher salt
3 tablespoons finely grated Parmigiano-Reggiano cheese

Bring a pot of salted water to a boil over medium-high heat. Have ready a bowl of ice water.

Blanch the basil leaves in the boiling salted water for 30 seconds. Remove the leaves with a spider (or other handheld strainer) and quickly shock them in the ice water bath to stop the cooking (this sets the chlorophyll and helps keep the vibrant green color).

When the leaves are completely cool, remove them from the ice water and gently squeeze them to remove excess moisture. Be careful not to squeeze too hard, as you don't want to remove the delicate and flavorful essential oils. Let dry on paper towels.

Put the basil leaves, olive oil, and garlic in a blender and puree until completely smooth, about 90 seconds. The blending step will also warm the puree to nearly 120°F, which will bring out the bright green color. Transfer the puree to a mixing bowl and fold in the salt and Parmigiano-Reggiano. Fresh pesto should be served within a day of two after it's made. Store refrigerated.

Squid Ink Chitarra with Sea Urchin, Tomatoes, and Chiles

As much as I like to wax poetic about pasta mythology and get creative with new dishes, that's only a sliver of my job as a chef. At the end of the day, a restaurant is a business and it is my job as an owner to push, motivate and give direction to every member of the team.

Even though our restaurant doesn't open until 5:30 p.m. every day, my workday starts as soon as I wake up. It's a whirlwind. I touch base with managers, I meet with my chefs and cooks, I ignore calls from the media, I taste new dish ideas, I coordinate the night's menu, and I put out any fires—those are mostly metaphorical.

With any business, numbers matter. So when a dish isn't selling, something has to change. Part of that puzzle is knowing which ingredients are customer favorites and which ingredients are historically a harder sell. For example, you put pork belly on a dish in San Francisco, and boom, it's flying off the stoves. The same goes for slow-cooked eggs, bone marrow, prosciutto, and pretty much anything with the word "crisp" in the description.

Squid ink chitarra is typically a harder sell. It's such a delicious dish—the squid ink gives the dough its signature black color and a slight salinity—but diners are often afraid of the unknown. Maybe they're not enthralled with the idea of eating a cephalopod's ink, or maybe jet-black pasta simply isn't appealing. Or perhaps they're unfamiliar with chitarra, a pasta made with a *chitarra* (guitar), a badass pasta tool with a lute-like set of strings. When a sheet of dough is draped over the strings and pressed with a rolling pin, the *chitarra* cuts long, straight-edged noodles.

If we trotted out the *chitarra* tool tableside and sliced the pasta in the dining room, we'd have a best seller on our hands, but whatever the reason, squid ink pastas usually need a little "dressing up" on the menu. When we use squid ink in heartier shapes like corzetti stampati, we can pair it with top sellers like pork belly or sausage. But chitarra is a delicate noodle, at its best when paired with the light, coastal, summer flavors of its native Abruzzo like squid, crab, and tomato. So if pork belly isn't an option, the next best way to get a dish selling is by adding the pork belly of the ocean: sea urchin, which is what we've done here.

Squid ink and sea urchin are available at any reputable seafood counter. If you don't have a *chitarra*, you can cut the noodles by hand.

Serves 4

Equipment
Chitarra tool (optional) + Pasta machine
Rolling pin + Baking sheets

Store-bought option
Dried squid-ink spaghetti

Squid Ink Chitarra
⅓ cup squid ink (25 grams)
1 large egg
½ cup water (120 grams)
3 cups 00 flour (540 grams)

To Finish
12 ounces whole squid (340 grams)
6 tablespoons pure olive oil (106 milliliters)
3 cloves garlic, slivered
⅓ cup white wine (79 milliliters)
1 heirloom tomato, diced (140 grams/1 cup)
1 teaspoon minced chile (Calabrian)
1 cup water
8 ounces fresh squid ink chitarra pasta, or any thin long noodle (226 grams)
½ cup chiffonade of mint
Grated zest of ½ lemon
½ teaspoon freshly squeezed lemon juice
Purslane, for garnish (optional)
8 whole lobes sea urchin (70 grams)

Dust 2 baking sheets with semolina flour and set aside.

To make the pasta, in a bowl, mix the squid ink, egg, and water. When thoroughly mixed, make the pasta dough following the instructions for standard egg dough (see page 7). Using a pasta machine, roll out the dough to the thick setting (see page 10) slightly over $\frac{1}{16}$-inch.

If you are cutting the dough with a *chitarra*, first cut a section of rolled dough that is the same length as your *chitarra* and place it atop the strings. Using a rolling pin, lightly press (but don't cut) the dough, forming a slight indentation—enough to set it so it won't slide. Then, press with more force to cut the dough through the strings into noodles. Put the noodles on the prepared baking sheet. Repeat with the remaining dough.

If you are cutting the dough by hand, cut a 2-foot section of the rolled-out dough sheet, and cover the rest of the dough with plastic wrap.

Using a knife, cut the dough into 12-inch segments. Make two stacks of strips, with four strips per stack and dusting between layers with semolina flour. Allow the dough to dry until it has a leathery texture, 30 to 45 minutes. It should still be pliable. Fold each stack like a letter, forming three even layers. Cut individual square-edged, long noodles by slicing segments off the edge of the folded dough that are the same width as the dough's thickness. Shake off the excess semolina and form into small nests on the prepared baking sheets.

Bring a large pot of seasoned water to a boil (see page 18).

To finish, prepare the squid. To clean the squid, wearing rubber gloves, remove the head from the body. Directly below the eyes, use a knife to separate the tentacles from the remainder of the head. Remove the beak from the tentacles. Remove the innards and cartilage from the body. Discard the head, innards, and cartilage.

Slice the body into ¼-inch rings. For small squid, leave the tentacles whole. Otherwise, find the smallest tentacle and cut everything to that size to allow for even cooking time. Put the pieces on a paper towel to dry off excess moisture before searing. You want the squid as dry as possible when you cook it.

Heat 1 tablespoon of the olive oil in a 12-inch sauté pan over high heat until the oil is shimming and slightly smoking, a little over a minute. Quickly sear half of the squid in the hot oil until caramelized, about 1 minute. Remove to a platter and set aside. Heat another tablespoon of the olive oil and repeat with the remaining squid. Remove to the platter with the rest of the squid and set aside.

Add another tablespoon of the olive oil and cook the garlic until it's fragrant and tender but not browned, about 1 minute. Add the white wine, reduce by half, and fold in the squid. Add the tomatoes, the chile, and the 1 cup water; bring to a simmer, cover, and gently braise the squid until tender, about 15 minutes.

Drop the pasta in the boiling water.

Add the remaining 3 tablespoons of olive oil to the sauté pan and stir quickly to emulsify the sauce. Decrease the heat to low.

Once the pasta is cooked 80 percent through, until almost al dente, 2 to 3 minutes, add it to the pan and increase the heat to high. Reserve the pasta water. Cook until the pasta is tender, about 1 minute more. If the pasta is too dry at this point, you can add a splash of reserved pasta water, so that the sauce coats the back of a spoon. Remove from the heat and fold in the mint, lemon zest, and juice.

To serve, divide the pasta and sauce between four plates. Garnish with purslane and 2 lobes of sea urchin per serving.

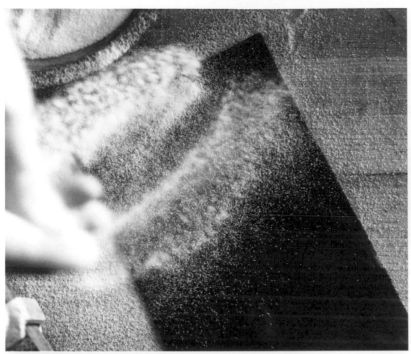

Ricotta and Tomato Tortelletti in Brodo

On my last night in Bologna, when my initial stint working in Italy was winding down, my friend Marcello called me into his kitchen. Taking me aside with a dead serious look on his face, he sat me down and pulled up a chair.

"Tom," he said, speaking slowly in his broken English. "I need to talk to you."

Like a kid in the principal's office, I thought I had done something terribly wrong.

"Your restaurant," he continued, unflinching. "When you go back there . . . it is very important to me . . . that you must promise . . . that you will never . . . ever serve . . . a tortellini . . . ever! . . . that is not in brodo."

The people of Emilia-Romagna, especially Bologna, take their tortellini very seriously. The only way it's ever served is in capon broth—their brodo. Every respectable salumeria in Bologna sells fresh tortellini; along with mortadella, tortellini in brodo might as well be the city's official food. We serve a fairly traditional tortellini in brodo during the colder months (page 164) but it's a little too heavy for the summer, so I decided to do a new version.

The idea for this dish started with the tomato water that takes on the role of the "brodo" in the bowl. Incidentally, the idea for the tomato water was a utilitarian one: We always seem to have too many tomatoes during the height of the season, so we invented a vegetarian summertime riff on that old wintry Emilia-Romagna classic.

Honestly, the lovely people of Bologna would probably be horrified at this version of their sacred dish, which is why we don't use the traditional tortellini shape. And so, the tortelletti—which is the original name for the shapes that would eventually be called tortellini.

But, hey, at least the "tortelletti" are technically in brodo.

You should prepare the tomato water 1 to 2 days ahead of time.

If you opt to buy ricotta instead of making it, I recommend getting some from your local dairy—raw, if possible.

Serves 4

Equipment
Food processor + Pasta machine + Rolling pin + Fluted wheel cutter + Piping bag + Spray bottle + Baking sheets + Vegetable peeler

Store-bought option
Any fresh, cheese-stuffed tortellini

Tomato Water (Brodo)
5½ pounds extremely ripe tomatoes, cored and coarsely chopped
2 tablespoons kosher salt

Cow's Milk Ricotta
8 cups whole milk (1.9 liters)
1 cup heavy cream (237 milliliters)
1 tablespoon kosher salt
¼ cup freshly squeezed lemon juice (59 milliliters)

Filling
2 cups cow's milk ricotta (435 grams)
½ cup freshly grated Parmigiano-Reggiano cheese (50 grams)
½ cup extra-virgin olive oil (118 milliliters)
Grated zest and juice of 1 lemon
2 tablespoons minced chives
1 tablespoon kosher salt
1 teaspoon cracked black pepper

Tortelletti
1 recipe Rav Dough (page 7)

To Finish
1½ cups cherry tomatoes, halved (235 grams)
2 tablespoons extra-virgin olive oil
1 cup chervil leaves, for garnish
Chunk of Parmigiano-Reggiano cheese, for shaving

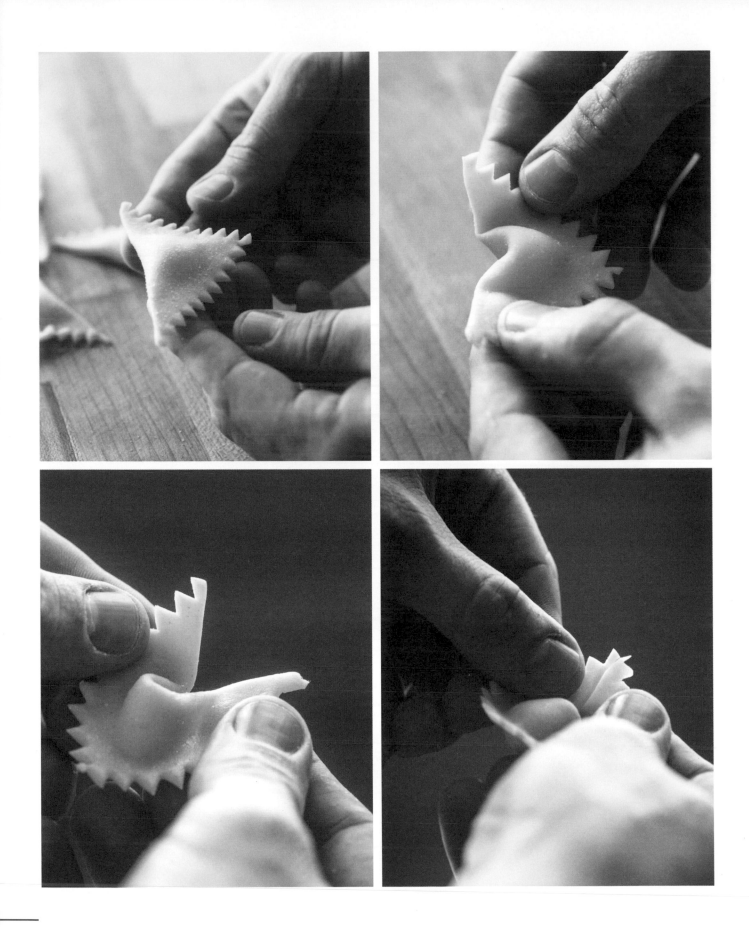

Line a strainer (or colander) with cheesecloth and set it over a large bowl.

To make the tomato water, combine the chopped tomatoes in a bowl with the salt.

Working in about four batches, using about 4 cups at a time, gently pulse the tomatoes in the work bowl of a food processor fitted with the steel blade. You only want to coarsely chop the tomatoes, not fully puree them. The more you puree them, the lower the yield. Depending on your machine, it should only take about five big pulses to give you the ideal chunky texture.

Pour the chopped tomatoes into the prepared strainer, refrigerate, and allow to rest for 18 to 24 hours to allow the liquid to fully extract. Don't let the liquid strain for more than 24 hours or the tomato water will taste dull and stale. You should have about 4 cups tomato water. It will keep up to 48 hours, refrigerated.

To make the ricotta, place a colander inside a larger bowl, line the colander with cheesecloth, and set aside.

Slowly bring the milk, cream, and salt to simmer in a heavy 6-quart pot over medium-low heat, stirring occasionally, about 15 minutes. When the milk barely begins to simmer (about 180°F to 200°F), add the lemon juice. Stir constantly until the mixture starts to curdle, about 4 more minutes.

Remove the pot from the heat. It is very important that you do not simmer the milk after the curds begin to separate or the curds will become dense and dry. Allow the curds to rest for 10 minutes.

Pour the milk mixture into the lined colander to strain. The milk will have already formed hard curds—ricotta cheese. It is ready to be used after 5 minutes because not much more moisture will be extracted by further draining. Reserve the liquid for another use.

To make the filling, in a large mixing bowl, combine the ricotta, Parmigiano-Reggiano, olive oil, lemon zest and juice, chives, salt, and pepper. (Personally, I like this filling to weigh heavier on the black pepper, especially when paired with tomatoes.) Set aside.

Dust 2 baking sheets with semolina flour and set aside.

To make the pasta, using a pasta machine, roll out the dough until the sheet is just translucent (see page 10). Cut a 2-foot section of the dough sheet and cover the rest of the dough with plastic wrap. Cut the sheet of dough into 2½-inch squares with a straight wheel cutter, or a knife and a ruler. Using a piping bag or spoon, place a heaping teaspoon of filling in the middle of each square, leaving ¼ inch of dough bare around the edge.

Fold the filled square so the opposite corners meet, pressing to create a triangle. Use a quick spritz of water from a spray bottle to help seal it if necessary. Gently but firmly seal the top corner and remove the air pocket by moving your fingers down the sides from the point down simultaneously, caressing the filling to make a tight, airless pillow.

With a fluted cutter, trim the two sealed edges, leaving about ¼ inch of pasta around the filling. Then, with the point of the triangle toward you, connect the facing corners, overlapping them while pushing the outer edges up. Working quickly, place the tortelletti on the prepared baking sheets, spaced apart. Don't let the tortelletti touch each other or they may stick together. Repeat until you run out of dough or filling. You should get 45 to 50 pieces.

To finish, bring a large pot of seasoned water to a boil (see page 18).

In a smaller pot, bring the tomato water to a gentle simmer over medium heat.

Drop the pasta in the boiling seasoned water. When using brodo, we cook the pasta half in the water and half in the brodo, so after about 2 minutes in the pasta water, transfer the tortelletti to the simmering tomato water. Cook the pasta until al dente, another 1 to 2 minutes.

Remove from the heat and add the cherry tomatoes.

To serve, divide the pasta and brodo between four bowls. Finish each portion with a light drizzle of olive oil and a generous heaping of chervil. Using a vegetable peeler, shave large ribbons of Parmigiano-Reggiano over the finished dish.

PARMIGIANO-REGGIANO

Some of the best meals of my life have come in fancy restaurants, but more have turned up unexpectedly in memorable places that serve simple food. I have fond memories of eating cured meat and cheese on a wall overlooking a centuries-old vineyard, engrossed in conversation with a good friend and drinking good wine. On more than one of those occasions, a crumbly chunk of Parmigiano-Reggiano was involved.

Real, legit Parmigiano-Reggiano—not domestic "parmesan" or Grana Padano or any other copycats—gets grated on top of nearly every one of our finished pasta dishes. There are a few exceptions, like seafood dishes, but for the most part, the recipes in this book are topped off with a healthy grating of Parmigiano-Reggiano. At the restaurant, we go through one wheel a week, no small feat considering that the wheel is a giant 80-pound chunk of cheese.

Anointing pasta with Parmigiano-Reggiano is an Italian tradition that goes back centuries. Not long after Dante famously wrote of purgatory and paradise in the *Divine Comedy*, a fellow Italian poet named Giovanni Boccaccio devised imaginary fourteenth-century worlds of his own. In the *Decameron*, Boccaccio describes a society of hedonists who live in Bengodi, where there is a mountain of grated Parmigiano cheese. At the top of the mountain, a group of people do nothing but make macaroni and ravioli—and then roll the pasta down the hill, dusting them with grated cheese for people below to pick up and eat as they pass by. I am very sad that this place does not exist.

Parmigiano takes its surname from the province where it is made, Reggio-Emilia. That official designation didn't come until the twentieth century, though the cheese has been relatively unchanged since the thirteenth century. The actual production of one wheel of Parmigiano-Reggiano—not to mention the strict geographic and production regulations that surround it—is impressive.

It starts with the source: giant white cows that get milked twice a day—every night and every morning—365 days a year. The evening milk sits overnight as the fat separates from the rest of the liquid. In the morning, the skimmed milk is combined with whole milk fresh from the cow just minutes earlier.

The two milks—1,200 liters worth—are mixed with calf rennet and the previous day's whey in a massive copper vat. The milk coagulates in a few minutes and is then cooked.

The *casaro* (cheesemaker) uses a traditional tool called a *spino*—basically a giant whisk—to break up the curds. As the milk cooks and undulates in the vat, the granules sink to the convex bottom. An hour later, two cheesemakers use a wooden paddle to bring the soft, solid mass to the surface. It's drained in cheesecloth and sliced in two, meaning each wheel of Parmigiano-Reggiano has an identical twin floating around somewhere in the world.

It takes 600 liters of milk and roughly 12 cows to make one wheel of Parmigiano-Reggiano. That said, even in light of the strict regulations, *casaros* will swear that the finished product is a direct result of their skill. Most of the cheesemakers have been doing the same job for decades, repeating the same process morning after morning.

Once removed from the cooked milk, each mass of cheese is stuffed into a cylindrical mold with the familiar markings, which denote the cheese's individual number, month of production, and so on. Throughout the entire process, inspectors from the consortium—the governing body of the Parmigiano-Reggiano world—check the cheeses; if there are any irregularities, the wheel is discarded. The cheese is moved from the humid production room into a side room, where, still warm to the touch, it dries for a few days before being submerged in a saltwater brine. After nearly a month under water, the cheese is moved to its final resting place on a shelf among thousands of other wheels. There, in a sprawling, dark, temperature-controlled storage room filled with row upon row of cheese, it ages for anywhere from 12 months to years. When it's ready to eat, the wheel is cracked open with a trio of chubby, short cheese daggers.

A wheel of Parmigiano-Reggiano, like any other naturally aged cheese, is alive right to the day that you cut into it. To this day, the best cheese course of my life took place in the massive aging room of a Parm house as the boss cracked into a three-year-old wheel. It was the first time that oxygen had touched the aged curds in over three years, and tasting the unoxidized center was a moving experience, akin to eating a freshly sliced watermelon in the height of summer.

When buying Parmigiano-Reggiano, always try to get a chunk that is freshly cut from the wheel, and use it as soon as possible. Once cut, cheese begins to oxidize, and in turn, the flavors and aromas gradually dissipate over time. Try to avoid buying cheese that has been Cryovac-packaged in plastic, as it mutes the complexity of the cheese.

Corn and Crescenza Cappelletti with Bitter Honey

I have nightmares about taking this dish off the Flour + Water menu. We introduced it during our first summer of business, somehow, during that first summer, the corn and crescenza cappelletti became our signature. Aside from the pasta shape (cappelletti means "little hats"), the dish isn't based on any specific Italian tradition. It's a labor-intensive dish; nonetheless, it was a best seller, so we trudged through and served the dish throughout the summer.

And then we decided that the dish was done. No more. We wanted to keep things fresh. And so, the dish was gone forever . . . until it came back the next year, that is.

The ban lasted only a week the following summer. We resurrected it due to popular demand, and at the end of the day, our restaurant is for our guests. Now it's firmly entrenched as a summer staple.

Why is it so popular? Partly because the American palate responds to sweetness in savory dishes—look at ketchup with French fries. The natural sweetness of corn pairs nicely with the fresh tang of crescenza cheese, which gives the pasta filling what we like to call the "perfect ooze" factor.

Bitter honey is different from normal honey; it's more balanced and pairs well with the sweet corn in the dish. It's a handy condiment to have around the kitchen and worth experimenting with. If you don't have bitter honey, just omit the honey drizzle; do not use normal honey. See Sources, page 250, for online retailers.

Serves 4

Equipment
Blender + Pasta machine + Rolling pin
3-inch ring mold or cookie cutter + Piping bag
Baking sheets + Spray bottle

Store-bought option
Any fresh, cheese-stuffed ravioli or tortellini

Filling
2 tablespooons pure olive oil
1 medium yellow onion, diced (255 grams)
Kosher salt
1 medium clove garlic, minced
3 cups white corn kernels (from about 3 ears), cobs reserved (450 grams)
1⅓ cups crescenza cheese (336 grams)
½ cup freshly grated Parmigiano-Reggiano cheese (50 grams)

Corn Stock
3 cobs of corn (left over from the filling), cut into thirds
½ medium yellow onion, thinly sliced (128 grams)
6 whole black peppercorns
1 bay leaf
4 cups water (946 milliliters)

Cappelletti
1 recipe Rav Dough (page 7)

To Finish
6 tablespoons unsalted butter (85 grams)
1 cup corn kernels, from about one ear of corn (150 grams)
1 cup corn stock (235 milliliters)
2 tablespoons minced fresh chives
Freshly squeezed lemon juice
Kosher salt
Freshly grated Parmigiano-Reggiano cheese, for finishing
Bitter honey, like chestnut, cardoon, or artichoke, for drizzling
Nasturiums for garnish, optional

To make the filling, heat the olive oil in a 12-inch sauté pan over medium heat. Once the oil is hot, add the onion and a pinch of salt. Sweat the onion until it is completely translucent and tender, 12 to 15 minutes. Add the garlic and the corn, stirring constantly. Cook until the corn is translucent, about 10 minutes. Remove the pan from the heat and add the crescenza cheese, stirring so it melts. Immediately transfer the corn mixture to the jar of a blender and puree until smooth. It's important to puree while the corn is still warm to get the smoothest texture possible.

Transfer the puree to a bowl and stir in the Parmigiano-Reggiano cheese. Season with salt, keeping in mind that both the Parmigiano-Reggiano and crescenza cheeses are salty. The end result should have the consistency of a thick sauce. Refrigerate, covered, until fully cooled.

To make the corn stock, in a large stockpot combine the cobs, onion, peppercorns, and bay leaf. Cover with water. Bring to a boil over high heat. Decrease the heat to medium and simmer for 45 minutes, checking occasionally to make sure it's not scalding. Strain, discard the solids, and refrigerate or freeze, covered, in an airtight container until ready to use. Makes about 3 cups. The stock will last 2 to 3 days refrigerated.

Dust 2 baking sheets with semolina flour and set aside.

To make the pasta, using a pasta machine, roll out the dough until the sheet is just translucent (see page 10). Cut a 2-foot section of the dough sheet and cover the rest of the dough with plastic wrap.

Using a 3-inch ring mold, cut out rounds of dough. Using a piping bag or a spoon, place one teaspoon of the filling in the middle of each dough round, leaving ¼ inch of dough around the edge bare. Fold the circle in half to create a half-moon shape. Use a spritz of water from a spray bottle to help seal it if necessary.

To form the shape, hold the half-moon pasta parallel to the ground with both hands. With the curved side of the pasta closest to you, bring the points together, moving the edges away from your body (not up) while gently nudging up the outer flap to form a circular shape that resembles an old-fashioned sailor hat (which is where the shape gets its name). Seal the points together. Place the pasta firmly on the work surface, making sure the finished "hat" will stand up on a plate. Working quickly, place the cappelletti on the prepared baking sheets, spaced apart. Don't let the cappelletti touch each other or they may stick together. Repeat until you run out of dough or filling. You should get 35 to 40 pieces.

To finish, bring a large pot of seasoned water to a boil (see page 18).

Add the butter, corn kernels, and the stock to a cold 12-inch sauté pan and place over high heat. Bring to a simmer, swirling constantly to create an emulsion.

At the same time, drop the pasta in the boiling water.

Once the pasta is cooked 80 percent through, until almost al dente, 2 to 3 minutes, add it to the sauté pan. Reserve the pasta water. Continue cooking over high heat until the pasta is fully tender and the sauce coats the back of a spoon. Add the chives and season with the lemon juice and salt.

To serve, divide the pasta and sauce between four plates. Finish with Parmigiano-Reggiano and drizzle with bitter honey.

AUTUMN

I LOVE COOKING IN AUTUMN, probably more than any other season. When summer turns into fall, the season always reminds me of my childhood on the East Coast, when the leaves began to turn and a crisp nip in the air punctuated the increasingly shorter days.

Summer is, in my opinion, the easiest season to cook in. During that time, the Flour + Water menus often have more southern Italian influences, simply due to the abundance of gorgeous vegetables at the market. As this bounty dries up and the temperatures drop (usually after San Francisco's annual weeklong October heat wave), we find ourselves looking northward for inspiration.

Our autumnal menus start to take on the darker shades of the meat and produce that come into season. Sauces are made with red rather than white wine and Prosecco. The vibrant reds, greens, and yellows of summer slowly give way to the dark, rich ingredients of fall: kale, cauliflower, mushrooms, Brussels sprouts, and warm spices.

Long braises start to figure more prominently. No matter whether you grew up in New Jersey or San Francisco, Marrakech or Munich, odds are you have memories of a house filled with the rich aromas of a dish that has been cooking all day. Braises are a distinctly cold weather staple, and the results are noticeable; low and slow cooking methods will always bring a nuance of flavor that is impossible to achieve from quick cooking.

Agnolotti dal Plin

This dish hearkens back to the lavish feasts thrown by Italian dukes once upon a time. During these celebrations, copious amounts of roasted meat were made; the leftover roasted meat was used the next day for agnolotti dal plin.

Centuries later, we're basically employing that same mindset. Agnolotti dal plin are a great way to utilize meat trimmings from the previous night's meal, and to be honest, that's the main reason that this dish is on the menu throughout the year at Flour + Water. We get whole animals all the time, and we never want to squander anything; everything gets used.

Agnolotti dal plin is one of the most classic, by-the-book pastas we do at the restaurant; it's a dish that I learned while working under chef Michael Tusk at Quince. It's a slightly different shape from the standard ravioli-like agnolotti that are usually filled with vegetables, cheese mixtures, or both. Whenever *plin* ("pinch") is involved, tradition calls for a meat filling. The pinch is essential to this pasta's shape, a little well that is agnolotti dal plin's trademark "pocket," perfect for catching sauce.

In this recipe, we use equal amounts of pork, chicken, and rabbit for depth of flavor. But the thing about meat fillings like this is you can tweak the ratios depending on whatever meat you have available, as long as the total amount of meat (here, 9 ounces) is maintained. For example, if you have some chicken left over from the night before, mix it with some leftover prosciutto. The idea is that you use what you have—nothing goes to waste. It's what they do in Italy, and it's what we do in the restaurant.

Serves 4

Equipment
Meat grinder or food processor + Pasta machine
Rolling pin + Straight wheel cutter (optional) + Fluted wheel cutter
Piping bags (optional) + Baking sheets + Spray bottle

Store-bought option
Any small, fresh, meat-stuffed pasta, like tortellini

Filling
3 ounces pork shoulder, cut into 1-inch cubes (85 grams)
3 ounces boned chicken thighs, cut into 1-inch cubes (85 grams)
3 ounces rabbit loin, cut into 1-inch cubes (85 grams)
Kosher salt
2 tablespoons neutral oil, like canola, grapeseed, or vegetable oil
2 tablespoons pure olive oil
1 small onion, diced (90 grams)
½ cup red wine (120 milliliters)
2 cups loosely packed spinach, coarsely chopped
¼ teaspoon sherry vinegar
1 large egg
¾ cup freshly grated Parmigiano-Reggiano cheese)
1½ teaspoons grated nutmeg
Freshly ground black pepper

Agnolotti dal Plin
1 recipe Rav Dough (page 7)

To Finish
1 cup chicken stock (235 milliliters; page 169)
½ cup unsalted butter (113 grams)
4 whole sage leaves
Freshly grated Parmigiano-Reggiano cheese, for finishing

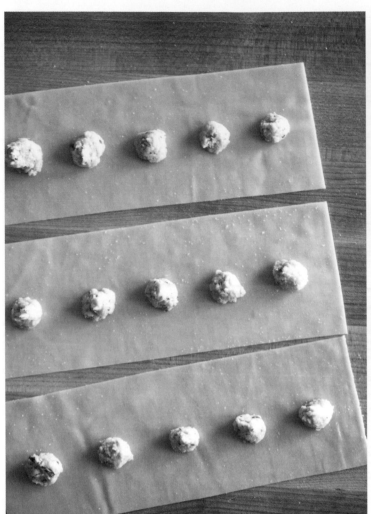

To make the filling, in a large bowl mix the pork, chicken, and rabbit and season with a few pinches of salt. Allow to rest for about 30 minutes. Heat the canola oil in a 12-inch sauté pan over high heat. Once hot, add the seasoned meat and cook, stirring occasionally, until the meat is caramelized and deeply browned, about 5 minutes. Remove the meat to a plate and set aside.

In the same pan over high heat, add the olive oil and the onion. Cook for about 4 minutes, scraping the bottom of the pan with a wooden spoon to release the fond (the caramelized meat on the bottom of the pan) until the onions are well caramelized, about 10 minutes. Add the red wine and cook until the pan is almost dry, 1 to 2 minutes. Add the spinach and cook until just wilted, about 1 minute. Remove the vegetables to a bowl and set aside until completely cool.

Combine the onion mixture with the browned meat in a bowl and stir until well incorporated. Put the warm meat mixture through a grinder, using a medium die, into a bowl. If you don't have a meat grinder, use a food processor to grind it to a smooth texture or chop it as finely as you can by hand.

Once the meat is ground, add the vinegar, egg, Parmigiano-Reggiano, and nutmeg and season with black pepper and salt. Mix well. This will make about 1 cup of filling.

Dust 2 baking sheets with semolina flour and set aside.

To make the pasta, using a pasta machine, roll out the dough until the sheet is just translucent (see page 10). Cut a 2-foot section of the dough sheet and cover the rest of the dough with plastic wrap.

With a straight wheel cutter or a knife and a ruler, cut the sheet of dough in half lengthwise, forming two strips that are about 3 inches wide. Using a piping bag or a spoon, place 1 teaspoon of filling onto the sheet in a row, leaving ½ inch between dollops. Each inch of dough should have one dollop of filling in the center. Take the edge closest to you and fold it over—

away from you—to comfortably cover the filling but still leaving about ¼ inch of dough bare at the far edge. Use a spritz of water from a spray bottle to help seal it if necessary.

To form the individual agnolotti dal plin, hold your thumb and index finger perpendicular to the table and pinch the dough between the lumps of filling. Start on the right side of one strip and work your way down the line, one shape at a time. Once the pinch is created, seal each agnolotti individually by gently pressing the rest of the dough over the filling and removing any air pockets in the front edge.

Using a fluted cutter, trim the entire edge directly in front of the filling, cutting as close as you can get to the filling without breaking the seal. For the final agnolotti-forming cuts, using a fluted cutter, quickly and with some force, cut them one by one directly in the middle of the "pinch." The trademark pocket should form with the swipe. Place the agnolotti on the prepared baking sheet, spaced apart. Don't let them touch or they might stick. Repeat until you run out of dough or filling. You should get about 75 pieces.

To finish, bring large pot of seasoned water to a boil (see page 18).

Drop the pasta in the boiling water. In a cold 12-inch sauté pan add the chicken stock, butter, and sage leaves. Turn the heat to high and bring the mixture to a simmer.

Once the pasta is cooked 80 percent through, until almost al dente, about 2 minutes, transfer to the sauté pan. Stirring constantly but gently so as not to break the agnolotti, finish cooking the pasta in the sauté pan, still on high heat. This should take about 3 minutes. Toward the end of cooking, swirl the pan vigorously to create an emulsion and keep the sauce from breaking. The sauce should coat the back of a spoon.

To serve, divide the pasta and sauce between four plates. Finish with freshly grated Parmigiano-Reggiano.

A CULTURE OF PORK

The story of pork in Emilia-Romagna is the story of salumerias. And the story of salumerias is the story of Franco Macchiavelli—a lifelong salumeria owner and worker. Every morning Franco arrives for work at Bruno e Franco la Salumeria, his business on the cobblestone path of Via G. Oberdan, nestled in the heart of Bologna. He wears the same ensemble every day: a maroon cap, maroon bow tie, and maroon apron, set against a starched white collared shirt. He takes pride in his appearance, keeping the apron clean and perfectly folded.

At his salumeria, he works with skill and grace behind the counter, smoothly slicing prosciutto and cutting off perfectly imperfect chunks of Parmigiano-Reggiano as he chats with customers. He's the kind of guy who easily conducts conversations with all his customers, whether he knows them or not. Maybe they'll talk about the latest issue in local politics, or maybe Franco will drop some knowledge about one of the olive varieties in his shop. His manner is not brash; he is soft-spoken, with Old World charm, almost deferential to his customers. His hospitality comes alive when discussing his favorite topic, the history of salumerias in Bologna.

In the back of his salumeria—a small stockroom with shelves of olive oil, jugs of wine, jarred tuna, and canned mortadella—Franco puts out a tray of sliced meat, pours some Lambrusco in paper cups, and tells the tale that is fundamental to understanding the tradition of fresh pasta in Bologna: the story of pork in Bologna.

Emilia-Romagna is one of the richest regions in all of Europe, thanks to a vibrant economic history that has given birth to industry giants like Ferrari, Maserati, Ducati, Lamborghini, and even Barilla. Then there are the region's worldwide food contributions, many of which are now tightly regulated by the state: balsamic vinegar, Parmigiano-Reggiano cheese, mortadella, prosciutto di Parma, and so on.

But none of that would have been possible without a little black pig. The fathers of the great-grandfathers of those heads of industry, the Lamborghini executives, Maserati suits, and Barilla bosses? Once upon a time, they all washed pigs. Pork built Emilia-Romagna; it's embedded in their society. And according to many old-timers there, these big industries threaten to flatten the old traditions. But we're getting ahead of ourselves.

Centuries ago, before the Middle Ages or Renaissance, little black pigs roamed the region's acorn-filled forests and hills. It sounds like some idyllic fairy tale, but it's true. The indigenous spiky-haired pigs known as Mora Romagnola were much smaller than the hogs of today; they were omnipresent, both wild and cultivated. Things stayed that way until the early twentieth century, when the more familiar pale and hairless breed of pigs was imported into Italy from England. These new pigs—appropriately dubbed "Large Whites"—were much bigger and grew faster than their black-haired predecessors. Since the farmers could get more bang for their buck with the English imports, the Mora Romagnola breed was cast aside. In a matter of decades, they were assumed to be all but extinct until a small herd was found in the forest in the 1950s. Now there's a movement to preserve the indigenous heritage pigs.

Like most successful endeavors, a little luck was also involved in the rise of Emilia-Romagna's pork culture. There was a second component: salt.

In Bologna, the city's governors during the Middle Ages—the signori—ruled the town and created guilds, which were the trade organizations that regulated all the components of the local economy. Two guilds were dedicated to the pork industry: one was the salaroli and the other was the lardaioli.

The salaroli controlled the salt, an industry that sparked many a war in Italy and elsewhere in the world. A network of canals once pulsed through Bologna, not unlike Venice to the north. Bologna is not directly on a major river thoroughfare, so those canals were essential to trading with the outside world. Boats were loaded with salt in nearby cities (Venice was one common trade partner) and then traveled to Bologna. The salaroli were the only group in the city that was allowed to work with salt, and hence pigs. In a world sans refrigeration, meat had to be preserved in salt. Only the salaroli could butcher the pigs, and in turn, they also preserved them. The salaroli's emblem was a mortar, a reference to Bologna's prized meat, mortadella.

Once the pork was salted by the salaroli, it went off to the lardaioli, the group that sold the pork. And living up to the name, the lardaioli also received the lard from the butchers and made candles and soap for the city. The two guilds were separate, but they worked together.

The lardaioli were the precursors to the salumeria. The traditional Bolognese salumeria acts as a curator, handpicking the best artisan goods—meats, cheeses, olives, pastas—from local producers. Even going back to the age of guilds in Bologna, the salumeria never cured its own meat; it only sold the meats provided by the salaroli. It's a system that lasted for centuries, until Napoleon did away with the guilds at the turn of the eighteenth century. By then, the culture of pork was already firmly established in Emilia-Romagna. In subsequent

centuries, technology—namely, electricity—changed the production of pork products, but the culture remains—and so does the salumeria. To this day, salumerias like Franco's are the place for Bolognese citizens to buy local goods, including prosciutto, mortadella, and fresh pasta.

Everything in Bologna is connected through the salumeria.

This is the history that permeates Bologna, and the world into which Franco was born. He grew up in the country, well outside the walls that encircle the city. His family was poor, like many others in the first half of the twentieth century. All fifteen of his family members were crammed into one little mountain cottage. They grew up on polenta. More familiar Bolognese staples of today, like tortellini and mortadella, were fancy foods, reserved for special occasions. He snacked on chestnuts from the fields. The rest of the year it was polenta, polenta, polenta.

Growing up in Italy when Franco did, kids had a choice: study or choose a profession. Franco did not want to study. But then again, he didn't want to work, either. He yearned for a life of singing and painting. Neither of those were possible

for a peasant boy in the hills of Emilia-Romagna. (A half century later, those artistic inclinations don't seem so far-fetched; Franco practically speaks in poetry. Sure, the sonnets might be about cured pig parts, but the guy was born with romanticism in his blood.)

Franco chose work and began as an apprentice in a salumeria well outside the city limits. And, as he puts it, once he put on that apron, he never took it off again.

He didn't think much of working in a salumeria at first. It was a job, nothing more, nothing less. As time passed, however, he found his passion. He explains that in the same way that he yearned for an artistic life once upon a time, he soon found ways to express himself—through the salumeria.

Unlike the other work alternative, in a factory, the job was dynamic. For the first four years he worked at the salumeria, young Franco never talked to a customer. He didn't even get to work near the counter. He was in the back of the salumeria, cleaning, grinding, and basically doing all the grunt work.

Eventually his boss let him handle one customer. He did well, so he got another, and another, and so on. Success in hospitality, as explained by Franco, is making sure that customers leave happy. His work was noticed. One day, an older man and established salumeria owner named Bruno Bellotti came looking for this boy in the countryside who was so good at serving customers. They went into business together and eventually opened a new salumeria in the center of Bologna. It was 1985. Their plan was to safeguard the salumeria tradition that was slipping away from an Italy under siege from McDonald's, supermarkets, and microwaves. Decades later, their salumeria is still carrying the torch for Bolognese traditions, preserving its culture. Franco was gracious enough to take me in and let me work in his shop. It was there that I embraced a culture of pork that would prove essential to Flour + Water's own restaurant culture, and the model also inspired us to open a salumeria of our own in San Francisco, just down the street from the restaurant.

At Flour + Water, pork quickly became a driving force for the restaurant. If pigs can support an entire region like Emilia-Romagna, why not a restaurant?

More than any other animal, pigs speak to how we want to cook in the restaurant. Between the three restaurants on our block, we usually get four pigs a week, roughly twelve hundred pounds total. With the possible exception of a duck, no other animal lends itself so completely to full utilization; the skin of the pig is as valuable as the leg. We don't have the capacity to break down a side of beef in the restaurant, but a whole pig or two fits perfectly—and it sells in the dining room.

Pork's versatility is also key. One week the pork loin might be chopped up into a tortellini filling; another week it might be roasted whole for a group in the private dining room. Much of that improvisation comes from the pig's characteristics. The more we work with local ranchers, the more we understand the intricacies of the products we buy. With pigs, the variations of region, diet, and species are paramount.

We get pigs year-round from Devil's Gulch Ranch, a family farm north of the city, in Marin County. Devil's Gulch produces pigs that are both muscular and fatty—and also delicious. Owners Mark Pasternak and Myriam Kaplan-Pasternak, who have run the farm since 1971, cross Yorkshire sows with Duroc or Berkshire boars. The sows are pastured along with their piglets until the piglets are weaned, and the piglets are then finished with local Nicasio Valley cheese, whole-grain breads, brewers' grain, and tortillas. Even pigs of the same breed in another place in America, like South Carolina, will taste different from our pigs. Ours are the pigs of Northern California, raised on the hills of the North Bay, with flavors that reflect our terroir.

We're lucky to have forged a long-lasting relationship with Mark. We've even colonized a spare area of his apple orchard to grow herbs and produce for the restaurant, and when I go up to visit the ranch, I'll often bring a few fallen apples to the pigs. Aside from the activity being oddly enjoyable for me—kitchen work gets claustrophobic, and I'll take every opportunity I can to get out of the city—it's just pretty cool that I can be tossing apples to a dozen pigs, knowing that in time, a couple will be coming to the restaurant.

Above all, the culture of pork at Flour + Water is a fundamental example of what makes the restaurant special and sustainable. When we opened the restaurant, using the whole pig was the starting point for our entire cooking style. We planned dishes around it, and as we grew, those same principles carried over to other facets of the business.

A culture of pork was the basis for Flour + Water, both in Emilia-Romangna and in our early days in the Mission, but from that, an entirely new culture arose in the restaurant: our own.

MORTADELLA

"Il colore è roseo, il profumo inebriante, il sapore unico."

That's how mortadella is poetically described on the menu at Franco's salumeria in the center of Bologna. It roughly translates to a haiku-like phrase along the lines of "The color is rosy, the perfume intoxicating, and the flavor unique." Maybe it's the gentle lilt of the language, but poetry seems to appear around every corner in Italy. Political graffiti on the streets comes in verses, and the sweaty guy who pulls your espresso at the local cafe is ready to quote Dante.

Sliced, cubed, or whipped, on bread or in pasta, mortadella has always been king in Bologna. It's a food that is inextricably linked with the city itself, so much so that centuries ago a city law stated that mortadella could only be made within the stone walls of Bologna. Every log of the mortadella bore an official stamp, and that exclusivity made it a food for the rich, not the poor.

The limited production of that era, though, wasn't the only factor in its exclusivity. Whereas prosciutto, for example, was made from the small legs of the indigenous black pigs that roamed the countryside, the more exclusive mortadella was made from the pigs' more prized fatty cuts. It wasn't until centuries later that the bigger legs of the enormous English white pigs sparked the rise of prosciutto's stock. But for centuries, mortadella trumped prosciutto in value.

No one knows for sure where the name "mortadella" originated, but there are a few theories. One school of thought holds that the name stems from *"mirto"* (myrtle), a Sardinian spice used in cured meat. But according to my salumeria friend and mentor, Franco, there is a "more true version": the word comes from *"mortaio,"* the mortar and pestle used to grind the spices that go into mortadella.

Despite mortadella's exclusivity to Bologna, it is found throughout the world, thanks to one key factor: the Università di Bologna. Since the eleventh century, students from around the world would come to the University of Bologna, billed as the world's oldest continuously operating university. While in the city, students would, of course, fall in love with the local delicacy. When they completed their university studies, the students would scatter to their homes across the globe—bringing mortadella back with them. Thus, mortadella spread, basically going viral in its own medieval way and cementing Bologna's fame as a culinary mecca. To this day, the motto of the city is *Bologna la dotta, Bologna la grassa*, which translates to "Bologna the doctor, Bologna the fat." The phrase speaks to the city's two claims to fame: its university and its rich culinary tradition.

Mortadella is different from many other Italian salumi in that it's first cooked and whipped before casing, similar to hot dogs. It starts with the same pork cuts used in sausage or salami: a combination of meat and fat back, finely ground together in a food processor at a stable temperature to ensure emulsification. In the Middle Ages, early versions of mortadella were made with cinnamon, nutmeg, and other strong spices that were used essentially to mask the flavor of subpar meat (similarly overwhelming spices were used with prosciutto at the time).

Mortadella remains a pantry staple in Emilia-Romagna. It's most often eaten sliced and unadorned as a cold antipasto, but it's also a handy filling for tortellini, fattisu, and other straightforward meat-stuffed pastas. It's cubed, cooked, and incorporated into sauces; oftentimes in restaurants, you'll see it whipped with cream into a silky mousse.

Mortadella Fattisu with Pistachios

Mariquita Farm near Watsonville, about 90 miles south of San Francisco, is one of the few local farms that provides produce to the restaurant on a year-round basis. We get all kinds of fruits and vegetables from them, from strawberries to orange Cheddar cauliflower. During the cooler months, they always bring us tons of beautiful savoy cabbage. At first, I didn't always know what to do with it, but as the Flour + Water pasta program evolved and grew, I wanted to find a pasta that would specifically highlight this exceptional cabbage.

Problem was, I couldn't think of a pasta shape that uses cabbage in a starring role, so we did some research. As it turned out, there was one right under my nose, one from Emilia-Romagna that was literally *built* for cabbage: fattisu.

Fattisu is a stuffed pasta with a candy wrapper–like shape, but fatter and rounder compared to the similar caramelle (page 228). It's found especially in Piacenza, one of the region's northernmost cities, along the Lombardy border.

There, savoy cabbage grows along the Po River and is a staple ingredient of the city. Like the area's famous ham, culatello, the cabbage also relies on the river's famous fog to flourish. It's a fog unlike any other I've seen. San Francisco's fog tumbles over arching hills and violently whips through the postcard bridges; the Po is protected by a lurching, low fog that slowly rolls off the peaceful river and kisses the crops every morning at sunrise. The cool, wet breezes that come off the river make the cabbage heads clam up and close the leaves. That is the best time to pick the cabbage.

Ingredients that rely on fog? Sounds like a dish that would do well in San Francisco.

Serves 4

Equipment
Food processor + Pasta machine + Rolling pin
Straight wheel cutter (optional) + Fluted wheel cutter
Piping bag (optional) + Spray bottle + Baking sheets

Store-bought option
Any fresh, meat-stuffed pasta

Filling
2 tablespoons olive oil
1 pound mortadella, cut into ½-inch cubes (450 grams)
1 small yellow onion, cut into small dice (150 grams)
1 tablespoon unsalted butter
1 large savoy cabbage, cut into 1-inch dice (360 grams)
½ teaspoon kosher salt
⅓ cup white wine (75 milliliters)
1 tablespoon whole-grain mustard
1 tablespoon apple cider vinegar
1⅓ cups freshly grated Parmigiano-Reggiano cheese (142 grams)

Fattisu
1 recipe Rav Dough (page 7)

To Finish
1½ cups pork or chicken stock (355 milliliters; page 169) or store-bought
5 tablespoons unsalted butter (71 grams)
2 teaspoons whole-grain mustard
1 tablespoon minced fresh Italian parsley
1½ teaspoons apple cider vinegar
Kosher salt
Freshly grated Parmigiano-Reggiano, for finishing
2 tablespoons pistachios, toasted and coarsely chopped

To make the filling, in a 12-inch sauté pan, heat the olive oil on medium-high heat until hot but not smoking. Add the mortadella and cook, stirring occasionally, until lightly browned, about 4 minutes. Remove the mortadella and reserve. Add the onion and cook until tender, about 8 minutes. Add the butter, cabbage, and salt and cook over medium heat for 2 minutes. Add the white wine and cook until the pan is almost dry, about 12 minutes. Transfer the cabbage to the work bowl of a food processor fitted with the steel blade and pulse until it's finely diced; add the mortadella and onion-cabbage mixture and continue pulsing until the filling is coarsely pureed. Fold in the mustard, apple cider vinegar, and Parmigiano-Reggiano and let cool completely before using. Once cooled, refrigerate or freeze, covered in an airtight container, until ready to use. Frozen filling can be thawed in refrigerator for 24 hours. You should have about 4 cups. The filling will last 2 to 3 days refrigerated.

Dust 2 baking sheets with semolina flour and set aside.

To make the pasta, using a pasta machine, roll out the dough until the sheet is just translucent (page 10). Cut a 2-foot section of the dough sheet and cover the rest of the dough with plastic wrap.

Using a straight wheel cutter or a knife and a ruler, cut the pasta sheets into rectangles measuring 2¼ inches by 2¾ inches. Using a piping bag or a spoon, place 1 teaspoon of filling in the center of each rectangle. Fold one long edge just over the filling (like you are folding a letter) and then roll through to finish the fold. Use a spritz of water from a spray bottle to help seal it if necessary. Gently press out the air around the filling by running your fingers from the tip of the triangle downward, creating one airtight lump in the middle. Twist each end of the pasta 180 degrees (one half turn) in opposing directions and flatten the ends so the pasta looks like a wrapped caramel.

Trim the edges using a fluted wheel cutter. Working quickly, place the fattisu on the prepared baking sheets, spaced apart, until ready to cook. Don't let the fattisu touch each other or they may stick together. Repeat until you run out of dough or filling. You should have about 50 to 60 pieces.

To finish, bring a large pot of seasoned water to a boil (see page 18).

Bring the stock to a simmer in a 12-inch sauté pan over high heat and reduce by half. Once the stock has been reduced by half, add the the butter.

At the same time, drop the pasta in the boiling water.

Add the mustard and the parsley to the pan. Once the pasta is cooked 80 percent through, until almost al dente, about 2 to 3 minutes, add it to the pan, swirling until the sauce coats the back of a spoon. Add the apple cider vinegar and cook until the pasta is tender, about 2 minutes. Season with salt.

To serve, divide the pasta and sauce between four plates. Finish with grated Parmigiano-Reggiano and toasted pistachios.

Cocoa Tajarin with Brown Butter–Braised Giblets, Butternut Squash, and Sage

I was eating dinner at my friend Franco's house in a small village outside Bologna. At the time, I was in the midst of working at the salumeria owned by Franco and his wife, Grazia. That night they served a cocoa pasta. Despite my bias against gratuitous sweetness in savory dishes, I had to admit the cocoa gave the dish an earthy flavor, with an underlying bitter kick.

Fast forward a few years to an October Sunday night at Flour + Water. We had just gotten through a crazy busy weekend, and thanks to two super-busy nights in a row, we basically ran out of food. As we were writing up that night's menu, we realized we needed a new pasta. Scrounging through the walk-in refrigerator, we could only find duck giblets. Duck giblets! What to do with duck giblets? The cooks started the process of brainstorming a dish around the giblets: What combination of flavors work? What makes sense in the restaurant and is practical for the kitchen? Braising the hearts and gizzards in nutty brown butter was a natural fit, but it needed balance, via some sweetness (butternut squash!) and an herbaceous hit (sage?).

The final piece was the pasta itself. The tajarin shape was an easy call—it's a very thin, traditional Piedmontese pasta that's traditionally accompanied by a ragu of organ meats, though usually from rabbits or chickens. (The word *tajarin* is regional dialect for "tagliarini," a long, thin egg noodle common throughout Italy). And then I had a flashback to that night at Franco's house: what if we tried to make a cocoa-flavored pasta? Sure enough, the cocoa component fit perfectly to complete the puzzle, and a version of the dish has become a mainstay at the restaurant.

Serves 4

Equipment
Pasta machine + Rolling pin + Baking sheets

Store-bought option
An extremely thin noodle, like angel hair or spaghettini

Cocoa Tajarin
1 recipe Standard Egg Dough (page 7)
1¼ ounces cocoa powder

Roasted Butternut Squash
¼ cup unsalted butter (56 grams)
½ pound butternut squash, peeled and cut into
    ¼-inch cubes (227 grams)
4 sprigs sage
Kosher salt
Cracked black pepper

Braised Giblets
8 ounces duck giblets, cleaned and silver skin removed (227 grams)
1 teaspoon kosher salt
¼ cup unsalted butter (69 grams)
1 small red onion, cut in small dice (70 grams)
4 cloves garlic, minced
½ teaspoon tomato paste
½ cup red wine (118 milliliters)
3½ cups chicken stock (828 milliliters; page 169)

To Finish
½ cup unsalted butter (137 grams)
3 ounces duck livers, cut into ½-inch cubes (85 grams)
Kosher salt
6 leaves fresh sage, cut in chiffonade
2 teaspooons sherry vinegar
Freshly grated Parmigiano-Reggiano cheese, for finishing

Dust 2 baking sheets with semolina flour and set aside.

To make the pasta, follow the instructions for Egg Dough (see page 7), incorporating the cocoa powder with the dry ingredients.

Using a pasta machine, roll out the dough to slightly thinner than $\frac{1}{16}$ inch (see page 10). With a sharp knife, cut the dough into 12-inch-long strips. On the prepared pan, make two stacks of strips, four strips per stack; thoroughly dust between the layers with semolina flour. Allow the dough to dry until it has a slightly dry, leathery texture but is still pliable, 30 to 45 minutes.

Fold the dough into thirds. With a knife, cut the edge of the folded dough into strips as thin as you can make them while maintaining whole noodles; the final thickness should be similar to that of angel hair pasta (which is a good dried substitute). Shake off the excess semolina and form into small nests on the prepared baking sheets.

To prepare the squash, heat a 12-inch sauté pan over high heat. Add the butter and cook until it is bubbling and slightly golden-brown. Add the squash, the sage, and a pinch of salt and cracked black pepper; cook, stirring every few minutes, until the squash is tender, 8 to 10 minutes. The squash should be slightly golden brown and caramelized. Remove from the heat and set aside to cool.

To prepare the giblets, season them with salt.

Heat a 3-quart saucepan over medium heat. Add the butter and stir. Once it starts to bubble and brown, add the giblets. At this point you're browning the butter while lightly coloring the giblets. Stir with a wooden spoon, constantly moving the giblets gently in the brown butter, almost as if you're basting them. Cook until slightly crisp on the outside, about 8 minutes. Transfer to a plate and set aside to cool.

Discard half the butter from the pan. Add the red onion and increase the heat to medium-high. Cook for 2 minutes, then add the garlic and cook 1 more minute. Add the tomato paste and cook for 1 minute. Add the red wine, stir well, and cook until the pan is almost dry, 2 to 3 minutes. Add the chicken stock and the giblets and increase the heat to high. Bring to a simmer, then decrease the heat to low to obtain a gentle simmer. Cover and let simmer until the meat is tender and almost falling apart, about 1½ hours. You should be able to cut the meat with a fork or spoon. Remove from the heat and cool the meat in the braising liquid until it comes to room temperature. Remove the giblets from the pan and chop them into ½-inch dice; add them back to the braising liquid and cool until ready to use.

To finish, bring a large pot of seasoned water to a boil (see page 18).

Heat a 12-inch sauté pan over high heat. Add 2 tablespoons of the butter and cook until browned, 1 to 2 minutes. Add the duck livers and a pinch of salt and sear them in the brown butter for about 1 minute, being careful not to overcook the livers. Remove the livers and set them aside on a plate, leaving the brown butter in the pan. Add the braised giblets and braising liquid to the pan and deglaze, bringing the liquid to a simmer over high heat.

Drop the pasta in the boiling water. Once the pasta is cooked 80 percent through, until almost al dente, about 30 seconds, transfer the pasta to the sauté pan. (Tajarin is a very thin noodle and will cook very quickly.) Add the roasted squash, sage, sherry vinegar, and the remaining butter and cook until you achieve a thick, sauce-like consistency, about 1 minute. Fold in the duck livers and remove from the heat.

To serve, divide the pasta and sauce between four plates. Finish with freshly grated Parmigiano-Reggiano.

Pumpkin Tortelloni with Sage and Pumpkin Seeds

The sweet and savory filling for the tortelloni—a bigger version of tortellini, closer to a dumpling—is traditionally made with pumpkin, nutmeg, and Parmigiano-Reggiano. But beyond that starting point, the regional variations are countless, differing even between neighboring villages. Every town puts their own spin on the same dish. In Imola they incorporate crushed amaretti cookies in the filling; 30 minutes down the road you might find raisins or candied fruits mixed in. In Modena, the dish is drizzled with copious amounts of their signature balsamic vinegar. It goes on.

Our twist: toasted pumpkin seeds in the sauce, to give a little crunch and nuttiness. And brown butter sauce to coat the pasta.

We have a large variety of heirloom pumpkins in Northern California, so we use the best pumpkins directly from the farm. We often opt for Cinderella pumpkins in the restaurant, which are great for purees and fillings because they are naturally low in water. Pumpkin is the most classic option, but butternut squash will work well if you can't find a fancypants heirloom pumpkin.

Serves 4

Equipment
Blender + Pasta machine + Rolling pin
Straight wheel cutter (optional) + Baking sheets
Piping bag (optional) + Spray bottle

Store-bought option
Any fresh pumpkin, squash, or cheese-stuffed pasta

Filling
6 tablespoons butter (85 grams)
2¼ pounds Cinderella pumpkin (1 kilogram), halved, seeded, and stringy fibers removed (seeds reserved)
Pure olive oil
Kosher salt
¼ teaspoon ground cinnamon
¼ teaspoon ground nutmeg
1 tablespoon apple cider vinegar
2½ cups freshly grated Parmigiano-Reggiano cheese (185 grams)
1 tablespoon honey (optional)

Tortelloni
1 recipe Rav Dough (page 7)

To Finish
3 tablespoons pumpkin seeds
½ teaspoon pure olive oil
Kosher salt
5 tablespoons unsalted butter (75 grams)
6 fresh sage leaves, cut in chiffonade
Freshly grated Parmigiano-Reggiano cheese, for finishing

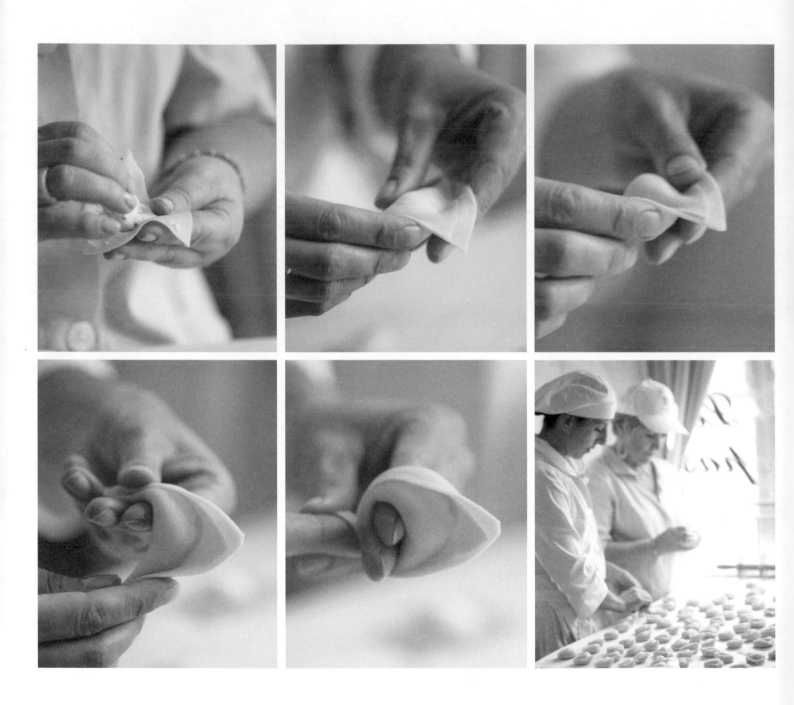

Preheat the oven to 350°F. Line a baking sheet with parchment paper.

Heat a sauté pan over medium heat and add the butter. Once the butter has melted and the foam has subsided, cook, stirring constantly, until the butter becomes a light tan color. Smell the butter; it should have a nutty aroma. Remove from the heat and set aside.

To make the filling, cut the pumpkin in half, drizzle olive oil over it, and season liberally with kosher salt. Place the pumpkin, cut side down, on the prepared baking sheet. Roast the pumpkin until fully tender when pierced with a knife, 45 to 60 minutes. The pumpkin should be soft to the touch but not mushy or deflated. Scoop out the flesh of the pumpkin and discard the rind. Add the warm pumpkin to the jar of a blender along with the brown butter, cinnamon, nutmeg, and vinegar. Puree until smooth and season with salt. The puree should have a nice balance of sweetness and acidity. If the pumpkin lacks sweetness and depth of flavor, add 1 tablespoon of honey to balance the flavor. Spoon the puree into a bowl and fold in the Parmigiano Reggiano. You should have about 3½ cups filling. Cool in a refrigerator, covered.

Dust a 2 baking sheets with semolina flour and set aside.

To make the pasta, using a pasta machine, roll out the dough until the sheet is just translucent (see page 10). Cut a 2-foot section of the dough sheet and cover the rest of the dough with plastic wrap.

Using a straight wheel cutter or sharp knife and a ruler, cut the dough into 2¾-inch squares. Using a piping bag or spoon, place 2 teaspoons of filling into the middle of each square. Fold the pasta in half so the opposite corners meet, forming a triangle. Use a spritz of water from a spray bottle to help seal it if necessary. Gently press out the air around the filling by running your fingers from the tip of the triangle downward. With your thumbs along the base of the triangle and your index fingers halfway down each side of the triangle, gently pinch your index fingers and thumbs together and rotate your left index finger to fit under the base of the triangle. Wrap the corners around your left index and middle fingers and pinch them together to seal. You should have a small gap between the filling and the pinched dough, like a ring.

Working quickly, place the tortelloni on the prepared baking sheets, spaced apart, until ready to cook. Don't let the tortelloni touch each other or they may stick together. Repeat until you run out of dough or filling. You should have 30 to 40 pieces.

Preheat the oven to 350°F.

To finish, bring a large pot of seasoned water to a boil (see page 18).

In a small bowl, combine the pumpkin seeds with the olive oil and a pinch of salt. Evenly distribute the seeds on a baking sheet and roast until golden brown, about 11 minutes. Remove to a plate and set aside.

Drop the pasta into the boiling water.

Heat a 12-inch sauté pan over high heat. Add ¼ cup of the seasoned pasta water and the butter and bring to a simmer. Once the pasta is cooked 80 percent through, until almost al dente, about 2 to 3 minutes, add it to the pan along with the sage and swirl until the sauce coats the back of a spoon. Reserve the pasta water. If needed, add a few more tablespoons of pasta water to keep a saucy consistency and continue cooking until the pasta is tender, about 90 seconds. Season with salt.

To serve, divide the pasta and sauce between four plates. Finish with freshly grated Parmigiano-Reggiano and toasted pumpkin seeds.

Celery Root Tortelli with Brown Butter, Balsamico, and Walnuts

Not every recipe in this book has a type of pasta as its starting point. This dish began with the sauce.

Traditionally, a classic brown butter sauce is made by toasting butter in a pan and then adding lemon juice to halt the browning of the milk solids and also to act as an acidic balance. Citrus, however, isn't the only way to apply acid to a dish; another way is vinegar. With this in mind, we experimented making brown butter sauce with balsamico condimento, a variation of balsamic vinegar made in Modena (see page 159 for more on balsamic vinegars). The results pretty much blow our minds. Since the acid level of balsamic is lower than that of lemon juice, a larger volume can be added, essentially creating a thick, dark (almost black) emulsion.

Although the other components of this dish change frequently, it always includes a combination of a root vegetable–stuffed pasta with some sort of nut and the balsamic brown butter sauce. We make this sauce every autumn and then tweak the rest of the players, whether it be rutabaga and pistachio, sunchokes and hazelnuts, or, as we have here, celery root and walnuts.

Serves 4

Equipment
Blender + Pasta machine + Rolling pin
Straight wheel cutter (optional) + Fluted wheel cutter
Piping bag (optional) + Baking sheets

Store-bought option
Any fresh, cheese-stuffed pasta

Filling
1 tablespoon pure olive oil
3 small celery roots, peeled and cut into small dice (455 grams)
10 sprigs thyme
1 medium yellow onion, cut into small dice (255 grams)
3 cloves garlic, minced
Kosher salt
1½ cups heavy cream (355 milliliters)
½ cup freshly grated Parmigiano-Reggiano cheese (50 grams)

Tortelli
1 recipe Rav Dough (page 7)

To Finish
6 tablespoons unsalted butter (85 grams)
1 teaspoon kosher salt
2 tablespoons coarsely chopped walnuts
1 tablespoon balsamico condimento
1 tablespoon minced fresh Italian parsley
Freshly grated Parmigiano-Reggiano cheese, for finishing

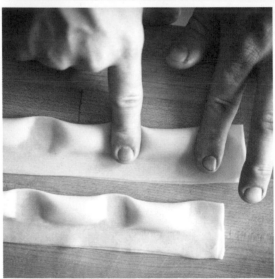

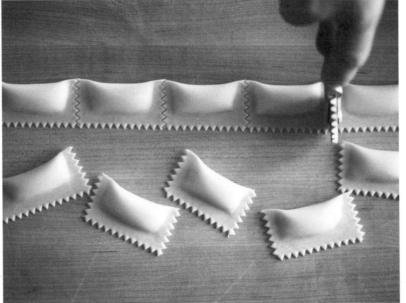

To make the filling, heat the olive oil in a 12-inch sauté pan on high heat until almost smoking. Add the celery root and thyme and cook until the celery root is golden brown, about 8 minutes. Add the onion, garlic, and a pinch of salt. Decrease the heat to low and cook gently until the celery root is completely soft, about 30 minutes.

Add the cream and increase the heat to high. Remove the thyme sprigs and immediately transfer the mixture to the jar of a blender. Puree until smooth. Transfer to a mixing bowl and, while still hot, fold in the grated Parmigiano-Reggiano. Adjust the salt to taste and cool completely. You should have about 2½ cups filling.

Dust 2 baking sheets with semolina flour and set aside.

To make the pasta, using a pasta machine, roll out the dough until the sheet is just translucent (see page 10). Cut a 2-foot section of the dough sheet and cover the rest of the dough with plastic wrap.

With a straight wheel cutter or a ruler and a knife, halve the pasta sheet lengthwise into two 3-inch-wide strips. Using a piping bag or a spoon, place 1¼-inch logs of filling in the middle of each strip, keeping an inch of separation between each log of filling. Fill both strips.

Gently fold the dough over the filling, bringing the two edges together to completely cover the filling. Use a spritz of water from a spray bottle to help seal it if necessary. Using your thumb, seal the top edge of the pasta, but just the very edge. To form the individual tortelli, start on the right side of one

strip and press down along the pasta with your index finger, sealing the pasta and pushing out all the air, creating a vacuum between the filling and the pasta dough. You want to create a tight capsule of dough around the log of filling. Move down the line, pressing down around one log at a time.

Using a fluted cutter, trim the edges, leaving ¼ inch of pasta between the filling and the cut. Working quickly, place the tortelli on the prepared baking sheet, spaced apart, until ready to cook. Don't let the tortelli touch each other or they may stick together. Repeat until you run out of dough or filling. You should get about 50 tortelli.

To finish, bring a large pot of seasoned water to a boil (see page 18).

Heat a 12-inch sauté pan over high heat. Add the butter and salt and cook until the butter is browned, 2 to 3 minutes.

When the butter is just starting to color around the edges and bubble, add the walnuts, stir to incorporate, and then turn off the heat. Add the balsamico condimento.

Drop the pasta in the boiling water. Once the pasta is cooked 80 percent through, until almost al dente, about 2 to 3 minutes, add it to the pan. Reserve the pasta water. Add a few tablespoons of pasta water and increase the heat to high. Toss to combine. When the pasta is tender—in less than 1 minute—add the parsley and toss. Remove from the heat.

To serve, divide the pasta and sauce between four plates. Finish with freshly grated Parmigiano-Reggiano.

THE BOAR HUNT

The boar hunt has become a rite of initiation of sorts at the restaurant. Every few months, David White and I leave San Francisco around 3 a.m. for a three-hour drive south. If we can, we usually bring a cook or two from the restaurant so they can experience the hunt as well. By dawn, we arrive at Paso Robles, where our friend—a heavily accented Turkish man named Attila—waits for us at a sprawling ranch.

With the rising sun peeking over the hills, the morning chill still lingering, and the mystique of nature in full effect (all sensations often intensified by lack of sleep, a hangover, or both), we set off in search of wild boars. Sometimes we might go hours without seeing anything; sometimes shots get fired within minutes.

But as soon as a boar comes into view, adrenaline quickly takes over. You see a shadow. You chase. You fire. You miss. Or maybe you nicked it. Someone yells. It's running. Your heart races out of your chest. Quick breaths. Neither thoughts nor sounds register. You try to steady your sweaty hands and squint through the scope. You fire again. The morning air is no longer frozen and you're no longer tired from that 3 a.m. wake-up call. Blood is pumping. The boar collapses. You feel slaps on the back and the roars of celebration. The hunt is over.

A few minutes after the boar goes down, you get up close, look down at the motionless animal, and suddenly the sport ends. Reality sets in: you killed something.

Moments after I shot my first boar—not long after I had actually held a *gun* for the first time, mind you—Attila ran up to the dead 350-pound beast, sliced a cut in its wound, and smeared its blood on my face. He said it was a family tradition to respect the death of the animal. I *think* I believed him.

Staring down at the dead boar, I did not feel a sense of pride or triumph; the adrenaline had drained, and I felt only a sense of responsibility. Suddenly, that boar—nasty and vicious as all hell just moments ago—had become *mine*. In the kitchen, if you overcook a lamb chop, it sucks because you screwed up, but there's another one waiting to replace it. But if that's your animal, there is only one of each cut. Screwing up isn't an option.

We gut and skin the boar at the ranch and then butcher it back at the restaurant. From that point, it's open season with the meat. We'll use it in sugos, cure some of it, and make fresh terrines with it. Pretty much anything we do with pork, we can do with boar. To date, the best prosciutto I've ever made was from a wild boar leg, cured with the black hairs still on for dramatic effect.

Not only does boar regularly find its way onto the menu nowadays, but it was a part of Flour + Water even before Flour + Water existed. Before the restaurant was even open, we were trying to raise the final financing, so I was tasked to cook a special dinner for potential investors. We held it in the restaurant-to-be—and made it an all-boar dinner. The restaurant was still a construction site, so we built a makeshift kitchen, cooking on propane burners. It must have been an acceptable dinner, because the investors came aboard. So in a way, we're all here because of a wild boar; the restaurant owes itself to boar.

Wild Boar Strozzapreti

Of the many various origin stories of strozzapretti ("priest
stranglers"), my favorite involves the one that dictates the pasta
shape should resemble a twisted dish towel. Back in medieval
times, the legend goes that a town's gluttonous priest was
taking advantage over the village people. This not-so-kind
priest would regularly invite himself to dinner at houses, picking
and choosing the home—or homes—with the best dinner that
night. The villagers eventually got sick and tired of the priest's
freeloading. During one of the self-invited dinners, the host
snuck up behind the unwelcome guest and strangled the priest
with a twisted dish towel. Hence, the name strozzapretti.

   Cooking wild boar is not easy; like other wild game, it's very
lean and therefore prone to overcooking. But a gentle braise
with red wine, chicken stock, and maybe some juniper berries
does it right.

   When blistered in a cast-iron pan, sweet fuyu persimmons
get a smoky depth that pairs quite nicely with the gaminess
of wild boar. Just make sure you get the right kind of
persimmons. And if you don't like persimmons, feel free to
use apples instead.

Serves 4

Equipment
Extruder

Store-bought option
Dried rigatoni, fusilli, or any short pasta

Wild Boar
1 pound boar shoulder or pork shoulder (453 grams)
1 tablespoon kosher salt
2 tablespoons pure olive oil
½ stalk celery, diced
1 medium yellow onion, diced (255 grams)
½ carrot, diced
2 cloves garlic, chopped
2 teaspoons tomato paste
½ cup red wine (118 milliliters)
Herb Sachet: 1 tablespoon black peppercorns, 1 teaspoon dried
    juniper berries, 3 sprigs thyme, and 2 bay leaves, wrapped
    in cheesecloth and tied with kitchen string
7 cups chicken stock (1.66 liters; page 169)

To Finish
1 tablespoon pure olive oil
1½ cups diced Fuyu persimmon (150 grams)
10 ounces homemade dried strozzapretti (see Extruded Dough,
    page 16) or store-bought dried strozzapretti (283 grams)
½ cup unsalted butter (113 grams)
2 teaspoons minced fresh thyme leaves
1 tablespoon apple cider vinegar
Kosher salt
Freshly grated Parmigiano-Reggiano cheese, for finishing

To make the boar, generously season the meat with the salt. Preheat a Dutch oven on high heat. Add the olive oil and heat until almost smoking. Add the seasoned shoulder and sear, caramelizing the meat and creating a fond on the bottom of the pan to create the base. Don't stir or shake the meat. Just let it be, as it cooks for about 8 minutes, then turn occasionally to give it an even sear on all sides, about 20 minutes total. Remove the meat to a platter and set aside.

Remove all but 2 tablespoons of fat from the Dutch oven. Quickly add the celery, onion, and carrot to the pan. Stir constantly, scraping the bottom of the pan. You want to caramelize the mirepoix and achieve a little bit of browning. Cook for 3½ minutes and then stir in the garlic and tomato paste. Cook for 30 seconds, being careful not to let the ingredients scorch. Add the red wine and the herb sachet. As you add wine, you want to scrape the bottom of the pan with a wooden spoon to remove any remaining fond and tomato paste on the bottom. Cook down until the pan is almost dry, about 1 minute. Then add the chicken stock and return the boar to the pot. When you put the boar in the pot, make sure to include any residual juice from the platter.

Bring the braising liquid to a boil, then decrease the heat to a simmer. Cover and gently simmer until the meat is fork-tender and almost falling off the bone, 3 to 4 hours. Cool the boar in the braising liquid until it's cool enough to handle. Remove and discard the sachet. Pull the meat from the bone and chop it into coarse cubes (about 1½ inches). Discard the bone, return the meat to the braising liquid, and cool until ready to use. Refrigerate, covered in an airtight container, until ready to use. The braise will last 2 to 3 days refrigerated.

To finish, bring a large pot of seasoned water to a boil (see page 18).

Heat a 12-inch sauté pan over high heat. Add the olive oil and heat until the oil is smoking. Add the persimmons and sear over high heat, stirring occasionally, until the persimmons are deeply blistered but not burned, about 2 minutes.

Bring the braising liquid and meat back to a simmer in the Dutch oven, then decrease the heat to low.

Meanwhile, drop the strozzapretti in the boiling water and cook until 80 percent cooked through, or almost al dente, about 10 to 12 minutes. Transfer the pasta to the Dutch oven along with the butter. Fold in the persimmons, thyme, and apple cider vinegar and adjust the salt.

To serve, divide the pasta and sauce between four plates. Finish with freshly grated Parmigiano-Reggiano.

Spaghetti with Black Trumpet, Poached Egg, and Cured Yolk

In this day and age, just about everyone in San Francisco has been exposed to squid ink pasta, and it's something we often showcase in the restaurant as well (see page 78). The black appearance is stunning, a negative-like snapshot of what a customer expects pasta to be. By mixing standard spaghetti with a black trumpet mushroom puree, we're toying with those same visual expectations, but in a new way. The pasta *looks* black, but instead of the salty sea flavor of squid ink, this dish exudes the intense earthy terroir of black trumpet mushrooms.

Spaghetti is an extruded semolina noodle, which means that it's not made with any egg in its dough; it's just flour and water. To make up for that ovoid deficiency, we finish the dish with two more colors that provide a stark contrast to the black pasta: the white of a slow-cooked egg and the bright yellow shavings of a cured egg yolk.

Serves 4

Equipment
Blender

Store-bought option
Dried spaghetti

Mushroom Brodo
1 medium yellow onion, halved (255 grams)
4 tablespoons unsalted butter (57 grams)
1 pound button mushrooms, stemmed and quartered, stems reserved (455 grams)
1 cup thinly sliced shallots (92 grams)
5 cloves garlic, thinly sliced
½ cup white wine (118 milliliters)
1 celery root, peeled and cut into medium dice (218 grams)
½ bunch thyme
3 large chunks Parmigiano-Reggiano cheese rind (200 grams)
8 cups cold water (1.9 liters)

Black Trumpet Mushroom Puree
⅔ pound black trumpet mushrooms (302 grams)
2 tablespoons pure olive oil
Kosher salt
½ cup Mushroom Brodo (118 milliliters)

To Finish
1 cup Mushroom Brodo (237 milliliters)
1 tablespoon unsalted butter
1 teaspoon sherry vinegar
8 ounces dried spaghetti (227 grams)
4 poached eggs
Freshly grated Parmigiano-Reggiano cheese, for finishing
Cured Egg Yolk (page 135), optional

To make the brodo, heat a small sauté pan over medium-high heat. Add the onion halves, cut side down, to the dry pan and cook until evenly blackened on the bottom, 8 to 10 minutes. Transfer the onion to a 4-quart stockpot.

Heat two 12-inch sauté pans over high heat. Add 2 tablespoons of butter to each pan, then add half the quartered button mushrooms to each pan and sear until deeply browned, about 5 minutes. Add half of the shallots and garlic to each pan and continue to cook until softened, about 2 minutes. Turn off the heat and transfer the mushrooms, shallots, and garlic to the stockpot. Deglaze the pans with the white wine, scraping with a wooden spoon to release as many of the browned bits as possible. Transfer the white wine to the stockpot.

Add the mushroom stems, celery root, thyme, cheese rinds, and the 8 cups cold water to the stockpot. Bring the brodo to a boil, decrease the heat to a simmer, and cook for 45 minutes. Remove from the heat and allow to rest for 15 minutes. Strain through a fine-mesh strainer into a large bowl and reserve. You should have about 6 cups, which is more than you need for this recipe, so reserve the excess for other uses.

To make the mushroom puree, first clean the black trumpet mushrooms. There will often be pine needles and grit trapped inside, so it's important to clean the mushrooms well. Tear them in half lengthwise to expose the inner layer. Wash the pieces thoroughly in a large bowl of water. Lift the mushrooms out of the water and drain in a colander. Blot gently with paper towels to remove excess moisture.

Heat a 12-inch sauté pan over high heat and add the olive oil. Once the oil is almost smoking, add the mushrooms. Cook until all of the water has evaporated and the pan is dry, about 5 minutes. Season with salt. You should have about 1½ cups cooked mushrooms.

Reserve ½ cup of the cooked mushrooms and set them aside.

Combine 1 cup of the cooked mushrooms and ½ cup of the brodo in the jar of a blender and puree until smooth. Adjust the seasoning with salt. Set aside.

To finish, bring a large pot of seasoned water to a boil (see page 18).

Heat a 12-inch sauté pan over high heat. Add 1 cup of the brodo, the reserved ½ cup cooked mushrooms, the butter, the mushroom puree, and the sherry vinegar. Bring to a simmer.

Drop the pasta in the boiling water. Once the pasta is cooked 80 percent through, until almost al dente, about 2 to 3 minutes, add it to the pan and continue cooking until you achieve a thick, sauce-like consistency, and the sauce coats the back of a spoon, about 2 minutes.

To serve, divide the pasta and sauce between four pasta bowls and top with a warm, poached egg. Finish with freshly grated Parmigiano-Reggiano and a liberal grating of cured egg yolk.

Black Pepper–Cured Egg Yolks

Every night after dinner service, the chefs at Flour + Water converge to discuss the next day's menu, line up deliveries and market visits, and recap what dishes did well in the night's service. The gathering takes up a little more of everyone's time, and maybe a beer or two, but the meetings have proven to be an invaluable source of ideas and inspiration, as well as a reinforcement of the way we want to cook at Flour + Water.

It was during one of these late-night sessions that we were brainstorming ways to increase our repertoire, as we felt the need to stack our shelves with culinary ammo in anticipation of a slow market season.

Someone randomly brought up cured egg yolks, so we started experimenting with a few recipes. It's a technique that took a few days to complete, but when we were done, the kitchen was almost immediately infatuated. We wanted to shave the cured yolk on everything: pasta, salads, bruschetta . . . our mouths.

Our favorite recipe cures the yolks in a mixture consisting primarily of salt, with additions of black pepper and thyme. Despite spending days buried in salt, the cured eggs are not used to add salinity to a dish; they add richness, more like garnishing a dish with Parmigiano-Reggiano than sea salt.

Note: This recipe will yield nine cured egg yolks. Once made, the yolks will keep indefinitely, so I think it makes sense to cure several at once, since it's barely any extra work. That said, if you want to make a smaller batch, simply keep the salt/pepper ratio the same. Once you have a few, keep them in an airtight container and grate them over any completed dish you want to get an extra hit of umami.

Makes 9 cured egg yolks

6 cups kosher salt (680 grams)
¼ cup finely ground black pepper
8 sprigs thyme
9 large eggs (450 grams)

In a mixing bowl, combine the salt and black pepper. Lay the sprigs of thyme on the bottom of an 8-inch square baking pan or another small container with a flat bottom and spread three-fourths of the salt mixture evenly on top of the thyme. Reserve the remainder.

Make individual "beds" for the egg yolks on the salt by using a whole, uncracked egg to form wells in the salt, pushing down gently with the egg's rounded bottom to create a well the size of an egg yolk. Crack the egg, reserving only the yolk and letting the whites drain off.

Carefully slip the yolk into the salt well without breaking it. Repeat the process with as many yolks as you can comfortably and spaciously fit in the pan. An 8-inch square pan should be able to accommodate nine eggs.

Cover the yolks with the remaining salt. Cover the pan with plastic wrap and put in the refrigerator for 2 days.

After 2 days, the yolks should be dry and firm to the touch. At this point, remove them from the salt, flip them upside down, and lay them out on a tray at room temperature. Let them dry for another day.

Store in an airtight container. The cured yolks will keep for up to 2 months at room temperature.

Chestnut Maltagliati with Porcini and Celery Root

Staging—the restaurant equivalent of an unpaid internship—
is a thankless task, but for a young, eager-to-learn cook, it's an
invaluable one. It's an experience that is equal parts culinary
training and life experience. A fledgling cook hopping around
Europe from stage to stage often doesn't have a plan or
schedule; he or she stays at each restaurant as long as possible,
absorbing as much as possible.

The byproduct of those unpaid gigs? You're utterly broke.

I suppose there's a certain irony to going home to bargain
bites following a long day in a Michelin-starred kitchen, but
cooks are often not a philosophical folk. During my winter stint
in northern Italy, I found salvation in the country's ubiquitous
cold-weather street food: steaming fire-roasted chestnuts,
served up in a newspaper cone. For a monetarily challenged kid
like me, a handful of chestnuts was sustenance on those bitter
winter days; walking to and from work, they were as much a part
of my routine as my daily espresso stop.

I like to bring that creamy chestnut flavor into the pasta
dough itself. Pairing it with mushrooms creates a sort of riff
on mushroom cream soup—with an earthy chestnut twist.

We use fewer egg yolks in this recipe than in most egg
doughs because the chestnut flour has a higher moisture
content than zero zero flour. If the standard number of yolks
was used, the dough would be too wet.

Serves 4

Equipment
Pasta machine + Rolling pin + Straight wheel cutter (optional)
Baking sheets + Mandoline (optional)

Store-bought option
Dried lasagna sheets, broken up into two-inch irregular shapes

Chestnut Maltagliati
270 grams 00 flour (3¼ cups)
90 grams chestnut flour (¾ cup)
275 grams egg yolks (about 11 to 12 yolks)
1¼ teaspooons kosher salt
1½ teaspoons extra-virgin olive oil

Braised Porcini
4 medium porcini mushrooms, very thinly sliced (280 grams)
2 tablespoons unsalted butter
¼ cup thinly sliced shallots
2 cloves garlic, thinly sliced
1 teaspoon kosher salt
¼ cup white wine (59 milliliters)
1 cup Mushroom Brodo (page 132) or chicken stock
    (page 169; 237 milliliters)
2 sprigs thyme

Braised Celery Root
1 large celery root, peeled and thinly sliced (232 grams)
2 cups water (473 milliliters)
2 tablespoons unsalted butter
½ teaspoon kosher salt

To Finish
1½ cups Mushroom Brodo (page 132), or chicken stock
    (page 169; 355 grams)
½ cup unsalted butter (113 grams)
1 tablespoon sherry vinegar
2 tablespoons heavy cream
Freshly grated Parmigiano-Reggiano cheese, for finishing

To make the pasta, follow the instructions for Egg Dough (see page 7), mixing the two flours together and incorporating the flour mixture as directed.

Dust 2 baking sheets with semolina flour and set aside.

To make the pasta, using a pasta machine, roll out the dough to $\frac{1}{16}$ inch thick (see page 10). The edges of the dough may crack as you work it through the pasta machine. Don't worry; this is normal. The chestnut flour makes the dough a bit drier, so it usually cracks a bit around the edges, but you will be trimming the edges when you cut the maltagliati, so it's not a problem.

Using a straight wheel cutter or a ruler and a knife, cut the dough into 12-inch long segments. Lay the segments on the prepared baking sheets, thoroughly dusting the pasta with semolina flour between each layer, in stacks of four pasta sheets each. Allow the dough to dry until it has a leathery texture but is still pliable, 30 to 45 minutes.

To shape the maltagliati, cut each stack into 2½-inch horizontal strips. Stack the strips and, with a sharp knife, cut them into rough triangles. Return them to the semolina-dusted baking sheets. You should get about 12 ounces of maltagliati.

To braise the porcini, clean them well with a damp paper towel or mushroom brush and quarter each mushroom lengthwise. Slice the mushroom quarters into very thin slices.

Heat a 12-inch sauté pan over high heat until almost smoking. Add the butter and mushrooms and cook until golden brown, about 5 minutes. Add the shallots, garlic, and salt and continue cooking until soft, about 3 minutes. Add the white wine and cook until almost dry, then add the brodo and thyme and bring to a boil. Decrease the heat to a simmer and continue cooking until the pan is almost dry, about 10 minutes. Reserve.

To make the celery root, peel the celery root and cut it in half down the middle. Reserve one half and set aside for another use. Place the other half, cut side down, on a cutting board and halve it. The resulting quarter should have a rough triangular shape (the same shape as the pasta). Thinly slice the celery root with a mandoline (or a knife) into ⅛-inch-thick "triangles." The celery root slices should be about twice as thick as the pasta. You should get about 2½ cups of sliced celery root.

Combine the celery root, the 2 cups water, butter, and salt in a shallow 8-inch saucepan over high heat. Bring to a boil, decrease the heat to a simmer, and cook, uncovered, until the liquid is almost completely evaporated and the celery root is tender, 15 to 20 minutes.

To finish, bring a large pot of seasoned water to a boil (see page 18).

In a 12-inch sauté pan bring the brodo, braised porcini, and celery root to a simmer over high heat. Add the butter and sherry vinegar and swirl the pan to create an emulsion.

Meanwhile, drop the pasta in the large pot of boiling water and cook until it's 80 percent cooked through, until almost al dente, 1 to 2 minutes (depending on how dry the pasta is).

Transfer the pasta to the sauté pan and continue cooking until you achieve a sauce-like consistency, and the sauce coats the back of a spoon, about 3 minutes. Add the cream and season with salt.

To serve, divide the pasta and sauce between four plates. Finish with freshly grated Parmigiano-Reggiano.

Pici with Vin Santo–Braised Squab, Pancetta, and Cabbage

Anytime I ask an Italian over the age of sixty what kind of pasta he or she ate growing up, nearly every single one replies in the same way: in the countryside, pasta meals consisted of simple noodles like spaghetti or maltagliati, served with either butter or oil, or with vegetables. Meats, and often eggs, were too expensive to have on an everyday basis during the post-war years.

The region of Tuscany does not have a rich pasta tradition in comparison to its immediate neighbors Emilia-Romagna and Liguria. Tuscan culinary fame lies elsewhere, in the peasant foods that permeated its hills and villages: olive oil, rosemary, hearty bean soups, wood-grilled steaks, tripe, and the wines of Chianti. Pici, however, it is a pasta shape that comes from southern Tuscany, and it is particularly common in Siena.

Pici is a very labor-intensive shape, but the hard work results in an amazing texture. It is a fatter version of spaghetti, made with semolina-based dough (no eggs) that has to be rolled by hand, one strand at a time. It expands when cooked to become a fat udon-like noodle. It's unique and delicious, but in a restaurant setting, where we have to make hundreds of pici for one night of service, it can be a little overwhelming.

Like many pasta dishes born from peasant traditions, pici were often served in the meatless sauces of bread crumbs, egg, and garlic that were popular with the Sienese—and also with modern-day students in Siena. Two fancier traditional Tuscan varieties of pici involve pancetta or some sort of game bird (usually duck). Here we combine those two preparations, with a little dose of sweet vin santo to offset the saltiness of the pancetta and the gaminess of the squab.

Serves 4

Equipment
Pasta machine + Rolling pin + Baking sheets

Store-bought option
Any fat, long noodle, like bucutini or liguine

Pici
1 recipe Hand-Rolled Semolina Dough (page 14)

Braised Squab
3 pounds whole squab, about three birds total (1.36 kilograms)
4 ounces pancetta, cut in small dice (113 grams)
Kosher salt
Cracked black pepper
1 red onion, diced (255 grams)
½ carrot, finely diced
3 cloves garlic, minced
1 tablespoon tomato paste
1 sprig rosemary
1 bay leaf
½ cup vin santo or any sweet wine like Marsala (118 milliliters)
½ cup white wine (118 milliliters)
2 cups chicken stock (473 milliliters; page 169)
1 tablespoon unsalted butter
½ cabbage, coarsely julienned (172 grams)

Braised Cabbage
1 tablespoon unsalted butter
½ cabbage, coarsely julienned (172 grams)
½ cup white wine (118 milliliters)
Kosher salt

To Finish
½ cup unsalted butter (113 grams)
1½ teaspoons minced fresh rosemary
2 tablespoons chopped fresh Italian parsley
Freshly grated Parmigiano-Reggiano cheese, for finishing

Dust 2 baking sheets with semolina flour and set aside.

To shape the pasta, divide the dough in half. Working with half of the dough at a time, using your hands, flatten it on a clean surface as much as possible to a rectangle that's about ¼ inch thick and about 4 inches wide. Cut into slices about ¼ inch thick.

On a clean wooden surface, using your fingers, roll out individual noodles from the individual slices: Start in the middle of one slice, moving your hands out quickly toward the edges and consistently stretching the dough as you roll the noodle back and forth. When your hands get to the edges of the noodle, start again in the middle, and repeat until the noodle is about 16 to 18 inches long. Don't be too gentle; you need to whip the pasta out to get it long enough. Try to keep the noodles all the same size so they cook evenly.

Place the noodles on the prepared baking sheets and sprinkle with additional semolina flour; set aside until ready to cook. You should get about 48 pieces of pici.

To make the squab, remove the wings first, then the legs, giblets, livers, and breasts. Or, if you prefer, ask the butcher to do this for you. Reserve the carcasses and wings to make squab stock, if desired.

Heat a Dutch oven over medium heat. Add the pancetta and cook until lightly browned and crisp, about 5 minutes. Remove the pancetta with a slotted spoon and set aside on a plate, leaving the fat in the pan.

Season the breasts with salt and pepper and sear them, skin side down, until all the fat beneath the skin is rendered and the skin is brown and crisp, 8 minutes. Flip the breasts over and cook on the other side until just rare, about 3 minutes more. Remove the breasts and set aside on a plate. Season the legs with salt and pepper and sear them, skin side down, until brown and crisp, about 4 minutes. Flip the legs and brown the other side completely, about 3 minutes more. Remove from the pan and set aside on a plate.

Season the livers and giblets with salt and sear until rare, about 4 minutes. Remove and set aside, keeping all of the rendered fat in the pan.

Add the onion and carrot to the fat and cook until deeply browned, about 4 minutes. Add the garlic and cook for 1 more minute. Add the tomato paste, rosemary, and bay leaf and cook for another minute. Add the vin santo and the white wine and reduce until the pan is almost completely dry. Return the pancetta, giblets, and squab legs back to the pan along with any reserved squab juices. Add the butter and the cabbage, cover the pot, and braise gently on the stovetop until the meat is tender about 45 minutes.

Remove from the heat. When the squab is cool enough to handle, pick the meat and skin off the leg bones, reserving the braising liquid. Discard the bones. Coarsely chop the meat and skin and return them to the pot.

Halve the breasts lengthwise, and then slice crosswise into ¼-inch slices. Set aside on a plate.

To braise the cabbage, heat an 8-inch sauté pan over medium heat. Add the butter, cabbage, white wine, and a pinch of salt. Cook until the cabbage is tender when pierced with a knife and the liquid is completely evaporated, about 20 minutes.

To finish, bring a large pot of seasoned water to a boil (see page 18).

Bring the braising liquid and meat back to a simmer in the Dutch oven, then decrease the heat to low. Add the braised cabbage.

Meanwhile, drop the pici in the boiling water and cook for 3 minutes. Transfer the pici to the Dutch oven. Stir thoroughly, then add the butter. Cook until the pasta is tender and the sauce coats the back of a spoon, about 7 minutes.

Stir in the squab breast and the rosemary; warm through. Remove from the heat. Fold in the parsley.

To serve, divide the pasta and sauce between four plates. Top with freshly grated Parmigiano-Reggiano.

Toasted Farro Garganelli with Short Ribs, Hazelnuts, and Radicchio

Just about everyone in America has grown up on dried penne pasta; garganelli is penne's fresh pasta cousin.

The creation myth of garganelli goes something like this: Once upon a time, a Bolognese housewife was making tortellini for a dinner party. She made the dough as usual and cut the pasta sheet into the typical squares. As she went to get the tortellini meat filling in the other room, she had a shock: Her cat had its face in the bowl of meat. The cat had eaten all of the filling. The housewife's guests had already arrived, and she had to serve something, so she improvised. She took the already-made pasta squares, rolled them around a stick to form a tube, and then pressed the stick on a hemp loom to create ridges on the pasta tube. Garganelli was born.

Making garganelli requires a dowel (*bastoncino*) and a ridged garganelli board. Both can easily be found for a few bucks online, usually sold together (see Sources, page 250). If you're lucky, you'll be able to find a real garganelli hemp comb (*pettine*).

All those people who have been eating penne for their entire lives? As soon as they try garganelli, their outlook changes. Garganelli behave similarly, in terms of grabbing sauces along ribbed edges and within a tube, but since they're made with an egg-based dough, the flavor is different.

That said, if you don't have the time to make fresh garganelli, dried penne is a fine substitute. Actually, the braise in this particular dish is even delicious without *any* pasta; the toasted farro dough certainly adds a lot to the final product, and the braise of short ribs—served alongside wilted radicchio, maybe atop a bed of soft polenta—is a quintessentially autumnal, cozy one-pot dish on its own.

Serves 4

Equipment
Pasta machine + Pasta roller + Spice grinder or coffee grinder
Straight wheel cutter (optional) + Baking sheets
Garganelli comb (or gnocchi board) + Dowel

Store-bought option
Dried penne or ziti

Toasted Farro Garganelli
½ cup faro (90 grams)
2 cups 00 flour (270 grams)
12 to 13 egg yolks (300 grams/1 cup)
2 big pinches kosher salt
1½ teaspoons extra-virgin olive oil

Braised Short Ribs
2 pounds bone-in short ribs (900 grams)
Kosher salt
Cracked black pepper
2 tablespoons pure olive oil
3 carrots, cut into 3-inch chunks (204 grams)
½ onion, quartered (128 grams)
2½ celery stalks, cut into 3-inch chunks (170 grams)
3 cloves garlic, minced
1 tablespoon tomato paste
1½ cups red wine (355 milliliters)
6 cups chicken stock (1.42 liters; page 169), or store-bought
2 bay leaves
¼ bunch thyme
½ sprig rosemary

Blistered Radicchio
2 tablespoons pure olive oil
8 ounces radicchio, cut into 1-inch strips (227 grams)
Kosher salt
1 tablespoon balsamic vinegar

To Finish
¼ cup unsalted butter (57 grams)
2 teaspoons sherry vinegar
Kosher salt
Cracked black pepper
¼ cup plus 2 tablespoons coarsely chopped toasted hazelnuts
Freshly grated Parmigiano-Reggiano, for finishing

Dust 2 baking sheets with semolina flour and set aside.

To make the pasta, toast the farro in a dry pan over medium heat until you achieve a deep golden brown color, about 5 minutes. Remove from the heat and cool completely. Grind the farro into a fine powder using a spice grinder or coffee grinder. Follow the instructions for Egg Dough (see page 7), incorporating the farro with the dry ingredients. (Note: standard egg dough, without the addition of farro, will work just fine as well.)

Using a pasta machine, roll out the dough to $\frac{1}{16}$ inch thick (see page 10).

Cut a 2-foot section of the pasta sheet and cover the rest of the dough with plastic wrap. With a straight wheel cutter or knife and a ruler, cut the pasta dough into 2-inch squares. Place one square on the garganelli comb, positioned diagonally, so two corners are at the top and bottom.

Place the dowel on the bottom of the comb. Using your fingers if necessary, curl up the corner so it curls up around the dowel to help get the tube started. In one smooth but firm motion, roll the dowel away from you from the bottom corner to the top corner, forming the tube-like garganelli.

Place the garganelli on the prepared baking sheets, uncovered, to air dry at room temperature until ready to cook. Repeat with the remaining dough.

Preheat oven to 325°F.

To make the short ribs, preferably 24 hours in advance, season the short ribs with salt and black pepper. Heat a Dutch oven over high heat. Add the olive oil and heat until almost smoking. Add the short ribs and sear on all sides until deeply browned and caramelized, about 15 minutes. Remove the short ribs and

set aside on a plate. Add the carrots, onion, and celery and cook until translucent, about 8 minutes. Add the garlic and cook for 1 more minute. Add the tomato paste and cook for another minute to remove the raw tomato flavor. Deglaze the pan with the red wine and reduce until the pan is almost dry. Return the short ribs to the pan and add the chicken stock, bay leaves, thyme, and rosemary. Bring to a boil, decrease the heat to a simmer, cover, and cook in the oven until the meat is tender and almost falling off the bone, about 5 hours. Allow the short ribs to cool to room temperature in the braising liquid, then pick the meat from the bone and tear it into ½-inch chunks. Coarsely chop the carrots and celery and reserve. You should have about 4 cups (791 grams) of picked meat. Add the meat and chopped vegetables back to the braising liquid and refrigerate until ready to use.

To make the radicchio, heat a 12-inch sauté pan over high heat. Add the oil and heat until almost smoking. Add the radicchio and a pinch of salt and cook, stirring constantly, until the radicchio is blistered and wilted, about 5 minutes. Deglaze the pan with the balsamic vinegar and set aside to cool.

To finish, bring a large pot of seasoned water to a boil (see page 18).

Add the short ribs along with the chopped vegetables and braising liquid to a 12-inch sauté pan, and bring to a simmer.

Drop the pasta in the boiling water. Once the pasta is cooked 80 percent through, until almost al dente, 2 to 3 minutes, add it to the pan along with the butter and cook until the sauce coats the back of a spoon. Add the sherry vinegar and adjust seasoning with salt and freshly cracked black pepper. Remove from the heat and fold in the radicchio.

To serve, divide the pasta and sauce between four plates. Garnish with the hazelnuts and Parmigiano-Reggiano.

WINTER

I THINK OF BOLOGNA WHEN I ROLL OUT PASTA. I think of Bologna when I fold and twist tortellini. I think of Bologna when I slice mortadella. But most of all, I think of Bologna during the winter months. It's the season when I worked in the pasta *laboratorio*, and it's the busiest time of the year for their pasta production, the time of the year when the pasta ladies are in overdrive and taking on any extra help they can as they make tortellini for the holidays. In 5½ hours of work, they'll make 60 kilograms of fresh tortellini—which is over 120 pounds—and each and every kilo will be sold that day downstairs in the salumeria.

The pillars of Bolognese cuisine—like tortellini in brodo, lasagna, and tagliatelle Bolognese—are, in essence, cold weather comfort foods. Hearty, warm, and rich, they are at home during wintry months. It was in Bologna, among those women, that I truly grasped the importance of passing along traditions—culinary and otherwise—from one generation to the next. That generational knowledge is something that crystallized over a late-night November dinner in the heart of Bologna. By chance, I found myself at a funky little trattoria, Drogheria della Rosa. After ordering half the menu, the owner, Emanuele Addone, came out, plopped down a bottle of grappa, took a chair, and waxed philosophic with us. When I eventually introduced myself as a chef interested in fresh pasta, his eyes lit up. He passionately explained in that quintessentially Italian way (hands waving) how handmade pasta was a dying art in Italy, a tradition in danger of slipping through the sands of time.

Honestly, I wasn't quite sure if our little neighborhood restaurant deserved a cookbook, but when the idea of a pasta book was broached by David Steele, I realized that I did have something to share: The traditions and science behind pasta, the intricacies of the doughs and the shapes—and most of all, the stories of those ladies that work in the laboratorio.

Near the end of my conversation, as the grappa was waning, Emanuele—gripping a cigarette in one hand and a wine glass in the other—held up a stubby index finger and looked me in the eye, dramatic as can be: "Now this is important: Teach someone else."

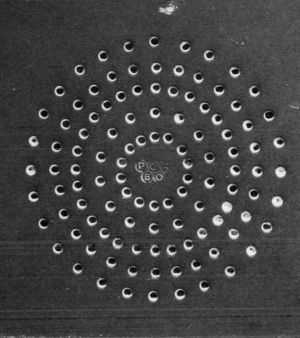

la Salumeria

LABORATORIO

Tagliatelle Bolognese

The maxim in Bologna goes that you don't measure a pasta shop by its tortellini, as sacred as that dish is there. You measure it by its tagliatelle. That's the test of great handmade pasta. With tortellini, the dough itself is obscured by the meat filling and the broth. Tagliatelle, on the other hand, is thicker and sans filling; you can actually taste—and critique—the pasta itself.

Bolognese ragu is a taste memory that most people have in common. Eating spaghetti with a thick meat sauce—whether it's called sugo, gravy, or ragu—is something that has been a part of a lot of childhoods. In fact, the sauce has become so common throughout the world that it has been bastardized into all kinds of unfortunate iterations.

A good Bolognese is all about the melding of flavors, neither too dry nor too wet. When you twirl your noodles together, there should be just enough sauce to bind the noodles together. The meat and tomato flavors come together through the addition of milk, which acts as the sauce's binding agent. The most important ingredient in Bolognese is something we all should make a point to discover: *time*. The sauce is a combination of simple ingredients that come together over hours—five hours, in our case—to create something greater than the sum of its parts.

Tagliatelle Bolognese is so beloved—and protected—in Italy that the recipe was codified and made official by the city during the 1970s. Even the size of tagliatelle was standardized: $5/16$ inch wide and $1/32$ inch thick. This is another recipe that is adapted from Bruno e Franco la Salumeria.

Serves 4

Equipment
Pasta machine + Rolling pin + Baking sheets

Store-bought option
Dried tagliatelle

Tagliatelle
1 recipe Standard Egg Dough (page 7)

Bolognese Ragu
2 tablespoon extra-virgin olive oil
1 medium onion, finely chopped (255 grams)
1 celery stalk, finely chopped (68 grams)
1 carrot, finely chopped (136 grams)
12 ounces ground beef (340 grams)
5½ ounces ground pork (156 grams)
3½ ounces pancetta, chopped (99 grams)
3 cups chicken stock (710 milliliters; page 169) or store-bought
2 tablespoons tomato paste
1 cup milk (237 milliliters)
Kosher salt
Freshly ground black pepper

To Finish
½ cup unsalted butter (137 grams)
Kosher salt
Freshly grated Parmigiano-Reggiano cheese, for finishing

Dust 2 baking sheets with semolina flour and set aside.

Using a pasta machine, roll out the dough to $\frac{1}{16}$ inch thick (see page 10). With a knife, cut the dough into 12-inch strips. Make two stacks of strips, four strips per stack, thoroughly dusting between the layers with semolina flour. Allow the dough to dry for 30 to 45 minutes, or until the dough has a slightly dry, leathery texture but is still pliable. Fold each stack like a letter, forming three even layers. Cut the folded dough into ¼-inch strips, shake off the excess semolina, and form into small nests on the prepared baking sheets. Set aside.

For the Bolognese ragu, heat the oil in a large, heavy pot over medium-high heat. Add the onion, celery, and carrot. Sauté until soft, 8 to 10 minutes. Add the beef, pork, and pancetta; sauté, breaking up with the back of a spoon, until browned, about 15 minutes. Add 2½ cups of the stock and the tomato paste; stir to blend. Reduce the heat to very low and gently simmer, stirring occasionally, about 2 hours. Season with salt and pepper.

Bring the milk to a simmer in a small saucepan; gradually add to the sauce. Cover the sauce with a lid slightly ajar and simmer over low heat, stirring occasionally, until the milk is absorbed, about 1 hour, adding more stock by ¼ cupfuls to thin if needed.

To finish, bring a large pot of seasoned water to a boil (see page 18).

Transfer the ragu to a 12-inch sauté pan and bring to a simmer. Add the butter and begin swirling to combine.

At the same time, drop the pasta in the boiling water.

Once the pasta is cooked 80 percent through, until almost al dente, about 2 to 3 minutes, add it to the pan. Reserve the pasta water. Continue to simmer, stirring constantly, until you achieve a sauce-like consistency, about 3 minutes. Season with salt. Remove from the heat.

To serve, divide the pasta and sauce between four plates. Finish with Parmigiano-Reggiano.

Taleggio Scarpinocc with Extra-Vecchio Balsamico

Cheese in Italy defines a place just as much as pasta does, if not more. Cheese is served before, during, and after meals. The local specialty is nearly always intertwined with some component of the town's history, whether it's the Fiore Sardo of Sardinia, where sheep outnumber people in the hot, dry climate, or Lombardy's famously pungent blue-veined Gorgonzola, which was born when, twice a year, tired cattle stopped in the town of Gorgonzola for milking en route to and from their summer pastures.

Lombardy's cheese resumé rivals that of just about any other region in Italy, maybe even Europe. It is one of Italy's northern regions, just down the hill from Switzerland. It's also home to a loaded roster of cheeses, many of them delightfully stinky. The aforementioned Gorgonzola leads the way, but it's flanked by strachino, scamorza, Bel Paese, ricotta, mascarpone, and one seemingly tailor-made for stuffed pasta: taleggio.

Taleggio is a washed-rind cow's milk cheese. It's creamy, tangy, salty, and, most importantly for our pasta purposes, it melts really well. When picking out taleggio in your local cheese shop, make sure that it's slightly bulging with a dry rind.

The cheese and pasta traditions of Lombardy come together in the region's indigenous pasta shape: scarpinocc. The name stems from the word "shoe" (*scarpa*) because the odd shape apparently resembles old-fashioned wooden shoes from Parre, a town in the province of Bergamo, just north of Milan. Usually filled with some sort of cheese mixture, scarpinocc have a defining little indentation in the middle that is perfect for holding sauce—or, even better, balsamico. When you eat the scarpinocc, the sauce releases into your mouth and mingles with the gooey cheese within.

Serves 4

Equipment
Food processor + Pasta machine + Rolling pin
Straight wheel cutter (optional) + Piping bag (optional)
Baking sheets + Spray bottle

Store-bought option
Any fresh, cheese-stuffed pasta

Filling
10½ ounces taleggio, cut into 1-inch cubes, rind removed (300 grams)
½ cup heavy cream (118 milliliters)

Scarpinocc
1 recipe Rav Dough (page 7)

To Finish
½ cup unsalted butter (137 grams)
Kosher salt
Freshly grated Parmigiano-Reggiano cheese, for finishing
1 tablespoon extra-vecchio balsamico, or more if desired, for drizzling

To make the filling, add the taleggio and the cream to the work bowl of a food processor fitted with the steel blade. Process the cheese and cream until you get a consistently smooth filling, 2 to 3 minutes. You want a nice, emulsified, thick consistency, similar to Greek yogurt. It should be a touch thicker than mayonnaise.

Dust 2 baking sheets with semolina flour and set aside.

To make the pasta, using a pasta machine, roll out the dough until the sheet is just translucent (see page 10). Cut a 2-foot section of the dough sheet and cover the rest of the dough with plastic wrap.

Cut the pasta sheet into rectangles that are 2 by 2½ inches with a straight wheel cutter, or a knife and a ruler. Using a piping bag or a spoon, place ¼ teaspoon of filling in the middle of each rectangle of pasta dough, leaving ¼ inch of dough bare around the edge.

Like a letter, fold the pasta from the side closest to you over one third. This should barely cover the filling. Use a spritz of water from a spray bottle to help seal it if necessary. Complete the fold (still folding away from you) so that you end up with a cannelloni-style pasta. You want to make sure the filling remains only in the center. With your thumb and index finger,

pinch in a "T" formation while still applying pressure to the bottom of the pasta. You should be forming a ridge at the top of the pasta. Press the center of the filling to form a dimple. It's important to create pressure on the bottom of the pasta while you shape it to form a strong seal. Working quickly, place the scarpinocc on the prepared baking sheets, spaced apart. Don't let the scarpinocc touch each other or they may stick together. Repeat until you run out of dough or filling. You should get 60 to 65 pieces.

To finish, bring a large pot of seasoned water to a boil (see page 18).

Drop the pasta in the boiling water. Heat a 12-inch sauté pan over high heat. Add 1 cup of the pasta water to the pan. Add the butter and swirl (or whisk) vigorously to create an emulsion. Once the pasta is cooked 80 percent through, until almost al dente, about 2 to 3 minutes, add it to the pan and continue swirling to continue creating an emulsion. Season with salt. When it achieves a sauce-like consistency and the sauce coats the back of a spoon, remove from the heat.

To serve, divide the pasta and sauce between four plates. Grate Parmigiano-Reggiano on top and drizzle liberally with extra-vecchio balsamico.

BALSAMICO

What America thinks is balsamic is far removed from the real stuff, which has been carefully curated for decades in the farmhouse attics of Modena. True balsamic vinegar is a prized commodity, a luxury ingredient that fetches triple-digit prices for a small bottle. Like Parmigiano-Reggiano and prosciutto di Parma, aceto balsamico tradizionale di Modena is a tightly regulated product and one of the primary reasons the Emilia-Romagna has the food reputation it does.

The decades-long process begins during the early fall grape harvest, when grapes—Trebbiano and Lambrusco are the most common varieties—are plucked from their vines and left out in the sun to boost sugar levels. They're pressed and then the juice is cooked, simmering for a day or more, until a syrupy reduction is all that remains. Unlike wine vinegar, which converts alcohol to acid, balsamic vinegar's acidity comes from sugar.

Then the concentrated must (the saba) is poured into the largest wood barrel, one of a set of progressively smaller barrels. Every year, the smallest barrel is emptied and refilled

by the second smallest barrel, which is refilled by the third smallest, and so on. It takes a minimum of twelve years for vinegar to age in the barrels; many spend thirty or more years in the battery, an amazing process that means that the person who started it might not even taste the finished product. The older the balsamic, the thicker (and more expensive) it is. Fist-sized bottles usually cost over one hundred dollars.

The end result is a harmonious ingredient that balances acid and sweet with the sloping viscosity of syrup. Like extra-virgin olive oil, real balsamic vinegar should never be cooked. It's only used as a finishing ingredient—in thick, syrupy drips atop pasta, meat, or fruit. We put large dollops on Parmigiano-Reggiano and on pasta like the Taleggio Scarpinocc (page 000). A more recent alternative is condimento balsamico, a younger, non-certified balsamic, often made in the same barrels. Though it's a completely different animal, it's cheaper and a nice alternative that can be used as real balsamic, or in salads or sauces.

THE *MATTARELLO*: ROLLING PASTA DOUGH BY HAND, BOLOGNESE STYLE

As I walked into the pasta lab one random morning, the ladies were all huddled up in a corner of the room. No one was rolling out dough by hand, and no one was making tortellini. Production was halted. They were all preoccupied. I couldn't understand what they were saying, but they were speaking urgently and in hushed tones. Someone eventually translated for me.

A scandal was afoot on the streets of Bologna: *The rival pasta shop had a pasta machine.*

This wasn't confirmed, of course. But someone heard that someone *else* heard that someone else's nephew saw a pasta machine in the other shop, or something like that. Now, given the Bolognese tradition of hand rolling pasta with the *mattarello*—the 4-foot-long, trophy-like rolling pin—this was a big scandal. For them, a blasphemous act.

The conversation soon shifted to how they knew all along that the rival shop's pasta was done by machine, not by hand. They could tell the difference, they said. The machine-made dough had streaks, sometimes even tears, they said. Then they went into their beliefs: Tortellini made by hand has dough that hugs the meat filling when cooked in the broth; the machine iteration allows the broth to swell inside the tortellini, creating an unenviable broth bubble. Tagliatelle made by hand absorbs the ragu and has what they call a "nervous attentiveness" in your mouth; tagliatelle made by machine is slippery and slimy, slipping down your throat.

Are they correct? Yes and no. Personally, I don't find pasta that is correctly rolled out from a machine and properly cooked to be inferior. In fact, I would wager that very few people could tell the difference between the finished results of both methods. I respect the art of the *mattarello*, but in the restaurant, we roll out the majority of our day-to-day pasta using an electric pasta roller. We have a careful process of rolling it out by machine (page 10), and I'm proud of the results. And, of course, once the sheet is rolled out, we form all our shapes by hand on a wood table.

The big difference between hand-rolled and machine-rolled pasta is not in the composition of the dough, but in the surface texture. When metal is the only thing that the dough touches, the pasta comes out smooth—too smooth—and, as the ladies noted, too slippery. Those mass-produced, vacuum-sealed tortellini in the refrigerated section of Safeway? The pasta feels as smooth as the plastic it comes in.

By comparison, rolling and forming pasta on porous wood creates a rougher surface, and one that catches the sauce better. That's why the big difference isn't so much a result of how the dough is rolled out but rather whether that the individual shapes are still made by hand. As long as the pasta touches hands, touches wood, it will get those coveted slight stretch marks and surface texture, which create a surface for sauce to adhere to.

There's no denying that rolling out fresh pasta with a *mattarello* is a beautiful thing to behold, and a beautiful thing to do. Making the *sfoglia*—the sheet of freshly rolled egg pasta dough—has always been a ritual reserved for the women of Bologna, be it the grandmother, the housewife (roughly translated to *razdoura* in the local dialect), or the young girl. Italian men tell bawdy jokes about how they were seduced by the sensual movements of their wives making the *sfoglia*, bending at the waist and leaning far over the table as their bodies moved back and forth over the pasta with the *mattarello*. (More than one will admit that this is the reason why their families are so big.) The movements must be harmonious, smooth, and sensual; if the sweeping pushes were too hard and brisk, the pasta would come out uneven, one side thicker or thinner than the other.

Making the *sfoglia* happens on a daily basis within each household, or at least did at one point. Every home has a large wooden table in the dining room or kitchen where the *razdoura* rolls the pasta dough. Though like many culinary traditions, making the *sfoglia* is an art that seems to fade with each subsequent generation.

It's a knowledge that has been passed down from mother to daughter, from aunt to niece. Paola Mazzetti, one of the longest-tenured women at the pasta lab, started making fresh pasta when she was eight years old. Growing up among the hayfields and farms outside the city, she was the oldest daughter in a family of fieldworkers. When her mother was away working, the task of making pasta for the family fell to her as the oldest daughter. Her father would even put out a step stool so she could work at the table.

Maria Grazia Foschini owns the pasta laboratory—and the downstairs salumeria—with her husband, Franco (page 104). She too learned how to make the *sfoglia* from her mother. Ask her for advice on how to make the *sfoglia*, and she'll shake her head with a smile before she drops wisdom: Making pasta is not a thing you understand immediately; it's a learned routine. It has to be done regularly, and it has to be done a lot. And then, once it's second nature, you understand the feel of the dough, the motion of the body, and how much rolling pin pressure needs to be applied to the dough to stretch it without ripping, and how thick each pasta should be. I think it is an Old World skill worth exploring, and one worth sharing.

A NONNA'S TOUCH

Unlike a normal rolling pin that you use with the heels of your hands, the *mattarello* is controlled with your fingers. The grip is formed by cupping your fingers and bringing your thumbs to the second knuckle of your index fingers, the fingertips and balls of the thumb resting on the upper portion of the rolling pin.

Place both hands over the *mattarello*, touching it only with your fingertips and the balls of your thumbs. Smoothly push the *mattarello* forward (not down) with the balls of your thumbs. As you move the *mattarello* back and forth over the dough, toward and away from your body, continually and fluidly move your hands back and forth from the ends of the mattarello to the center. Essentially, your hands are forming figure-eight motions. It is a motion very different from the normal, herky-jerky rolling pin motion; this is rhythmic. Very little pressure is placed on the *mattarello* and thus the dough; the dough is stretched by the weight of the *mattarello*, not your hands.

Sfoglia:

Makes 627 grams/22 ounces of dough

360 grams 00 flour (2 cups)
150 grams whole large eggs (½ cup/about 3 eggs)
125 grams egg yolks (½ cup/about 7 yolks)

Follow the basic directions for Egg Dough (page 6). Add the eggs and yolks in the middle of the well and stir carefully with a fork, trying to maintain the integrity of the walls. Incorporate the flour and knead until fully combined. Compared to the other egg doughs, this is much wetter and should come together more easily.

Once it's in a ball, knead for 10 to 15 minutes, then wrap tightly with plastic wrap. Let rest at room temperature for at least 30 minutes before using. If you're not using it after 30 minutes, put it in the refrigerator.

When ready to roll, remove the dough ball from the plastic wrap, sprinkle it with flour, and place on a wooden surface. Using a *mattarello*, roll the dough into a 12-inch circle, like a pizza. Sprinkle liberally with flour on both sides.

Hang one third of the dough circle over the edge of the table closest to your body. Set the mattarello parallel to the edge of the table and give it a little push away from you so it lightly rolls over the dough once to remove any air pockets.

At this point, begin using the *mattarello* to stretch and flatten the dough; apply light pressure but stay gentle.

When the sheet of dough feels uniform and has slightly expanded, move the *mattarello* to the very top edge of the dough. Press down gently and wrap the edge of the dough around the *mattarello*. Roll the dough around the wood as you roll the mattarello toward your body. When you have most of the dough wrapped around the *mattarello*, gently pick up the dough and rotate the mattarello 45 degrees. Unroll the dough into a smooth sheet, again leaving a (different) third of it hanging over the edge of the table. Bring the *mattarello* back parallel to your body and the edge of the table. Push the *mattarello* over the dough to smooth out any air pockets. Then roll again until the dough is a uniform thickness, and then rotate the dough again, continuing the entire process until the desired thickness is achieved.

Tortellini in Brodo

Even though it does not take the name of the city like tagliatelle Bolognese, tortellini in brodo is the signature dish of Bologna. Tortellini are found in every salumeria, every pasta shop, and every home in Bologna. They're the city's comfort food, not unlike clam chowder in Boston, or shrimp and grits in the American South. Tortellini are also at the heart of the pasta *laboratorio*, where the women huddle around the wooden table forming tortellini throughout the day, a sprawling sheet of four hundred at a time.

The myth goes that tortellini dates back to the days when gods roamed the earth, and Venus and Zeus happened to spend a night at an inn near Bologna (it's clearly a Bolognese myth). The innkeeper was so enthralled with the beauty of Venus that he couldn't resist taking one more glance at the goddess, so in the middle of the night, he cracked open the door to her room. He saw Venus lying on the bed, naked in all her glory. To pay homage to the beauty he just witnessed, the innkeeper created a new pasta shape inspired by her navel: tortellini.

The exact recipe varies from family to family—and naturally, every Bolognese *razdoura* will swear hers is the best. In the restaurant, our filling varies based on what meats we have available, but the recipe here is the same one that is used in the pasta *laboratorio*.

The *laboratorio* has been making the same tortellini filling for decades. Before the lab even existed, a pair of short Bolognese ladies—twins, actually—made fresh tortellini for Bruno e Franco Salumeria. Last time I was in Bologna, only one of them, Irena, was still working there, folding and twisting tortellini, head down at the table, as usual.

Their legacy will live on through their training, but also through their recipes. The twins' original tortellini recipe is still used in the *laboratorio* today. We thought it would be appropriate to share it here.

Serves 4

Equipment
Food processor or meat grinder + Pasta machine
Rolling pin + Straight wheel cutter (optional)
Piping bag (optional) + Spray bottle + Baking sheets

Store-bought option
Any meat-filled tortellini

Filling
5 ounces pork loin, finely minced (150 grams)
5 ounces mortadella, finely minced (150 grams)
2½ ounces prosciutto di Parma, finely minced (75 grams)
4½ ounces grated Parmigiano-Reggiano (125 grams)
1 egg (50 grams)
Ground nutmeg
Kosher salt

Tortellini
1 recipe Rav Dough (page 6)

Chicken Brodo
1½ pounds lean chicken meat, preferably breasts (680 grams)
1 medium leek (with green top), minced (145 grams)
1 stalk celery, minced (68 grams)
1 small carrot, minced (68 grams)
12 egg whites (360 grams)
1 cup tomato paste (237 grams)
    1 cup white wine (237 milliliters)
4 quarts cold chicken stock (3.78 liters; page 169 or store-bought)
Kosher salt

To make the filling, combine the pork loin, mortadella, prosciutto, Parmigiano-Reggiano, egg, nutmeg, and salt in a large bowl. Mix until fully incorporated. If you have a grinder, put the mixture through the grinder on the wide setting. If you don't have a grinder, run a knife through the meat mixture, mincing it as finely as possible, and then put it in a food processor until it has a pâté-like texture.

Dust 2 baking sheets with semolina flour and set aside.

To make the pasta, using a pasta machine, roll out the dough until the sheet is just translucent (see page 10). Cut a 2-foot section of the dough sheet, and cover the rest of the dough with plastic wrap.

Using a straight wheel cutter or a knife and a ruler, cut the dough into 1½-inch squares. Using a piping bag or a spoon, place 1 teaspoon of filling in the middle of each square. Rotate the square ninety degrees so the corner is facing your navel. Fold the corner over the filling to meet the opposing corner so you form a triangle. Use a spritz of water from a spray bottle to help seal it if necessary. Running your fingers from the tip of the triangle downward, gently press out the air around the filling. With your thumbs along the base of the triangle and your index fingers halfway down each side of the triangle, gently pinch your index fingers and thumbs together and rotate your left index finger to fit under the base of the triangle. Wrap the corners around your index and middle finger and pinch them together to seal. You should have a small gap between the filling and the pinched dough, like a ring. Place the tortellini on the prepared baking sheet, spaced apart, until ready to cook. Don't let the tortellini touch each other or they may stick together. Repeat until you run out of dough or filling. You should have about 75 pieces.

To make the brodo, add the chicken, leek, celery, and carrot to the work bowl of a food processor fitted with the steel blade and grind until it has the texture of mincemeat, 15 to 20 seconds. It should have some small chunks and not be fully pureed. Add the egg whites, the tomato puree, and the white wine and process for 30 seconds.

Transfer the mixture to an 8-quart stockpot. Add the chicken stock. Place the stockpot over medium heat. The goal is to slowly bring the stock to a simmer so the proteins in the ground meat and vegetables coagulate and form a "raft," which will flavor and clarify the stock. Using a rubber spatula, gently stir the mixture every few minutes until a raft starts to form on the surface, 15 to 20 minutes. Once the raft is set, stop stirring and allow the stock to gently simmer through the raft. Decrease the heat, if needed, and gently simmer for about 45 minutes, basting the raft every 5 minutes with a few ladles of the simmering broth. Basting the raft helps cook out the raw vegetables and egg whites at the top of the raft. If you don't baste the raft the brodo could become cloudy. Once the stock is clarified, turn off the heat and gently strain the brodo through a fine-mesh strainer lined with cheesecloth set over a large pot. Season with salt, roughly 1 tablespoon, but each batch may vary—so you should gradually add salt until you achieve the desired flavor. You should have about 3 quarts brodo.

To finish, bring large pot of salted water to a boil (page 18).

In a smaller pot, bring the chicken brodo to a gentle simmer over medium heat.

Drop the pasta in the boiling seasoned water. We cook the pasta half in the water and half in the brodo, so after about 2 minutes in the pasta water, transfer the tortellini to the simmering brodo. Cook the pasta until it is al dente, another 1 to 2 minutes.

Remove from the heat.

To serve, divide the pasta and brodo between four bowls. Finish each portion with a light drizzle of olive oil. Using a vegetable peeler, shave large ribbons of Parmigiano-Reggiano over the finished dish.

Shortcut Brodo

The great thing about tortellini in brodo is that it's quick and painless to prepare once you have the tortellini and the brodo. If you don't want to go the full nine yards of making a clarified brodo, here's our shortcut version that takes about a third of the time.

Yields 9 cups

½ yellow onion
2 tablespoons pure olive oil
1 chicken breast (8 ounces)
3 quarts chicken stock (opposite), preferably low-sodium
    if using store-bought stock (2.84 liters)
2 teaspoons whole black peppercorns
1 bay leaf

Heat a cast-iron pan on high heat. When hot, place the onion cut side down in the dry pan. Let it sit for five minutes on high heat. It will be blackened, but don't be alarmed. Set aside. Heat the olive oil in the pan and sear the chicken breast on both sides until it's well caramelized. In a stockpot, add the onion, chicken breast, chicken stock, peppercorns, bay leaf, and any aromatics you have lying around, like carrots, thyme, celery, and so on. Simmer for 30 to 45 minutes. Strain through a fine-mesh sieve lined with cheesecloth into a large bowl. Season to taste.

Our Chicken Stock

At Flour + Water, the usual fate of chicken stock is pasta dishes. Our chicken stock is very viscous, probably more viscous than the average version, thanks to the large amount of gelatin (chicken bones, chicken feet) incorporated into it. (The main ingredient, though, is chicken carcasses, so be sure to save them in the freezer). The thickness of the stock logically makes for a thick finished sauce—and one that coats the pasta particularly well.

If you have to buy a canned or boxed broth, go for the low-sodium version. You can also use that as a base to be fortified with vegetables and aromatics. (See our recipe for Shortcut Brodo, opposite).

Makes about 12 cups

3 chicken carcasses (about 2½ pounds)
6 chicken wings (1¼ pounds)
1½ cups white wine (355 milliliters)
4 chicken feet (144 grams)
1 tablespoon kosher salt
2 medium yellow onions (500 grams)
5 stalks celery, cut into 2-inch pieces (200 grams)
3 carrots, cut into 2-inch pieces (200 grams/2 cups)
7 cloves garlic, lightly smashed
2 bay leaves
1 teaspoon whole black peppercorns
½ bunch fresh thyme
½ bunch Italian parsley stems, leaves completely removed
4 quarts plus 2 cups water

Preheat the oven to 425°F.

Remove any excess fat from the chicken carcasses. Using a cleaver, cut each chicken carcass into 4-inch squares (roughly 5 pieces per carcass). Place the chicken carcasses and wings on a baking sheet and roast in the oven until all the fat has rendered and the bones are deeply golden brown, 45 to 60 minutes. Transfer the roasted bones to an 8-quart stockpot and allow to cool. The sheet pan will have lot of fond (brown bits) on the bottom. Place the sheet pan over a burner on medium heat. Add the wine and bring to a gentle simmer, scraping the fond with a wooden spatula or spoon to combine it with the wine. Once you've completely removed the fond, transfer the wine mixture to the stockpot with the bones to cool.

Cover the chicken feet with cold water in a small saucepan. Bring to a boil, decrease the heat to a simmer, add the salt, and cook for 5 minutes. This step draws out impurities from the chicken feet so they don't cloud the stock. Transfer the chicken feet to the stockpot with the bones to cool.

Halve one of the onions crosswise. Cut the other into 2-inch pieces and set aside in a bowl. Heat a 12-inch sauté pan over high heat. Place one of the onion halves, cut-side down, in the hot pan for 12 to 13 minutes. The browned onion not only adds sweetness and flavor to the stock, but also deepens the stock's rich golden color.

Add the browned onion and all remaining ingredients to the stockpot. Place over medium heat and slowly bring to a simmer. It's important that the stock never comes to a rolling boil or the fat and proteins in the stock will emulsify and make it cloudy. Once the stock is gently simmering, decrease the heat until gentle bubbles rise constantly to the surface. Skim the foam and the fat from the surface of the stock every 15 to 20 minutes. Simmer the stock for 3 to 3½ hours. Taste the stock as it cooks so you know when it's done; the finished stock should have a rich, meaty flavor. Strain the stock through a fine-mesh strainer and cool completely until ready to use.

The stock will keep 4 days refrigerated or 3 months frozen.

Tagliarini with Braised Hen, Lime, and Pistachio

Two components that are crucial to every pasta dish are acid and texture. Nearly every recipe in this book gets a splash of lemon juice or vinegar at some point (usually at the end). This recipe highlights the importance and utter simplicity of both acid and texture.

Bearrs limes—also called Persian or Tahitian limes—are sort of like the lime version of Meyer lemons, a little sweeter and more floral than your standard variety. With intensely green flesh, they are particularly well suited to growing in cold weather—unlike the more common Mexican limes—and as a result, they thrive in the San Francisco Bay Area.

On the other hand, our pistachios come all the way from Sardinia. Pistachios from Italy have a more vibrant green hue and distinct smooth flavor than the California variety. We pay a premium to stock foreign pistachios—something ridiculous like ninety-five dollars per pound, putting them on a par with luxury ingredients like truffles and morels. In Italy, you'll usually see pistachios in desserts, in mortadella, or as accompaniments on meat platters, but they are also used to finish pasta dishes.

Once you've got the acid and texture right, one more component pulls the flavors together at the end: a healthy dose of black pepper.

Serves 4

Equipment
Pasta machine + Rolling pin + Baking sheet

Store-bought option
Dried linguine, tagliatelle, or any other thin noodle

Braised Hen
1⅓ pounds chicken legs, including both thigh and drumstick, with skin on (580 grams, about 3 legs).
Kosher salt
Freshly ground black pepper
2 tablespoons pure olive oil
1 yellow onion, diced (255 grams)
1 small carrot, diced (68 grams)
½ fennel bulb, diced (68 grams)
2 cloves garlic, minced
1 bay leaf
½ cup dry white wine (118 milliliters)
3 cups chicken stock (710 milliliters, page 169 or store-bought)
Freshly squeezed juice of 1 Bearss or regular lime

Tagliarini
1 batch Egg Dough (page 6)

To Finish
½ cup unsalted butter (137 grams)
Kosher salt
Grated zest and juice of 2 small Bearss or regular limes
1 tablespoon chopped fresh Italian parsley
1 tablespoon pistachio oil
Freshly grated Parmigiano-Reggiano cheese, for finishing
Freshly ground black pepper
¼ cup toasted and chopped pistachios, for garnish

Preheat the oven to 325°F.

To braise the hen, season the chicken legs with salt and pepper. In a 12-inch sauté pan, heat the olive oil on medium heat. When almost smoking, decrease the heat to medium-low and sear the chicken on each side until deep golden brown, about 14 minutes total. Remove the chicken from the pan to a plate, reserving 3 tablespoons of the oil and rendered fat.

Add the onion, carrot, fennel and 2 pinches of salt. Cook on medium heat until tender, about 8 minutes. Add the garlic and bay leaf and cook for 1 more minute. Add the wine, increase the heat to high, and reduce until the pan is almost dry, about 1½ minutes. Add the chicken stock and lime juice and return the chicken legs to the pan. Bring the liquid to a simmer over medium heat.

Cover and braise in the oven until the meat is fork-tender, 45 to 60 minutes. Remove from the oven and let rest at room temperature until the chicken is cool enough to handle. Then, pull the meat from the bones and chop the skin into 1-inch pieces. Combine the skin and meat with the cooled braising liquid and cool at room temperature until ready to use. It should yield about 2 cups of meat (473 grams).

Dust 2 baking sheets with semolina flour and set aside.

To make the pasta, using a pasta machine, roll out the dough to ¹⁄₁₆ inch thick (see page 10).

With a knife, cut the dough sheet into 12-inch sections. Make two stacks of strips, four strips per stack, thoroughly dusting between the layers with semolina flour. Allow the dough to dry for 30 to 45 minutes, or until the dough has a slightly dry, leathery texture, but is still pliable. Fold each stack like a letter, forming three even layers. Cut the folded dough into ⅛-inch strips, shake off the excess semolina, and form into small nests on the prepared baking sheet.

To finish, bring a large pot of seasoned water to a boil (see page 18).

In a 12-inch sauté pan, bring the braised chicken and braising liquid to a simmer. Add the butter and begin swirling to create an emulsion.

At the same time, drop the pasta in the boiling water.

Once the pasta is cooked 80 percent through, until almost al dente, about 2 to 3 minutes, add it to the pan. Continue to simmer, stirring constantly, until the sauce coats the back of a spoon, about 3 minutes. Season with salt and fold in the grated lime zest, lime juice, parsley, and pistachio oil. Remove from the heat.

To serve, divide the pasta and sauce between four plates. Finish with Parmigiano-Reggiano, plenty of black pepper, and toasted pistachios.

Oxtail and Rosemary Lasagna with Spigarello and Fresh Horseradish

Elsewhere, I've stressed the importance of never adding olive oil directly to the cooked pasta, because adding a layer of fat to the pasta just means the sauce won't stick. When it comes to baked pastas like lasagnas or cannelloni, forget that piece of advice. In this situation, the pasta doesn't need to absorb the sauce. When making baked pasta, the cooked sheets of pasta must come to room temperature before assembly, and during that time, the starches in the pasta will stick to, well, anything. Dousing the sheets of pasta with olive oil avoids that problem, and also serves a secondary function: when the lasagna gets baked in the oven, the coating of olive oil will actually help fry the dough inside the oven, rendering a beautifully crispy texture.

Oxtails are my preferred meat in lasagna; during the winter, oxtails might be my favorite braised meat, period. Since they're cooked with the gelatinous bones, the finished product has an extra hit of sticky richness, transforming something so crude into something so divine. In the restaurant, we use oxtails in terrines every once in a while, but most of the time they're cooked slowly in a big pot and served in big, hearty pasta dishes.

Serves 4

Equipment
Pasta machine + Rolling pin + Baking pan
Baking sheets + Straight wheel cutter + 13x9 baking dish

Store-bought option
Dried lasagne

Oxtail
2⅓ pounds oxtail, bone-in, cut into about five 2-inch segments (1.06 kilograms)
Kosher salt
Freshly ground black pepper
1½ teaspoons chopped fresh rosemary
1 cup neutral cooking oil, like canola or grapeseed (235 milliliters)
1 tablespoon pure olive oil
2 tablespoons tomato paste
2 cups red wine (473 milliliters)
8 cups beef stock (1.89 liters)
½ onion, left whole (128 grams)
1 carrot, peeled and left whole (136 grams)
½ stalk celery, halved crosswise (68 grams)
4 cloves garlic
1 sprig rosemary
Sherry vinegar

Braised Spigarello
2 tablespoons pure olive oil
2 cloves garlic, thinly sliced
1 cup chopped spigarello or any hearty winter green or broccoli florets (156 grams)
1 teaspoon kosher salt
¼ cup red wine (59 milliliters)
¼ cup water (59 milliliters)

Lasagna Sheets
1 recipe Standard Egg Dough (page 6)

Assembly
Extra-virgin olive oil
Béchamel (page 201)
1 tablespoon finely chopped fresh rosemary
Freshly grated Parmigiano-Reggiano
Freshly grated horseradish

Preheat the oven to 325°F.

To make the oxtail, up to 24 hours ahead season the oxtail generously with salt, black pepper, and rosemary. Though not necessary, it's always best to season the oxtail as far in advance as possible, up to a day. This allows the seasoning to better penetrate the meat.

In a Dutch oven or heavy-bottomed pan, heat the canola oil on high heat until almost smoking. Add the meat and deeply caramelize on all sides, about 12 minutes total. Remove the oxtails to a platter and set aside. Discard the oil.

Return the same pot to the stove and decrease the heat to medium. Add the olive oil and tomato paste and cook for about 1 minute. You want to cook the paste as much possible without scorching it. Here, you're cooking out the raw acidity of the tomato paste, with the goal of enriching its natural sugars.

Add the red wine, increase heat to high, and reduce until the pan is almost dry, 8 to 9 minutes. It should achieve a thick consistency, enough to coat the back of a spoon.

Add the stock, onion, carrot, celery, garlic, and rosemary sprig. Bring to a simmer. Return the meat to the pan and cover. Decrease the heat to medium-low. Gently simmer until the meat is fork-tender and almost falling off the bone, 4 to 4½ hours. Cool the oxtail in the braising liquid until cool enough to handle. Remove the oxtails and set aside. Strain the braising liquid through a fine-mesh strainer set over a large bowl, reserving the vegetables.

Return the braising liquid to the Dutch oven and cook over medium heat until it reduces to 2 cups. Meanwhile, pick the meat from the bone; you should have about 3 cups of picked meat. Chop the reserved onion, carrot, and celery into medium dice. Combine the meat, the chopped vegetables, and 1 cup of the reduced braising liquid in a bowl. Season with salt and sherry vinegar. Reserve the remaining reduced braising liquid.

To make the spigarello, add the oil to a cold 12-inch sauté pan and heat over medium heat. Add the garlic and cook until golden, about 2 minutes. Add the spigarello and salt and cook until the greens are completely wilted and tender, about 5 minutes. Remove from the heat and add the red wine and water. Return to low heat and cook until the pan is dry, 5 to 6 minutes. The greens should be fully cooked and have that "braised greens" texture.

Line a baking sheet with parchment paper. Have ready a bowl of ice water. Liberally coat a baking sheet or large baking pan with olive oil.

To finish, bring a large pot of seasoned water to a boil (see page 18).

Using a pasta machine, roll out the dough to slightly over $\frac{1}{16}$-inch thick setting (page 10). With a straight wheel cutter or a knife and a ruler, cut the rolled-out dough into 12-inch sections. Quickly simmer the lasagna in the boiling water for about 30 seconds. You want to barely cook the pasta here; the final cooking will happen in the oven. Transfer the lasagna to the ice water bath and cool for 30 seconds. Transfer the cooled pasta to a mixing bowl, removing as much water as possible, and toss with about 2 tablespoons of extra-virgin olive oil. Lay them out on the parchment-lined baking sheet to dry.

In a small saucepan, over medium-heat, warm up the reserved braising liquid.

Preheat the oven to 400°F.

To assemble, into the bottom of a 13 by 9-inch baking dish, spread ⅓ of the béchamel sauce. Arrange the pasta sheets side by side, covering the bottom of the baking dish. Spread a thin layer of the béchamel on each (about 1 tablespoon per sheet). Add the rosemary (just a small pinch per sheet), the braised meat (about 2 tablespoons per sheet), the spigarello, the freshly grated Parmigiano-Reggiano, and the freshly grated horseradish, to taste. Make sure to leave about ⅛-inch of dry pasta on the outside of each layer. Repeat the layering step one more time.

Top the second layer with a third sheet of pasta. Top the last layer with the béchamel, rosemary, Parmigiano-Reggiano, and horseradish. Bake until the top layer and edges are bubbly and golden brown, 12 to 15 minutes. If after 15 minutes the lasagna is hot and bubbly but not browned on top, move the tray to the top oven rack, turn the broiler on high, and cook until well browned, about 30 seconds.

To serve, divide the lasagna into four portions. Plate and spoon some reserved braising liquid around each portion. At the restaurant we garnish with deep fried leaves of spigarello to play off of the crispy texture of the pasta.

Red Wine Rigatoni with Beef Cheeks and Parsnips

Cooking pasta directly in red wine is a common technique in Italy. Some cook pasta in red wine instead of water, while others cook it halfway in pasta water and finish it by submerging it in the boiling wine. Either way, the result of this incredibly romantic technique is striking: vibrant, bright purple pasta.

There's only one problem: pasta cooked in wine tastes disgusting. While visually stunning, wine-cooked pastas are overwhelmed by the wine's acidity and tannins—at least in my opinion.

But the general idea kept lingering. The more I thought about it, the more I really wanted to figure out a way to make it work, so we started toying with ideas in the restaurant. For the longest time, we tested technique variations every day. We tried different methods, adjusted ratios, tweaked recipes. But it still never saw the light of the menu. We couldn't get it right. It became our white whale.

Finally, I remembered a trick I learned earlier in my career while working at Gary Danko, a traditional fine dining restaurant. There, all the line cooks always had reduced wines on hand at our stations; we'd use the ready-to-use reduction—basically a wine syrup—to season our sauces. It was a brilliant, and easy, way to balance a dish on the fly. We could control it. And that's the problem with cooking pasta in the wine: you can't control how much flavor is imparted; once you drop the pasta in the wine, the floodgates open. But what if we put a controlled amount directly in the dough to rein in the flavor?

And that seed of an idea proved to be a winner. To make the wine rigatoni, we now use a reduced red wine as the hydrating agent in the extruded dough. Especially in the winter months, the resulting pasta gets paired with the classic flavor combination of red wine and beef.

Serves 4

Equipment
Pasta extruder + Baking sheet

Store-bought option
Dried rigatoni, fusilli, or any short shape

Red Wine Rigatoni
1 pint red table wine (450 grams)
1 tablespoon sugar
360 grams 00 flour (2 cups)
80 grams water

Braised Beef Cheeks
2½ pounds beef cheeks, trimmed of excess fat and cut into 1-inch cubes (1.13 kilograms)
Kosher salt
Freshly ground black pepper
½ cup neutral oil, like canola or grapeseed (120 milliliters)
½ onion, finely diced (383 grams)
½ carrot, finely diced (68 grams)
1 stalk celery, finely diced (68 grams)
4 cloves garlic, minced
1 bay leaf
2 tablespoons tomato paste
1 cup red wine (237 milliliters)
1 cup chicken stock (page 169, or store-bought) or beef stock (237 milliliters)

Parsnips
8 ounces parsnips, cut into ½-inch pieces (227 grams)
1 teaspoon chopped fresh thyme
1 teaspoon kosher salt
Freshly ground black pepper
2 teaspoons pure olive oil

To Finish
¼ cup butter (57 grams)
½ teaspoon red wine vinegar (optional)
Freshly grated Parmigiano-Reggiano cheese, for finishing

Preheat the oven to 325°F.

To make the meat, season the beef cheeks with salt and pepper. Though not necessary, it's always best to season the meat as far in advance as possible, up to a day. This allows the seasoning to better penetrate the meat.

In a Dutch oven or heavy-bottomed pan, heat the oil on high heat until almost smoking. Add the beef cheeks and caramelize on all sides until well browned, 10 to 11 minutes. If your pot does not have enough room for the meat to fit comfortably, work in two batches, adding fresh oil for the second batch. Remove the meat with a slotted spoon to a platter and set aside. Discard most of the oil, leaving about 1 tablespoon in the pan.

Decrease the heat to medium. Add the onion, carrot, celery, and 2 pinches of salt. Cook until tender, scraping the bottom with a wooden spoon, about 8 minutes. Add the garlic and bay leaf and cook for 1 minute. Add the tomato paste and cook for 1 more minute. Add the red wine, increase the heat to high, and reduce until the pan is almost dry, about 3 minutes.

Add the stock and return the beef cheeks to the pan. Bring to a simmer over medium heat. Cover and cook in the oven until the cheeks are fork-tender and almost falling apart, about 2 hours. Set aside to cool. You should have about 4 cups, liquid included.

To make the red wine rigatoni, make a reduction by cooking the wine and sugar over medium heat until it's reduced by half. Add 40 grams of the reduction to the flour and water. Mix the dough as instructed on page 16.

Increase the oven temperature to 350°F.

To make the parsnips, on a baking sheet, toss the parsnips with the thyme, salt, pepper, and olive oil. Roast in the oven until slightly caramelized and tender, 25 to 30 minutes. Set aside to cool.

To finish, bring a large pot of seasoned water to a boil (see page 18).

In a 12-inch sauté pan, bring the braising liquid and beef cheeks to a simmer.

Drop the pasta in the boiling water. Once the pasta is cooked 80 percent through, until almost al dente, 2 to 3 minutes, add it to the pan. Fold in the parsnips and butter and reduce until the sauce coats the back of a spoon. If using store-bought rigatoni, add the red wine vinegar for acidity. If using the red wine rigatoni, you don't need any additional vinegar because the wine is already in the pasta.

To serve, divide the pasta and sauce between four plates. Finish with freshly grated Parmigiano-Reggiano.

EMILIO MITIDIERI, THE MACHINE MAN

If a top-flight restaurant in America has fresh pasta on the menu, chances are that the man behind it is Emilio Mitidieri.

He's the secret weapon of nearly every restaurant that has a pasta extruder or laminator (rolling machine) in the kitchen, including ours. Emilio basically invented a job for himself providing customized machines that suit each chef's needs and creativity. He has a virtual monopoly on the game; not only is he a supplier, but he's an inventor as well.

When I was coming up in San Francisco kitchens, Emilio was a mythical presence to young cooks like me, an unseen pasta whisperer that all the staffers had heard of but none had ever actually met. His fingerprints were quite literally on nearly every San Francisco restaurant kitchen that I worked.

When we were in the process of building Flour + Water, I went to the local restaurant supply wholesaler to shop for pasta machines and related equipment. They had nothing. Not even a pasta roller. The salesperson called the supplier to ask about more machines. That particular conversation didn't seem to go anywhere, but for some reason I knew it was this infamous Emilio character on the other end of the line, so I swiped the number while they were still on the phone. Figuring it was best to eliminate the middleman, I later called the number myself.

As it turned out, Emilio's workshop was only two blocks from Flour + Water. It didn't even have a sign, but inside the humble industrial storefront was heaven for an Italian culinary geek like me: hundreds of pasta machines and meat slicers, wall to wall, floor to ceiling. And not just any run-of-the-mill pasta machines, but every shape and size imaginable (and then some): pasta extruders, rollers, ravioli machines, vintage pasta-making tools, and even a giant tortellini-making prototype that Emilio had built decades ago. I walked in cold, not knowing what to expect from this stranger; hours later, I walked out with more stuff than I could carry, thanks to a new friend.

Emilio is a rare breed, especially in a realm like pasta that is so steeped—some may say mired—in tradition. He has mastered a profession, and evolved into an innovator.

Emilio cut his teeth at the iconic (and now defunct) Cafferata Ravioli Factory in San Francisco's North Beach neighborhood. His mentor there was Gino Biradelli, who took over the business in 1966 from the founding Cafferata family. Biradelli is a Genovese mountain of a man who will tell stories about being a prisoner of war in Africa during World War II one minute and then somehow transition into his most important piece of advice for pasta-making ("Be clean!") in the next.

He and Emilio changed the landscape of fresh pasta in San Francisco. Together they modernized the Cafferata Ravioli Factory—a company established in 1886 in an old Victorian building—by bringing in new pasta machines. Until they came along, the factory only made pasta by hand or with hand-cranked machines. The old Italian ladies that made the pasta in the now-legendary factory basement—Biradelli's pals Frank Sinatra and Tony Bennett were rumored to have consumed a drink or two down there—were getting older still, and San Francisco was demanding more fresh pasta. Demand was skyrocketing, and Cafferata couldn't keep up.

So they made changes, bringing in new Italian machinery. Like the original computers that were the size of truck, the pasta machines of that era were oversized, bigger than a large communal table. The move to modernization worked, upping production from 50 pounds an hour to 350 pounds an hour. Using farm fresh eggs delivered daily from Petaluma, some forty miles north of San Francisco, Cafferata thrived, selling this novelty of fresh pasta to restaurants all over San Francisco. Even out-of-state restaurants wanted to serve fresh pasta. They were hustlers, in the best possible sense of the word. Once, Emilio struck a deal with a famous Vegas restaurant for a shipment of ravioli, but the restaurant wanted it immediately. Shipping so much fresh pasta across state lines was expensive, so Emilio bought a plane ticket to Sin City and loaded up all twenty boxes as his luggage. Instead of getting on the flight, he just let the pasta go solo and had a friend pick it up off the conveyor belt at the Vegas airport. It got there more quickly—and much more cheaply.

As Emilio puts it decades later, they were the only ones doing anything new at the time. Yes, they were following an established culture, but they were doing it their own way. They learned the traditional craft, assimilated it into the mainstream, and then developed something innovative. It's a mindset that he carried over when he started his own business years later. He describes his job today as providing chefs with tools to help them realize their visions and make their jobs easier. The first pasta machine he sold was to Larry Mindel in 1979. Mindel—the great Bay Area restaurateur who would go on to open Il Fornaio—was opening a new downtown restaurant named Ciao that would help usher in many modern trends, like a daily menu printed on a single sheet of paper, an open kitchen . . . and fresh housemade pasta.

My goal, however idealistic, is to make Flour + Water a pasta think tank. Within that spectrum, we have a wide range of pasta possibilities, both made by hand and made by machine. And at the end of the day, that's what Emilio wants to give the chefs he works with: He wants them to create, to learn and to think about pasta in a new light.

Pappardelle with Braised Goat Shoulder, Anchovy, and Kale

When it comes to ordering from the menu, a pasta with a strange name can be as intimidating as esoteric wines. Just like the guy on a first date is much more likely to order the Chardonnay rather than risk trying to pronounce "Ormeasco di Pornassio," so do our guests tend to avoid pasta dishes like cappellacci dei briganti or strozzapreti. Instead, more familiar household favorites like farfalle and tagliatelle are some of our best sellers. We have to write our menu accordingly, and the responsibility also falls upon our servers to demystify some of the less common pasta shapes, explaining things like tajarin or garganelli that are, in reality, quite simple and familiar behind their foreign names.

Pappardelle also falls under that "safe word" umbrella. Whenever it's on the menu, it's guaranteed to be a top seller for the night. The flip side of that popularity is that we have to be very careful as to which ragu it's paired with. And make no mistake, it always goes with a hearty ragu of some sort. A recurring joke in the kitchen is that pappardelle is the destination for our homeless lamb brain ragu, because that's the way we'll get people to order it. More often than not, though, pappardelle is matched with a less common meat, like goat.

Goat is one of the most underutilized and misunderstood meats around. It gets conflated with lamb in that it sounds gamey and exotic, but in reality, it's much milder. A nice goat ragu, laced with kale, is winter comfort food at its finest, especially paired with our thickest noodle.

Serves 4

Equipment
Pasta machine + Baking sheets

Store-bought option
Dried pappardelle or any wide noodle

Pappardelle
1 recipe Standard Egg Dough (page 6)

Goat Braise
1 whole goat shoulder (3½ pounds), bone in (1.62 kilograms)
Kosher salt
¼ cup plus 1 tablespoon pure olive oil (74 milliliters)
1 yellow onion, finely diced (255 grams)
1½ carrots, finely diced (170 grams)
2 stalks celery, finely diced (136 grams)
3 cloves garlic, sliced
1 tablespoon smoked paprika
1 tablespoon tomato paste
1½ cups red wine (355 milliliters)
5 anchovy fillets, rinsed and left whole (142 grams)
8 cups chicken stock (1.89 liters; page 169 or store-bought)

Kale
1 tablespoon pure olive oil
½ yellow onion, finely diced (128 grams)
Kosher salt
4 cloves garlic, sliced
5 ounces kale, stem removed, washed, and coarsely chopped (142 grams)
1 cup chicken stock (page 169, or store-bought; 237 milliliters)

To Finish
1 cups braising liquid (237 grams)
¾ cup unsalted butter (170 grams)
2 teaspoons sherry vinegar
Kosher salt
Freshly grated Parmigiano-Reggiano, for finishing

Dust 2 baking sheets with semolina flour and set aside.

To make the pasta, using a pasta machine, roll out the dough to slightly over $\frac{1}{16}$ inch thick (see page 10).

Cut the dough sheet into 12-inch sections. Layer each section on top of the other, thoroughly dusting with semolina flour between each layer. You should have about 8 layers total. Allow the dough to dry until it has a slightly dry, leathery texture, but is still pliable, 30 to 45 minutes. Fold each sheet into thirds, like a letter, creating three layers. Cut the folded sheet of dough into 1-inch wide strips of pappardelle, shake off the excess semolina, and form into small nests on the prepared baking sheets.

Preheat the oven to 325°F.

For the goat braise, season the goat shoulder liberally with salt. Heat ¼ cup of the olive oil in a Dutch oven on high heat until almost smoking. Add the goat shoulder, decrease the heat to medium-high, and sear on all sides until golden brown, 8 to 10 minutes. Remove the goat shoulder and set aside. Pour off any excess oil from the pot.

In the same pot, add the onion, carrots, and celery. Add the remaining 1 tablespoon of olive oil and sweat the vegetables on medium-low until tender, 8 to 10 minutes. Add the garlic and cook for 1 more minute. Stir in the paprika, tomato paste, and salt. Cook for another minute. Add the wine and increase the heat to high. Add the anchovies and return the goat shoulder to the pan. Cover the goat three-quarters of the way with chicken stock (you may not need to use all 8 cups). Bring to a simmer. Cover and braise in the oven until fork-tender, about 3 hours. Remove from the oven and let the goat cool in the braising liquid until cool enough to handle. Remove the goat meat and tear it into ½-inch pieces. Refrigerate until ready to use.

Skim the remaining fat from the cooking liquid. Strain the liquid through a fine-mesh strainer into a saucepan and reduce over medium heat to 1 cup.

To make the kale in a 12-inch sauté pan, heat the olive oil over medium-high heat until almost smoking. Add the onion and a pinch of salt. Cook until the onions are translucent but not browned, about 8 minutes. Add the garlic and cook for 1 minute. Add the collard greens and chicken stock. Bring the stock to a boil over medium-high heat, decrease the heat to a simmer, cover, and cook until the stock is almost completely evaporated, about 10 minutes. You should have about 1½ cups greens.

To finish, bring a large pot of seasoned water to a boil (see page 18).

In a 12-inch sauté pan, bring the braising liquid and butter to a boil over medium heat. Add the goat shoulder and the braised kale.

Drop the pasta in the boiling water. Once the pasta is cooked 80 percent through, until almost al dente, about 2 to 3 minutes, add it to the pan. Reserve the pasta water. Continue cooking until the sauce thickens, about 2 minutes. Season with sherry vinegar and salt.

To serve, divide the pasta and sauce between four plates. Finish with freshly grated Parmigiano-Reggiano.

Corzetti with Sausage, Clams, and Fennel

It's always exciting to see how the textures of various clams play so well with pasta. At the height of the season we have a gamut to choose from: manila clams, littleneck clams, cherrystone clams, and even razor clams. They're nearly always used in pasta dishes, because basically everything about clams—the fork-size bites, the briny flavor, the meaty nuggets of texture—pairs well with pasta.

When dealing with clams in pasta, I steer away from my East Coast roots and the classic Italian-American combination of linguini, whole clams, and a smothering cream sauce. I'm never high on including clam shells in pastas; I feel like it detracts from the rhythm of eating, and having a shell bowl on the table is just one more thing that the waitstaff has to worry about in our tiny dining room. So instead of Italian-American menus, we look to Spanish ones, where sausages and clams are a classic combination. Corzetti stampati—easy to make, but increasingly available dried in stores—are the logical pasta to use, though I suppose linguine is not a bad option either.

Serves 4

Equipment
Pasta machine + Rolling pin +
Corzetti stamp or 2-inch ring mold or cookie cutter
Baking sheets

Store-bought option
Dried corzetti, or any short noodle

Corzetti
1 large egg
½ cup white wine (118 milliliters)
360 grams 00 flour

Clams
1 tablespoon pure olive oil
1 shallot, thinly sliced
1 clove garlic, sliced
2 cups white wine (474 milliliters)
2 pounds Manila clams, scrubbed (907 grams)
1½ cups flour (360 grams)
2 tablespoons squid ink (26 milliliters)
1 egg
½ cup white wine (126 milliliters)

To Finish
1 tablespoon pure olive oil
8 ounces fresh pork sausage (page 189), broken into ¼-inch pieces (227 grams)
1½ medium red onions, finely diced (383 grams)
4 cloves garlic, thinly sliced
½ cup white wine (118 milliliters)
1 cup chicken stock (237 grams; page 169, or store-bought)
2 tablespoons extra-virgin olive oil
Kosher salt
Juice of ½ lemon
1 tablespoon chopped fresh Italian parsley
1 tablespoon finely minced chives

To make the clams, in a 12-inch sauté pan over high heat, add the olive oil and shallot. Cook until translucent, about 6 minutes. Add the white wine and clams to the pan, cover, and cook until the clams all open, about 8 minutes. Remove the clams and continue cooking until the liquid is reduced by half. Let the the liquid cool completely. Remove the clams from their shells, cover with the cooled liquid and refrigerate until ready to use.

To make the pasta, mix the dough together as instructed on page 6. Roll out the dough and make the corzetti stampati as instructed on page 74.

To finish, bring large pot of seasoned water to a boil (page 18).

In a 12-inch sauté pan over high heat, add the olive oil and the sausage. Brown all sides of the sausage, about 3 minutes. Add the red onions and cook until translucent, about 90 seconds.

Add the garlic and continue cooking until the garlic starts to brown, about 3 to 4 minutes. Add the white wine and cook until almost evaporated, about 30 seconds. Add the chicken stock, the clams, and their liquid. Bring to a simmer.

Drop the pasta in the boiling water. Once the pasta is cooked 80 percent through, until almost al dente, about 2 to 3 minutes, add it to the pan. Reserve the pasta water. Continue simmering the pasta over high heat until the sauce coats the back of a spoon, about 3 minutes. Drizzle with the extra-virgin olive oil. Season to taste with salt and lemon juice.

To serve, divide the pasta and sauce between four plates. Finish with the parsley and the chives.

Flour + Water Pork Sausage

This is our standard recipe for the sausage we make at Flour + Water, scaled down for home use.

The recipe here features pork shoulder, pork fat, and pork skin. The pork fat is included for moisture in the finished product, and the pork skin is there for texture. Beyond that, the sausage recipe can customized by substituting any lean protein for the pork shoulder: lamb, rabbit, goat, duck, chicken, turkey, or even a high-fat fish like salmon.

Makes 26 ounces/737 grams of ground sausage

Equipment
Meat grinder

2¼ ounces pork skin (65 grams)
1 pound pork shoulder (or leg), diced and chilled (450 grams)
½ pound pork fat, diced (225 grams) and chilled
2 tablespoons white wine
¾ teaspoon freshly ground black pepper
Pinch of red pepper flakes
Pinch of fennel pollen (see Sources, page 250)
1.29 grams dextrose
1 tablespoon plus 1 teaspoon kosher salt

In a stockpot, add the pork skin and cover with cold salted water. Bring to a simmer over medium heat. Skim off any residue and simmer until completely tender, about 45 minutes. Chill for 1 hour or up to 4 days and dice.

Making sure all your diced meat is very cold; mix all of the ingredients together in a large bowl. Quickly put through a meat grinder.

Mix the ground meat until the mixture is tacky and sticks to your hand. If you're using a stand mixer with a paddle attachment, put the ground meat in the bowl and mix for 4 minutes to get a cohesive texture. Keeps 4 days refrigerated or 3 months frozen.

Pizzoccheri with Speck, Braised Cabbage, Potato, and Fontina

In the same way that southern Italy's durum wheat bred a pasta culture dependent on semolina dough, so did the cuisine of the diminutive Valtellina region center around buckwheat. The Valtellina is an isolated area in the northernmost sliver of Italy, technically in the Lombardy region but on the alpine border of Switzerland. Buckwheat has been grown there for centuries, and it has been incorporated into its indigenous pasta.

Pizzoccheri are buckwheat noodles similar in thickness to pappardelle, only shorter. And in keeping with the mountain regions where they originate, they are often served with ingredients more commonly associated with Switzerland and Germany than Italy: cabbage, potatoes, and funky fontina cheese. The dish is baked in the oven until the cheese is bubbling and melted, at which point it's cooked under the broiler. In the restaurant, we have the luxury of finishing it in our wood-burning oven instead of a broiler to give it a hint of smoke, but the important part is that cap of burnt, crisp cheese that you'll get in either the pizza oven or under a broiler. It's like a pasta version of French onion soup.

Serves 4

Equipment
Baking sheets + Pasta roller
Straight wheel cutter (optional)

Store-bought option
Dried pappardelle, cracked in half before cooking

Pizzoccheri
¾ cup buckwheat flour (90 grams)
2 cups 00 flour (270 grams)
2 big pinches kosher salt
1¼ cups egg yolks, about 14 to 16 yolks (350 grams)
1½ teaspoons extra-virgin olive oil

Speck-Braised Cabbage
3 tablespoons unsalted butter
½ yellow onion, thinly sliced (128 grams)
Kosher salt
6 cloves garlic, thinly sliced
6½ ounces savoy cabbage, cut into ½-inch x 2½-inch strips (184 grams)
1¼ cups white wine (300 milliliters)
3¼ cups chicken stock (768 milliliters; page 169 or store-bought)
6 ounces speck, julienned (170 grams)

Boiled Potatoes
6 to 7 fingerling potatoes (180 grams)
1 bay leaf
8 whole black peppercorns
1 tablespoon kosher salt
1 tablespoon white wine vinegar

To Finish
1 tablespoon minced fresh thyme leaves
½ cup unsalted butter (113 grams)
1½ cups grated fontina cheese (170 grams)
4 ounces fontina cheese, cut into ¼-inch dice (113 grams)

To make the pasta, on a wooden board combine the flours and the salt. Create a well. Add the yolks and the olive oil and use the well method to bring the dough together (see page 14). The buckwheat flour is higher in protein and may require a few spritzes of water to bring it together. Knead for 15 to 20 minutes, then cover tightly with plastic wrap and let rest for at least 30 minutes before rolling.

Dust 2 baking sheets with semolina flour and set aside.

Using a pasta machine, roll out the dough to slightly over $\frac{1}{16}$ inch thick (see page 10).

With a straight wheel cutter or a ruler and a knife, cut the long sheet of dough into 12-inch segments. Stack the segments, dusting liberally with semolina between each layer. Allow the dough to dry until it has a slightly dry, leathery texture but is still pliable, 45 minutes. It should still be pliable. Cut the dough stack into strips that are ½ inch by 3 inches. Place the pizzoccheri on the prepared baking sheets until ready to cook.

To braise the cabbage, heat a Dutch oven over medium-high heat. Add the butter and heat until bubbling. Add the onions and a pinch of salt and cook until translucent, about 8 minutes. Add the garlic and cook 2 more minutes. Add the cabbage and a pinch of salt and cook for another 2 minutes. We aren't trying to brown the cabbage, just coat it with the hot fat. Add the white wine, bring to a boil, and reduce until the pan is almost

dry. Add the chicken stock, bring back to a simmer, and cook until the cabbage is fully tender and the braising liquid has reduced by half, about 10 to 15 minutes. Turn off the heat and fold in the speck.

To make the potatoes, combine all the ingredients in a small saucepan over medium heat. Bring to a boil, reduce to a simmer, and cook gently until fork-tender, about 12 minutes. Drain and cool the potatoes completely, then slice into ⅛-inch-thick rounds. Place in a bowl and set aside.

To finished, turn the broiler to high and place your oven rack so your Dutch oven is as close to the heat source as possible. On the stovetop, bring the cabbage and its braising liquid to a simmer in the Dutch oven. Add the thyme and the butter.

Bring a large pot of seasoned water to a boil (see page 18).

Drop the pasta in the boiling water and cook it for only 1 minute. The majority of the cooking time will be in the pan with the cabbage. Drain the pasta and add it to the cabbage and continue cooking until the sauce coats the back of a spoon, 5 to 6 minutes. Fold in the potatoes, 1 cup of the grated fontina, and all of the cubed fontina. Sprinkle an even layer of the remaining grated fontina cheese on top. Place under the broiler and cook until the top is deeply browned and bubbling, 5 to 10 minutes. Allow to rest for 10 minutes before serving. To serve, divide the pasta mixture into four plates.

Whole Wheat Campanelle with Anise-Braised Pork and Chard

At the end of the night, when all the cooks meet and talk about the next day's menu, the brainstorming doesn't begin with a pasta and accompanying ingredients. We mostly talk about flavor profiles, combinations that jive together and the textures that highlight them. In some ways, I liken the process to a jazz band riffing; there's no set song, but we all have an idea of what notes work together in a sequence.

Whole wheat and anise are flavors that groove together in a dish. It's not a flavor combination that stems from any particular pasta tradition, at least as far as I know; if anything, it's a pairing that has thrived in the baking world, with anise-flavored bread.

But instead of bread, we bring those flavors to pasta via campanelle ("bells"), an extruded pasta that has become common in American grocery stores. Also called gigli ("lilies") in Italy, they have thrived in the mainstream for the same reasons that farfalle have: they are functional, easy to eat, and good looking.

Serves 4

Equipment
Pasta extruder (optional) + Spice grinder

Store-bought option
Dried campanelle, or other short pasta

Fennel-Anise Salt
1 tablespoon finely ground fennel seeds
1 teaspoon finely ground star anise
3 tablespoons kosher salt

Braised Pork Shoulder
2 pounds pork shoulder, cut into 1-inch cubes (900 grams)
2 tablespoons Fennel-Anise Salt
1 tablespoon fennel seeds, toasted
2 bay leaves
2 tablespoons pure olive oil
1 pound leeks, cut into ½-inch dice (450 grams)
1 fennel bulb , cut into ½-inch dice (108 grams)
7 cloves garlic, minced
1 cup white wine (237 milliliters)
4 cups chicken stock (946 milliliters; page 169 or store-bought)

To Finish
¾ pound chard or spinach, coarsely chopped (82 grams)
¾ pound whole wheat campanelle or any other dried whole wheat pasta (340 grams)
½ cup unsalted butter (113 grams)
2 tablespoons crème fraîche
Kosher salt
Juice of ½ lemon
Freshly grated Parmigiano-Reggiano cheese, for finishing

To make the flavored salt, grind the fennel seeds and anise seeds in a coffee or spice grinder. Transfer to a small bowl and combine with the salt. You will have about ⅓ cup.

To make the pork shoulder, season the meat with the flavored salt 24 hours in advance, if possible. Put on a baking sheet, uncovered, and refrigerate.

Preheat the oven to 325°F.

Heat a small sauté pan over medium heat. Add the fennel seeds and stir constantly until toasted, about 45 seconds. Using a cheesecloth and kitchen string, make a sachet with the toasted fennel seeds and bay leaves.

Heat a Dutch oven over medium-high heat. Add the olive oil and heat until almost smoking. Working in batches, sear half of the pork, stirring every few minutes, until it is caramelized and has a deep golden-brown color, about 12 minutes. Remove the pork to a platter, set aside, and sear the second batch. Remove the pork and set aside, reserving the fat in the pan. Decrease the heat to medium, add the leeks and fennel, and cook until tender and translucent, about 8 minutes. Add the garlic and

cook for 2 more minutes. Add the white wine and reduce until the pan is almost dry. Add the chicken stock and the sachet and return the pork shoulder to the pan. Bring to a simmer. Cover and cook in the oven until the meat is fork-tender, about 2 hours. Cool to room temperature, discard the sachet, and refrigerate until ready to use. It can be store for 2 to 3 days. You should have about 5 cups.

To finish, bring a large pot of seasoned water to a boil (see page 18).

In a 12-inch sauté pan over high heat, bring the pork shoulder and its braising liquid to a simmer. Add the chard.

Drop the pasta in the boiling water. Once the pasta is cooked 80 percent through, until almost al dente, about 2 to 3 minutes, add it to the pan along with the butter and the crème fraîche, stirring until the sauce coats the back of a spoon. Adjust the seasoning with salt and lemon juice, if needed.

To serve, divide the pasta and sauce between four plates. Finish with freshly grated Parmigiano-Reggiano.

Rabbit Cannelloni with Sweet Potato and Thyme

Pasta al forno—pasta baked in our wood-burning oven, which is usually reserved for pizzas—is a relatively rare sight at Flour + Water. When those dishes make an appearance on the menu, the vibe of the restaurant is completely transformed. A new energy permeates the room.

Most diners can see the oven from their tables, which in turn means they can see the cannelloni, in all their glory, being slid in and out. The whole room smells like cannelloni as well; it's that familiar lasagna aura of blistered cheese fused with béchamel with a backdrop of slowly cooked meat. It's the kind of dish that turns heads as it goes out to a table. We cook them to order in the restaurant, about six minutes in the wood-fired oven.

The cannelloni itself is crisp, maybe even a little charred on the outside, so if you tap the pasta gently with the back of a spoon, it might delicately crack. Digging deeper, you get the tender meat bits and the accompanying sweet potato puree.

Our versions of baked cannelloni aren't drenched in red sauce or rolled the size of beer bottles. In a weird way, they almost resemble egg rolls or taquitos.

You can form the cannelloni a day ahead of time, and then crisp them up in the oven when it's go time.

Serves 4

Equipment
Blender + Baking sheets
Large baking pan or casserole dish + Pasta machine
Rolling pin + Straight wheel cutter

Store-bought
Dried cannelloni

Roasted Sweet Potatoes
6 ounces peeled and small-diced sweet potatoes (170 grams)
1 tablespoon pure olive oil
1 teaspoon kosher salt
½ teaspoon freshly ground black pepper
½ teaspoon finely chopped fresh thyme
1 tablespoon chopped fresh Italian parsley

Sweet Potato Puree
9 ounces coarsely chopped sweet potato (255 grams)
1 clove garlic, sliced
1½ cups whole milk (355 milliliters)

Braised Rabbit Filling
1 pound rabbit legs (455 grams, about 2 legs)
Kosher salt
Freshly ground black pepper
2 tablespoons pure olive oil
2 tablespoons plus 1 teaspoon minced fresh thyme
1 medium onion, diced (255 grams)
1 carrot, diced (80 grams)
1 stalk celery, diced (80 grams)
6 garlic cloves, minced
1 cup white wine (237 milliliters)
6 cups chicken stock (1.42 liters; page 169, or store-bought)
7 tablespoons Béchamel (page 201)
2 ounces minced prosciutto (55 grams, about 2 thin slices)
¼ cup freshly grated Parmigiano-Reggiano cheese

Fried Brussels Sprouts (optional)
8 ounces Brussels sprouts (227 grams)
Canola oil
Kosher salt

Cannelloni
Pure olive oil
1 recipe Standard Egg Dough (page 6)

To Finish

Béchamel (opposite)
Freshly grated Parmigiano-Reggiano cheese, for finishing
1 cup fried Brussels sprout leaves, for garnish (optional)

Preheat the oven to 350°F.

To make the roasted sweet potatoes, in a bowl, toss the sweet potatoes with the olive oil, salt, pepper, thyme, and parsley. Arrange in a single layer on a baking sheet and roast until tender and lightly browned, about 25 to 30 minutes. Set aside.

To make the sweet potato puree, combine all the ingredients in a medium saucepan. Simmer over medium heat until the sweet potatoes are tender. Drain, reserving the milk. In a blender, puree the sweet potatoes, adding just enough reserved milk to create a smooth puree (about ½ cup). Set aside.

To make the filling, preferably 24 hours in advance, season the rabbit with 2 tablespoons of the thyme, and salt and pepper. Preheat a Dutch oven over high heat. Add the olive oil and heat until almost smoking. Add the seasoned legs and sear, caramelizing the meat and creating a fond on the bottom of the pan, about 4 minutes. Remove and set aside.

Remove all but 2 tablespoons of fat from the Dutch oven. Add the onion, carrot, and celery and cook until translucent, about 8 minutes. Add the garlic and cook 1 minute more. Add the white wine and cook until almost dry. Then, add the chicken stock and return the rabbit to the pot. Bring the braising liquid to a boil, then decrease the heat to a simmer. Cover and gently simmer until the rabbit is tender and almost falling off the bone, about 1½ hours.

Cool the rabbit in the braising liquid until it's cool enough to handle. Pick the meat off the bones and tear it into ½-inch chunks. Discard the bones and set the meat aside in a bowl.

Strain the braising liquid into a large pan. Reserve the strained cooked vegetables (mirepoix) in a separate bowl and set aside. On medium heat, reduce the braising liquid to a sauce-like consistency, about 15 to 20 minutes. Remove from the heat and set aside.

In a large mixing bowl, combine the rabbit meat, the cooked mirepoix, béchamel, prosciutto, the 1 teaspoon of thyme, and the grated Parmigiano Reggiano. Mash and shred the mixture, using a spatula. Transfer to a crock or a glass jar with a lid.

Cover and refrigerate until ready to use. The rillettes can be refrigerated for up to one month. Keep the meat covered with a layer of fat. Rendered pork fat is available from farmer's market and butcher shops.

To make the pasta, bring a large pot of seasoned water to a boil (see page 18). Have ready a bowl of ice water to shock the pasta. Coat two large baking sheets and one large baking dish with olive oil.

Using a pasta machine, roll out the dough to slightly over ¹⁄₁₆-inch thick setting (see page 10).

Cut the rolled dough into 5 by 4-inch rectangles. Using a straight wheel cutter, or a knife and a ruler. Quickly simmer the sheets, 8 at a time, in the boiling water until barely cooked, 30 to 45 seconds. The final cooking will happen in the oven. Remove the pasta quickly from the boiling water and drop the pieces in the ice bath. Remove the pasta from the ice water as soon as they are cool (about 1 minute). Blot dry with a kitchen towel, then stack them on one of the prepared sheet pans, drizzling between sheets with more oil so they don't stick.

To fill the cannelloni, place one pasta sheet on a clean work surface, with the longer side horizontal. With a spoon, distribute about 2½ tablespoons of filling evenly in a row along the bottom edge of the noodle. Roll the noodle into a tube (like a burrito) around the filling, keeping it as tight as possible, with as little of the filling as possible bulging out from the open ends. Place the cannelloni on the second prepared baking sheet, with the rolled side down. Before you form the next cannelloni, quickly dry off any remaining oil from your rolling surface.

Arrange the 12 cannelloni in the oiled baking pan in four rows of three, each group tightly nestled together. These can be made ahead of time and will keep for up to 24 hours, covered, in the fridge.

To fry the Brussels sprouts if using, trim off the bottoms of the sprouts and discard the outermost leaves. Pull off the good leaves, reserving the hearts for another use. Pour enough oil into a medium pot so that the oil comes 3 inches up the sides. Heat the oil to 350°F. Fry the Brussels sprout leaves until the edges begin to curl and brown, about 60 seconds. Drain on a paper towel lined pan and season with salt.

To finish, preheat the oven to 400°F.

When the cannelloni are formed and arranged, spread the béchamel on the tops of the cannelloni, about 1½ tablespoons on each. I personally like to keep the edges of the cannelloni exposed so they become extra crisp in the oven. Grate a liberal amount of Parmigiano-Reggiano on top.

Bake the cannelloni until the tops are browned, about 30 minutes.

In a small saucepan, combine the reserved braising liquid and the diced sweet potato. Bring to a boil. Heat up the sweet potato puree in a separate pan.

To serve, place three cannelloni on a plate per person for a midcourse, or six per person for a large entree. Dollop a few spoonfuls of the sweet potato puree around them. Arrange the roasted sweet potatoes around the plate and on top of the cannelloni. Spoon the remaining braising liquid on top of the cannelloni and around the plate. Garnish with the fried Brussels sprouts leaves if using.

Béchamel Sauce

Makes ½ cup

5 tablespoons butter
4 tablespoons flour
3 cups milk
2 teaspoons salt
½ teaspoon freshly grated nutmeg
8 ounces Parmigiano-Reggiano, for grating

In a medium saucepan, heat butter until melted. Add flour and stir until smooth. Over medium heat, cook until light golden brown, about 6 to 7 minutes.

Meanwhile, heat milk in a separate pan until just about to boil. Add milk to butter mixture, 1 cup at a time, whisking continuously until very smooth and bring to a boil. Cook 30 seconds and remove from heat. Season with salt and nutmeg and set aside until ready to use.

SPRING

THROUGHOUT THE MONTH OF MARCH IN SAN FRANCISCO, spring creeps through the market with brief cameos, giving glimmers of hope that the winter has passed for good before squashing that optimism with a week of violent fog. Most of the winter citrus is long gone by this point, and diners (not to mention chefs) tire of root vegetables somewhere around Valentine's Day. As the warmer weather slowly lurches forward, some early asparagus appear one weekend. The next weekend, frost might delay the harvest, but fava beans make their debut. It's stop and go for a few weeks, just like the spring rains.

Then on a random sunny morning—maybe in late March, maybe in mid-April—the market explodes in a sea of colorful spring bounty. The market blooms overnight, suddenly emerging from its winter hibernation with bright green peas, fava beans, spring onions, fuzzy green almonds, green garlic, and asparagus of all sizes and colors. Soon there will be strawberries and cherries, and later, the summer windfall—tomatoes, stone fruits, corn.

Farmers' markets are the heart of the San Francisco food world, whether it's at the chef-heavy market in Marin, the classic Alemany Market (the oldest in California), or the mothership—the triweekly Ferry Plaza Market at the Ferry Building on the Embarcadero. We go to several markets regularly. There, we look for ideas, and we pick up from farmers who don't deliver directly to restaurants. Maybe with a wink and a handshake deal, we get the inside track on "off-menu" ingredients. (I won't discuss the "seedy" black market circuit of the market, but let's just say there was some grade-A raw goat's milk making the rounds for a while.)

The market is also a social place, a place to directly interact with the amazing farmers and purveyors who make our menus possible. And, just as important for me as a young chef, the market is a place for me to learn. The farmers know everything about their produce, the area's microseasons, and why (and when) it tastes the way it does. Chatting with the other chefs, we share tips on which produce is good, and how it can be utilized. For the most part, the San Francisco chef community is a small, supportive collective. The majority of our days are spent in hot, cramped kitchens—it's what we love, after all—but going to the market every few days, free of our chef whites for a few hours, clears our heads and gives us a little extra inspiration.

Goat's Milk Ricotta and Artichoke Triangoli

One of the first stuffed pastas ever offered at Flour + Water was artichoke triangoli. In the first several months of the restaurant's life, making stuffed pasta was a near impossibility, simply because we had neither the room nor the time. There was a dreadfully small pasta area, and I quickly figured out that spending half of a sixteen-hour day making hundreds of triangoli in a three-foot-square corner of the kitchen was not the ideal use of our time. We resolved that dilemma when we built our Dough Room, and over the years we've continued to evolve the dish.

Artichokes, like cardoons, their not-so-distant wild relatives in the thistle family, are native to the Mediterranean. Dating back to Roman times, they have always been farmed in Italy, but they came to the Bay Area with the wave of Italian immigrants during the early twentieth century. I've always maintained that the Bay Area is, in many ways, like another region of Italy, given its climate, geography, and seasonal cooking. The artichokes proved me right, as it turns out that they are tailor-made for growing along the foggy California coastline. These days, California grows most of the artichokes used in this country.

Artichokes are the harbingers of spring. We marinate them, or sometimes fry them. We slice them atop a pizza with prosciutto and potato, and we shave them raw and mix them in a simple salad of greens, Parmigiano-Reggiano shavings, and vinaigrette. And, of course, we put them in pasta. Pairing artichokes with goat's milk ricotta in a stuffed pasta is by far my favorite version. It's served with a sauce of whey and olive oil.

You can substitute fresh cow's milk ricotta, which is much easier to find, but the texture and tangy flavor of goat's milk ricotta works particularly well with artichokes. Besides, it's so easy to make. And when accentuated by the grated Pecorino Romano, the whole thing goes to another level.

Serves 4

Equipment

Blender + Pasta machine + Pasta roller
Straight wheel cutter (optional) + Piping bag (optional)
Fluted wheel cutter + Baking sheets + Spray bottle

Store-bought option

Any fresh, cheese-stuffed pasta

Goat's Milk Ricotta

8 cups whole goat's milk (1.9 liters)
1 cup heavy cream (236 milliliters)
1 tablespoon kosher salt
½ cup plus 1 tablespoon apple cider vinegar (133 milliliters)

Artichoke Puree

24 baby artichokes or 6 standard artichokes, cleaned and trimmed (303 grams)
½ medium yellow onion, thinly sliced (128 grams)
1½ cups white wine (355 milliliters)
1½ cups water (355 milliliters)
1 tablespoon salt
Juice of 1 lemon

Filling

2 cups goat's milk curds (439 grams)
¼ cup grated Pecorino Romano
1 tablespoon chiffonade of mint
Grated zest of 1 lemon
2 teaspoons freshly squeezed lemon juice
Kosher salt

Triangoli

1 recipe Rav Dough (page 6)

To Finish

2 cups goat's milk whey (473 grams)
½ cup extra-virgin olive oil (118 milliliters)
2 tablespoons minced fresh mint
2 tablespoons minced fresh Italian parsley
Kosher salt
Juice of ½ lemon
Freshly grated Pecorino Romano cheese, for finishing

In a heavy 4-quart pot over medium heat, add the milk, cream, and salt. Slowly bring to a rolling boil, stirring occasionally to prevent scorching. Add the apple cider vinegar and decrease the heat to low. Simmer until the mixture curdles, about 4 minutes. Turn off the heat. Let the milk mixture rest for about 15 minutes.

Line a large sieve or colander with a large piece of cheesecloth. Place the lined colander over a large bowl. Pour the milk mixture into the lined sieve and let it drain for 30 minutes or up to 12 hours in the refrigerator, uncovered. Refrigerate the curds and whey separately in airtight containers. The curds and whey will keep in the refrigerator for up to 3 days. You should have about 2 cups curds and 2 cups whey.

To make the artichoke puree, combine all the ingredients in a small saucepan and bring to a boil over medium-high heat. Decrease the heat to a simmer and cook until the artichokes are tender when pierced with a knife, about 20 minutes.

Drain the artichokes and onion over a bowl and reserve the braising liquid. Halve the artichokes lengthwise (from tip to base), remove and discard the choke, and slice them into ⅛-inch slivers. Reserve about one quarter of the artichoke slivers (about 1 cup) for the finishing steps and set aside.

Add the remaining artichokes and all of the onion slices to the jar of a blender and puree until smooth. Use some of the reserved braising liquid if needed to make a smooth puree. Season with salt, if necessary, and set aside. You should have about 1¼ cups of puree (290 grams).

To make the filling, combine the goat's milk curds, Pecorino Romano, mint, and lemon zest and juice in a bowl. Adjust the seasonings and transfer the filling to a bowl and set aside. The filling will keep in the refrigerator, covered, for 3 days.

Dust 2 baking sheets with semolina flour and set aside.

To make the pasta, using a pasta machine, roll out the dough until the sheet is just translucent (see page 10). Cut a 2-foot section of the dough sheet and cover the rest of the dough with plastic wrap.

Cut the sheet of dough into 3-inch squares with a straight wheel cutter or a knife and a ruler. Using a piping bag or spoon, place a heaping teaspoon of filling in the middle of each square, leaving ¼ inch of dough bare around the edge.

Fold the filled square so the opposite corners meet, pressing to create a triangle. Use a quick spritz of water from a spray bottle to help seal, if necessary. Gently but firmly seal the top corner and remove the air pocket by moving your fingers from the point down, caressing the filling to make a tight, airless pillow.

With a fluted cutter, trim the pasta along the two edges, leaving about ¼ inch of pasta around the filling.

Working quickly, place the triangoli on the prepared baking sheets, spaced apart. Don't let the triangoli touch each other or they may stick together. Repeat until you run out of dough or filling. You should get 30 to 40 pieces.

To finish, bring a large pot of seasoned water to a boil (see page 18).

In a 12-inch sauté pan, bring the goat's milk whey, olive oil, and the reserved 1 cup of slivered artichokes to a simmer.

Drop the pasta in the boiling water. Once the pasta is cooked 80 percent through, until almost al dente, about 2 to 3 minutes, add it to the pan and swirl to combine. You aren't looking to emulsify the whey and olive oil like a unified butter sauce; instead, the two components should stay separate. Fold in the mint and parsley. Season to taste with salt and lemon juice.

To serve, divide the pasta and sauce between four plates. Garnish with freshly grated Pecorino Romano cheese.

Stradette with Leeks and Fava Beans

The meaning of stradette—"little streets"—becomes evident when they are plated. When they are laid out one at a time, unlayered and unadorned, in stripes flat on a plate, it doesn't take much imagination to see how they resemble roads on a tiny map.

Stradette come from the region of Piedmont. Thicker than most flat noodles but shorter than pappardelle, they are made with a unique cornmeal dough and are most often served alongside another Piemontese staple, stewed leeks. It's a peasant pasta born of necessity; corn flour was cheaper than wheat flour in Piedmont, and leeks have long been a staple crop there.

The stradette dishes that I saw in Italy were slightly heavier than this one, in which the fava bean puree mimics creaminess and adds a new dimension of flavor. A few whole beans are tossed in for texture purposes, but it's the pasta itself that is the key texture component. It should be cooked al dente, so it still has some bite. It is tough pasta to cook because of its utter simplicity. It's so easy that it's difficult. Basic in both its composition and its appearance, it is, at its best, a beautiful and singular dish.

Serves 4

Equipment
Blender + Pasta machine
Rolling pin + Baking sheets

Store-bought option
Dried pappardelle, or any fat and flat noodle

Stradette
1¾ cups 00 flour (240 grams)
⅔ cup coarsely ground polenta (120 grams)
1 large egg
12 large egg yolks (300 grams)
1 tablespoon extra-virgin olive oil
1 tablespoon whole milk

Fava Puree
1 cup packed spinach (57 grams)
1 cup fava beans picked and peeled (145 grams)
⅓ cup whole milk (79 milliliters)

Leek and Fava Ragu
1 cup fava beans, picked and peeled (145 grams)
2 tablespoons unsalted butter
3 medium leeks, white part only, julienned (250 grams)
½ teaspoon kosher salt
2 cups prosecco (475 milliliters)
½ cup water (118 milliliters)

To Finish
½ cup unsalted butter (113 grams)
¼ cup minced fines herbes (a mixture of parsley, chives, tarragon, and chervil)
Grated zest of ½ lemon
Kosher salt
Freshly grated Parmigiano-Reggiano cheese, for finishing

To make the pasta, follow the instructions for Egg Dough (page 6), adding milk with wet ingredients. Note that this dough starts out very wet, but it will firm up as the polenta hydrates.

Dust 2 baking sheets with semolina flour and set aside.

Using a pasta machine, roll out the dough to slightly over $\frac{1}{16}$ inch thick (see page 10). With a sharp knife, cut the dough sheet into 12-inch sections. Layer each section on top of the other, thoroughly dusting with semolina flour between each layer. You should have about 8 layers total. Allow the sheets to dry until the dough has a slightly dry, leathery texture but is still pliable, 30 to 45 minutes. Cut the stack into strips 1¼ inches by 6 inches. Reserve on the prepared baking sheets until ready to use.

Bring a pot of salted water to a boil and have a bowl of ice water ready.

To make the fava puree, blanch the spinach in the boiling salted water for 45 seconds. Remove the spinach with a spider (or other handheld strainer) and quickly shock it in the ice water to stop the cooking. Drain the spinach and set aside.

Blanch the fava beans in the boiling water for 1 minute. Remove the fava beans with a spider and quickly shock them in the ice water to stop the cooking. Set aside.

Combine the spinach, favas, and milk in the jar of a blender and puree until smooth.

To make the ragu, bring a pot of salted water to a boil and have a bowl of ice water ready.

Blanch the fava beans in the boiling water for 1 minute. Remove the fava beans with a spider and quickly shock them in the ice water to stop the cooking. Set aside.

In a 12-inch sauté pan, melt the butter on medium heat. Add the leeks and salt, cover the pan, and sauté gently until translucent, 10 to 12 minutes. Add the Prosecco and bring to a boil. Decrease the heat to a simmer, cover, and continue cooking until the leeks are completely tender (or "melted") and the prosecco is completely evaporated, about 20 minutes more. Add the ½ cup water and let reduce again over medium-low heat until the liquid has completely evaporated. Fold in the whole fava beans and the fava bean puree and set aside.

To finish, bring a large pot of seasoned water to a boil (see page 18).

Drop the pasta in the boiling water.

Heat a 12-inch sauté pan over high heat. Add the butter and ⅔ cup of the pasta water and bring up to a simmer. At the same time, in a second small saucepan, heat up the ragu.

Drop the pasta in the boiling water. Once the pasta is cooked 80 percent through, until almost al dente, about 2 to 3 minutes, add it to the sauté pan with the butter and pasta water and cook until tender, about 4 minutes.

To serve, arrange the noodles flat on four warmed plates, mimicking streets. Add the fines herbes and lemon zest to the ragu; spoon the warm ragu onto the plate atop the pasta. Garnish with freshly grated Parmigiano-Reggiano.

Beet Casonsei with Poppy Seeds

More often than not, people assume that this pasta— filled with beets and ricotta, and then topped with poppy seeds—is one of our California-ized dishes. It's not. But it *is* a prime example of the incredible depth and ultra-regionalism of Italian cuisine, much of which is still undiscovered in American kitchens.

Casonsei is a very old stuffed pasta that hails from the northernmost reaches of Italy—all the way up past Venice, high in the Alps. The shape is very similar to that of tortelli (page 118), but with one final inward fold to create a fan-like formation.

Serves 4

Equipment
Blender + Baking sheets + Pasta machine + Rolling pin Straight wheel cutter (optional) + Fluted wheel cutter Baking pan + Piping bag (optional) + Spray bottle

Store-bought option
Any fresh, cheese-stuffed pasta

Beet Filling
25 baby beets, all a little smaller than golf balls (540 grams)
Pure olive oil, for roasting
Kosher salt
3 bay leaves
8 sprigs thyme
2 cups ricotta cheese (490 grams)
½ cup freshly grated Parmigiano-Reggiano cheese (50 grams)
Kosher salt
Freshly ground black pepper

Casonsei
1 recipe Rav Dough (page 6)

To Finish
½ cup unsalted butter (137 grams)
Kosher salt
Freshly grated Parmigiano-Reggiano cheese, for finishing
2 teaspoons poppy seeds
3 baby beets, peeled and shaved

Preheat the oven to 350°F.

To make the filling, in a small roasting pan drizzle the beets with a few tablespoons of olive oil. Add a generous pinch of salt, the bay leaves, and thyme. Toss to combine. Cover the pan tightly with aluminum foil and roast the beets until fork-tender, about 45 minutes. Peel the beets once they are cool enough to handle.

In the jar of a blender, puree the roasted beets with a small amount of water to achieve a smooth puree. You should have about 1 cup of beet puree.

In a large bowl, combine the roasted beet puree, the ricotta, and the Parmigiano-Reggiano. Season with salt and pepper. Refrigerate the filling until ready to use. The filling can be refrigerated up to 3 days. You should have about 4 cups of filling.

Dust 2 baking sheets with semolina flour and set aside.

To make the pasta, using a pasta machine, roll out the dough until the sheet is just translucent (see page 10). Cut a 2-foot section of the dough sheet and cover the rest of the dough with plastic wrap.

With a straight wheel cutter or a knife and a ruler, halve the pasta sheet lengthwise into two 3-inch-wide strips. Using a piping bag or a spoon, place 1¼-inch logs of the filling in the middle of each strip, leaving 1 inch between each log of filling. Fill both strips.

Gently fold the dough over the filling, bringing the two edges together to completely cover the filling. Use a spritz of water from a spray bottle to help seal it if necessary. Using your thumb, seal the top edges of the pasta, but just the very edge. To form the individual cansonsei, start on the right side of one strip and press down along the pasta with your index finger, sealing the pasta and pushing out all the air, creating a vacuum between the filling and the pasta dough. You want to create a tight capsule of dough around each log of filling. Move down the line, pressing down around one log at a time.

Using a fluted cutter, trim the edges, leaving ¼ inch of pasta bare between the filling and the cut.

With the serrated edge facing away from you, holding each corner with your thumb and index fingers, bump the filling upward and bring the corners close to each other, but not quite touching. The final shape will resemble a paper fan, with a slight arc on the top side and a slight pinch at the bottom. Place the casonsci on the prepared baking sheets, spaced apart, until ready to cook. Don't let the casonsei touch each other or they may stick together. Repeat until you run out of dough or filling. You should get about 50 pieces of casonsei.

To finish, bring a large pot of seasoned water to a boil (see page 18).

Drop the pasta in the boiling water.

Heat a 12-inch sauté pan over high heat. Add 1 cup of the pasta water to the pan. Add the butter and swirl (or whisk) vigorously to create an emulsion. Once the pasta is cooked 80 percent through, until almost al dente, about 2 to 3 minutes, add it to the pan and continue swirling to continue creating an emulsion. Season with salt. When the sauce coats the back of a spoon, remove from the heat.

To serve, divide the pasta and sauce between four plates. Grate Parmigiano-Reggiano on top and garnish with poppy seeds and shaved beets.

Lemon Farfalle with Spring Pea Ragu

"Spring pea ragu" is really just a fancy way of describing the melange of peas in this vegetarian dish. It's a vibrant, bright green sauce—really, a porridge—that combines all the different peas of the season, in all the ways that we use them. The sauce is a great base for spring flavors. At the restaurant, I might tell cooks to pick a bunch a wild greens from the roof and fold them in at the end. If you like spice, add red pepper flakes. If you've got preserved lemons lying around, toss a few pieces in.

I like to make the fresh farfalle with a lemon-parsley dough. It gives the dish a needed punch of acidity but without dulling the greens. Store-bought farfalle is a fine substitute, but using the flavored dough here is a great example of how flavor can be incorporated directly into the pasta to impart extra twists and turns.

Serves 4

Equipment

Baking sheets + Pasta machine + Rolling pin
Straight wheel cutter (optional) + Fluted wheel cutter
Spray bottle + Baking pan + Blender

Store-bought option

Dried farfalle

Farfalle

1 recipe Standard Egg Dough (page 16)
Grated zest of 6 lemons
⅓ cup minced parsley

Pea Stock

4 cups English peas, shells only, the shoots and
    peas reserved for the puree (239 grams)
1 yellow onion, thinly sliced (255 grams)
2 cloves garlic, smashed
2 small fennel bulbs, thinly sliced (248 grams)
Grated zest of 1 lemon
1 tablespoon whole black peppercorns
1 bay leaf
8 ounces Parmigiano-Reggiano cheese rinds (227 grams)

Pea Puree

2 cups tightly packed pea shoots (112 grams)
1½ cups shelled English peas (375 grams)
1 cup tightly packed spinach (67 grams)
½ cup Pea Stock (118 milliliters)

To Finish

2 cups Pea Stock (475 milliliters)
¾ cup English peas (100 grams)
½ cup snow peas, julienned
½ cup snap peas, stringed and cut diagonally into ¼-inch pieces
1 cup pea shoots
Grated zest of 2 lemons
Juice of 1 lemon
Extra-virgin olive oil
1 cup Pea Puree (210 grams)
Kosher salt
Freshly grated Pecorino Sardo, for finishing

To make the pasta, follow the instructions for Egg Dough (page 6), incorporating the lemon zest and parsley with the egg yolks.

Dust 2 baking sheets with semolina flour and set aside.

Using a pasta machine, roll out the dough until the sheet is just translucent (see page 10). Cut a 2-foot section of the dough sheet and cover the rest of the dough with plastic wrap.

Using a straight wheel cutter or a knife and a ruler, cut the pasta into 1½-inch-wide strips. With a fluted cutter, cut across the strips every 2 inches, creating rectangles.

Pick up a rectangle with both hands. Fold it in half, bringing the two flat, unfluted sides toward each other but not touching. Just as they are almost touching, create a seam in each quarter and move the edges away from each other. You are folding each half in half, like a letter, essentially forming a "W." Pinch the middle to hold its shape and form the familiar bowtie shape. Use a spritz of water from a spray bottle to help shape the farfalle if necessary. Place the finished farfalle on the prepared baking sheets, slightly apart. Don't let the farfalle touch or they might stick together. Repeat with the remaining dough. Let the farfalle sit, uncovered, to dry out slightly while you continue with the recipe.

To make the pea stock, in a 4-quart saucepan, combine all the ingredients and cover with cold water (about 8 cups). Bring to a simmer over medium heat and cook until, about 30 minutes. Remove from the heat and allow the stock to steep for 15 minutes. Strain through a fine-mesh strainer into a large bowl and set aside until ready to use. You should have about 6 cups.

Bring a pot of salted water to a boil. Have ready a bowl of ice water.

To make the pea puree, blanch the pea shoots in the boiling salted water for 40 seconds. Remove the shoots with a spider (or other handheld strainer) and quickly shock them in the ice water to stop the cooking. Repeat the blanching process with the peas and spinach.

Put the shoots, peas, and spinach in the jar of a blender. Puree until smooth, gradually adding the ½ cup stock as you blend. Refrigerate in an airtight container until ready to use. The puree can be stored for 2 to 3 days. You should have about 2 cups (475 milliliters).

To finish, bring a large pot of seasoned water to a boil (see page 18).

Drop the pasta in the boiling water.

In a 12-inch sauté pan, bring the 2 cups stock to a simmer. Add the English peas, snow peas, snap peas, and pea shoots. Once the pasta is cooked 80 percent through, until almost al dente, about 2 to 3 minutes, add it to the pan. Stir to incorporate over high heat. Add the lemon zest, lemon juice, and olive oil. Add the pea puree and stir to create a vibrant green sauce. Season with salt. Add the Pecorino Sardo to the pan and stir to incorporate. Remove from the heat.

To serve, divide the pasta and sauce between four plates. Garnish with more grated Pecorino Sardo.

Salt Cod and Potato Tortelli with Salsa Verde

Salsa verde can be used in *everything*. It's a versatile, eminently useful sauce that we've always made in the restaurant. In the summer, we use it in a salad with peaches, avocado, ricotta, and pistachio. And I particularly enjoy its piquancy with small fish like sardines or smelts that have been fried crisp and served alongside olives.

My love for salsa verde also means I'm quite particular about it. We make our version with chives, parsley, mint, tarragon, chervil, capers, garlic, and anchovy, but our little trick is the acidic ingredient: macerated shallots. We mince shallots and macerate them in white wine vinegar, but we don't fold them into the salsa until the very end so the fresh herbs don't steep in the acid for an extended period.

The other trick to keeping the salsa verde's punch is to leave the herbs' essential oils and chlorophyll intact. Don't mince or bruise the herbs. Chiffonade them all at once. When you work them with the mortar and pestle, it's important to work in small batches, not overcrowding the mortar. The pestle should be used gently; the more delicately you use it, the better.

Salt cod and potatoes are traditional partners in crime, but they're best in the spring, when the new potatoes arrive in the market. Freshly harvested new potatoes are completely different from the nearly-cured versions in the supermarket bin the rest of the year. New potatoes actually have flavor. They have moisture. They have snap. And it shouldn't surprise you that they go well in our pasta filling version of brandade—one that, in turn, pairs well with salsa verde.

Serves 4

Equipment
Ricer + Pasta machine + Rolling pin
Straight wheel cutter (optional) + Piping bag (optional)
Flutted wheel cutter + Baking sheets
Mortar and pestle or food processor + Spray bottle

Store-bought option
Any fresh, cheese-stuffed pasta

Filling
½ pound salt cod
2 cups whole milk (475 milliliters)
1 clove garlic, smashed, plus 4 cloves garlic, minced
1 sprig thyme
Small pinch of red pepper flakes
⅓ cup plus 2 tablespoons extra-virgin olive oil (104 milliliters)
1 yellow onion, minced (128 grams)
Kosher salt
2 small russet potatoes (or any non-waxy potato), peeled and cut into 1-inch cubes (530 grams)

Tortelli
1 recipe Rav Dough (page 6)

Salsa Verde
2 tablespoons minced shallots
Kosher salt
2 tablespoons red wine vinegar
1 bunch fresh chives
1 bunch fresh tarragon
¼ bunch fresh mint
½ bunch fresh chervil
½ bunch fresh Italian parsley
1¼ cups extra-virgin olive oil (296 milliliters)
½ clove garlic
1 tablespoon plus 2 teaspoons capers, drained
4 anchovy fillets (114 grams)
Grated zest of ½ lemon

To Finish
Fresh chopped chives, for garnish
Fresh tarragon leaves, for garnish
Fresh mint leaves, for garnish
Fresh chervil leaves, for garnish
Fresh Italian parsley leaves, for garnish

In a bowl or pot large enough to hold the salt cod comfortably, cover the cod completely with cold water. Soak the cod, changing the water several times, until it is pleasantly salted. This can take anywhere from overnight to a full 24 hours, or even a little more.

To make the filling, remove the salt cod from the water and add it to a small saucepan with the milk, smashed garlic, thyme, and red pepper flakes. Bring to a simmer over medium heat and cook until the salt cod is completely tender, about 25 minutes. Set aside to cool completely in the milk.

In a small pan over medium heat, heat ⅓ cup of the extra-virgin olive oil. Add the onion and a generous pinch of salt and sauté until completely tender and translucent, about 10 minutes. Add the minced garlic and cook for 2 more minutes.

Meanwhile, in a small saucepan, simmer the potatoes in salted water over medium heat until fork-tender, about 15 minutes. Drain the potatoes and pass through a ricer into a large bowl.

Strain the salt cod and discard the milk and smashed garlic. Add the salt cod mixture to the riced potatoes along with the remaining 2 tablespoons of extra-virgin olive oil. Season with salt. You should have about 3 cups filling.

Dust 2 baking sheets with semolina flour and set aside.

To make the pasta, using a pasta machine, roll out the dough until the sheet is just translucent (see page 10). Cut a 2-foot section of the dough sheet and cover the rest of the dough with plastic wrap.

With a straight wheel cutter or a knife and a ruler, halve the pasta sheet lengthwise into two 3-inch-wide strips. Using a piping bag, pipe 1¼-inch logs of fillings in the middle of each strip, leaving 1 inch between each log of filling. Fill both strips.

Gently fold the dough over the filling, bringing the two edges together to completely cover the filling. Use a spritz of water from a spray bottle to help seal it if necessary. Using your thumb, seal the top edge of the pasta, but just the very edge. To form the individual tortelli, start on the right side of one strip and press down along the pasta with your index finger, sealing the pasta and pushing out all the air, creating a vacuum between the filling and the pasta dough. You want to create a tight capsule of dough around each log of filling. Move down the line, pressing down around one log at a time.

Using a fluted cutter, trim the edges, leaving ¼ inch of pasta bare between the filling and the cut. Working quickly, place the tortelli on the prepared baking sheets, slightly apart, until ready to cook. Don't let the tortelli touch each other or they may stick together. Repeat until you run out of dough or filling. You should get about 50 tortelli.

To make the salsa verde, in a small mixing bowl, combine the shallots, ½ teaspoon of salt, and the vinegar. Allow the shallots to macerate for at least 1 hour. Pick all the herbs, discard the stems, and gently bundle them together. Chiffonade them all together, running the knife through only once to maintain the integrity and flavor of the herbs. Working in 4 small batches, combine the herbs with a pinch of salt in a mortar. Rub the pestle against the mortar in a circular motion, essentially smearing the herbs against the side of the mortar. You aren't trying to beat the herbs, but rather release their essential oils. Once the herbs have a paste-like consistency, remove them to a small container, adding just enough extra-virgin olive oil to cover the paste while you grind the remaining batches.

Add the garlic, capers, and anchovies to the mortar and pestle and grind them into a paste. Combine the caper mixture with the herb paste and add the lemon zest and enough extra-virgin olive oil to cover.

Drain the shallots, reserving the vinegar for another use (it's great for vinaigrettes). Make sure to keep the shallots separate from the garlic herb paste until you are ready to complete the dish; otherwise the acidity will discolor the herbs. You can make the salsa verde in a food processor, but the texture and flavor will not be the same as using a mortar and pestle.

To finish, bring a large pot of seasoned water to a boil (see page 18).

Drop the pasta in the boiling water. In a small mixing bowl, combine the drained shallots with the herb paste.

Heat a 12-inch sauté pan over medium heat and add ¼ cup of the pasta water. Once the pasta is cooked 90 percent through, until almost al dente, add it to the pan. Fold in the salsa verde and toss quickly to combine. You want to heat the salsa verde as little as possible.

To serve, divide the pasta and sauce between four plates. Combine the herbs and sprinkle over each portion for garnish.

Cappellacci dei Briganti with Quail and Green Coriander Gremolata

Tender bits of poultry, pasta, and carrots, plus chicken broth and a subtle hint of lemon? This dish is essentially chicken noodle soup, Flour + Water style.

Cappellacci dei briganti are different from the cappelletti on page 102. Both are named after hat-like shapes—hence the similarity in the names—but cappellacci dei briganti are not a stuffed pasta. Truth be told, they are probably the hardest shape to make in this book. Forming cappellacci dei briganti will probably take some trial and error before you can get the perfect slanted cone that defines the shape.

They're named after the hats worn by brigands in southern Italy during the political uprisings of the mid-nineteenth century that eventually unified Italy. The brigands were peasant workers fighting against the upper class; they ended up on the losing side of history, but their headgear was somehow immortalized as an edible wheat product. Small victories?

(Sidenote: Never discuss Italian politics in Italy. You will find yourself mired in a long complaint about pretty much everything.)

Serves 4

Equipment
Pasta machine + Baking sheets
2-inch ring mold or round cookie cutter
Piping tip (normally used with a piping bag)

Store-bought option
Any dried, short pasta shape

Cappellacci dei Briganti
1 recipe Standard Egg Dough (page 6)

Braised Quail
3 quail, deboned (5 ounces)
Kosher salt
Freshly ground black pepper
2 tablespoons pure olive oil
1 carrot, diced (68 grams)
1 yellow onion, diced (255 grams)
½ cup green garlic, cut into 1/8-inch ring (21 grams),
    or 2 tablespoons minced garlic
½ cup white wine (118 milliliters)
2 cups Quail Stock (recipe follows) or chicken stock (475 milliliters),
    page 169 or store-bought

Quail Stock
Bones from 3 whole quail
¼ cup white wine (59 milliliters)
4 cups water (946 milliliters)
½ yellow onion, diced (128 grams)
½ carrot, diced
2 sprigs fresh thyme
6 whole black peppercorns
1 bay leaf

Gremolata
2 tablespoons minced fresh cilantro
1 tablespoon minced fresh Italian parsley
Grated zest of 2 Meyer lemons

To Finish
½ carrot, thinly sliced into coins
¼ cup unsalted butter (57 grams)
Kosher salt
Freshly ground black pepper
Juice of ½ Meyer lemon
Freshly grated Parmigiano-Reggiano cheese, for finishing

To make the pasta, follow the instructions for the Egg Dough (page 6), adding the parsley to the egg yolks.

Using a pasta machine, roll out the dough to $\frac{1}{16}$ inch thick (see page 10). Cut a 2-foot section of the dough sheet and cover the rest of the dough with plastic wrap.

Dust 2 baking sheets with semolina flour and set aside.

Using a 2-inch round cutter, cut out rounds of dough. Put a piping tip on your left index finger. For each cappellacci, wrap a dough round around the piping tip, forming an open-tipped cone. Use your left thumb to seal the edges of the cone. Gently lift the bottom flap on the front of the cone (the side opposite the seam), like the brim of a hat. Carefully remove the cappellacci from the piping tip and place it erect on the prepared baking sheet. Repeat this process for each disk. You should have about 40 cappellacci dei briganti.

Preheat the oven to 350°F.

To prepare the quail, make a slit along the skin between the breast and the thigh and slice all the way to the bone, exposing all the meat to the thigh. Grab the thigh where it meets the backbone and snap the bone to expose the joint. Slice along the backbone to remove the leg. Remove the wings at the first joint (by the breast) and reserve for the stock. To remove the breast, slice along the side of the breastbone. Follow down the breast plate and ribs, making sure to keep your knife blade pointed toward the bones so you remove as much meat as possible. Rotate the quail 180 degrees and remove the other breast in the same way.

Separate the breasts and legs and liberally season both sides with salt and pepper. Reserve the bones for the stock.

To make the stock, place the quail bones on a small baking sheet and roast in the oven until deeply caramelized but not burned, about 45 minutes. Add the roasted bones to a stockpot. Deglaze the baking sheet with the white wine, scraping up the browned bits. Add the white wine to the stockpot. Cover the bones with water; they should be barely covered by the water. Bring to a boil over high heat and add the onion, carrot, thyme, black peppercorns, and bay leaf. Decrease the heat until the liquid is simmering. Simmer, uncovered for about 3 hours. Strain through a fine-mesh strainer into a large bowl and refrigerate until ready to use. The stock will keep refrigerated for 1 week or frozen for 3 months.

To make the braised quail, heat a 12-inch ovenproof sauté pan over medium-high heat. Heat the oil until it ripples but is not smoking. Sear the breasts, skin side down, until lightly browned, about 3 minutes. Remove the pan from the heat, flip the breasts, and just barely cook the other side. By the time you have flipped all the breasts you can begin removing them from the pan. We want the breasts to be rare at this point since they are going to be heated again. Store the breasts in the refrigerator until ready to use.

Return the pan to the heat and add the legs, skin-side down, to the pan and sear until browned, about 3 minutes. Flip the legs and sear until browned on the other side, about 3 minutes. Remove the quail legs from the pan.

Decrease the heat to medium-low and add the carrot, onion, and green garlic. Cook until the onions are translucent, about 5 minutes. Deglaze with the white wine and reduce by half. Add the stock and bring to a simmer. Add the reserved quail legs, tightly cover, and cook in the oven at 350°F until the legs are fully cooked but not falling of the bone, about 1 hour and 15 minutes.

Cool the braised legs for at least 1 hour at room temperature. If you pick the meat while it is hot it will shred too much. Using your hands, pick the meat off the bones and discard the bones. Reserve the meat and the braising liquid separately.

To make the gremolata, mix all ingredients in a small bowl. You should have about ¼ cup.

To finish, bring a large pot of seasoned water to a boil (see page 18).

Halve each breast lengthwise, making four pieces. Cut the meat again, crosswise, into ¼-inch pieces. In a 12-inch sauté pan heat 1½ cups of the braising liquid over medium-high heat until boiling and add the carrot. Drop the pasta in the boiling water. Once the pasta is cooked 80 percent through, until almost al dente, about 2 to 3 minutes, add it to the pan and toss to coat with the liquid, about 30 seconds. Add the butter and begin swirling and tossing to create an emulsion. Season with salt and freshly ground pepper. Fold in the quail and cook for 1 minute to completely heat through. Stir in the lemon juice.

To serve, divide the pasta and sauce between four plates. Sprinkle with gremolata and freshly grated Parmigiano-Reggiano.

Asparagus Caramelle with Brown Butter and Meyer Lemon

Like with any job, routine is inevitably part of chef's life. As much as cooking is fluid and the market fluctuates, there are some restaurant routines that I can depend on. Every year, usually on a random February morning, I get a text from Roscoe Zuckerman: "Two weeks."

Roscoe is a third-generation asparagus farmer. His property, Zuckerman's Farm, is located on an island in the Sacramento–San Joaquin River delta, north of San Francisco. The water is held at bay by levees that surround the farmland. Roscoe and his family have been growing the best asparagus in the country for years. When he sends the annual text, I know that asparagus is coming.

Artichokes and favas trickle into markets in the final, dying weeks of our California winter, but for all intents and purposes, the first "big" spring vegetable to hit is asparagus. Most asparagus in America—like the ones you see year-round in the supermarket—comes from Peru, but when the local asparagus comes in, San Francisco goes crazy. Chefs around town joke with each other about who's going to put it on the menu first, and before long, the A word is littering nearly every menu in town.

During peak asparagus season (March to May), we get four cases a week from Roscoe between Flour + Water and Central Kitchen. Generally speaking, we try to stay away from expected pairings at the restaurants, but brown butter and asparagus is one of those classic duos that is meant to be. This is a stuffed pasta with a filling that oozes out and mingles with the acidic brown butter. There's a reason why it's a classic flavor combination, and sometimes routines can be good.

Serves 4

Equipment
Blender + Pasta machine + Rolling pin + Piping bag (optional)
Baking sheets + Straight wheel cutter (optional)
Fluted wheel cutter + Spray bottle

Store-bought option
Any fresh, cheese-stuffed pasta

Filling
1 tablespoon pure olive oil
4 ounces spring onions (113 grams), trimmed and
    cut into ⅛ inch rings
¾ ounce green garlic), trimmed and cut into ⅛ inch rings
1 cup white wine (237 milliliters)
9 ounces asparagus, cut into 1-inch pieces
    (255 grams, about 18 to 20 spears, tips reserved)
1 teaspoon kosher salt
½ cup freshly grated Parmigiano-Reggiano cheese (50 grams)
Grated zest and juice of 1 Meyer lemon

Caramelle
1 recipe Rav Dough (page 6)

To Finish
½ cup unsalted butter (113 grams)
Juice of 1 Meyer lemon
1 teaspoon red pepper flakes
1½ ounces reserved asparagus tips
Kosher salt
Freshly grated Parmigiano-Reggiano cheese, for finishing

To make the filling, heat the olive oil in a 10-inch sauté pan over medium-low heat. Add the spring onions and cook until translucent, about 8 minutes. Add the green garlic and cook for 2 more minutes. Add the white wine. Increase the heat to high and cook until the pan is almost dry. Add the asparagus, salt, and enough water to barely cover the asparagus. Cook until all of the liquid is evaporated.

Transfer the solids to the jar of a blender and puree. Add cooking liquid as needed to make a smooth puree. Transfer the puree to a bowl and fold in the Parmigiano-Reggiano and lemon zest and juice. Season with salt. Refrigerate until completely cool. You should have about 2 cups of filling.

Dust 2 baking sheets with semolina flour and set aside.

To make the pasta, using a pasta machine, roll out the dough until the sheet is just translucent (see page 10). Cut a 2-foot section of the dough sheet and cover the rest of the dough with plastic wrap.

Using a straight wheel cutter or a knife and a ruler, cut the pasta sheets into rectangles 3 inches long by 2 inches wide. Using a piping bag or a spoon, place the filling onto the rectangles, forming a stripe of filling parallel to the long side about 2 inches long and ½ inch wide. Leave ½ inch of space on each side.

With the stripe of filling parallel to you, gently move the bottom edge of the rectangle to barely cover the filling. Roll the tube away from you, forming a wrap, like a cannelloni. Pinch the sides down, sealing the dough where the filling ends. You should have an enclosed tube of filled pasta with ½ inch of sealed dough on each end.

Now, to form the signature candy wrapper twists for the caramelle, use your thumbs to pinch both ends, right where the filling ends (not where the filling is, but where the two layers of dough touch). Give each side a 180-degree twist and pinch again, forming a candy-like wrapper.

Pinch and flatten the ends. Trim each end with a fluted cutter. Working quickly, place the caramelle on the prepared baked sheets, spaced apart, until ready to use. Don't let the caramelle touch each other or they may stick together. Repeat until you run out of dough or filling. You should get about 45 pieces of caramelle.

To finish, heat a 12-inch sauté pan over high heat. Add the butter and brown it until you achieve a deep brown color and nutty aroma, being careful not to burn the butter. Add the lemon juice, red pepper flakes, asparagus tips, and a pinch of salt.

Bring a large pot of seasoned water to a boil (see page 18).

Drop the pasta in the boiling water. Once the pasta is cooked 80 percent through, until almost al dente, 2 to 3 minutes, add it to the pan. Finish cooking the pasta in the brown butter for 2 minutes, stirring constantly. You are actually frying the pasta in the brown butter, which gives it a slightly chewy, pleasant bite.

To serve, divide the pasta and sauce between four plates. Finish with freshly grated Parmigiano-Reggiano.

Garganelli with Prosciutto and Peas

Especially if you swap out storebought penne for the garganelli, this recipe can come together in a matter of minutes. In the restaurant, I like to add in arugula at the end of cooking so that it wilts in the pan, and then garnish the finished plate with arugula flowers for an added dimension and a little spiciness. But really, it's the kind of dish that shouldn't be tweaked too much, because it's so straightforward. Just let it float. For that same reason, buy the best ingredients you can for this dish, because simplicity often exposes the quality of your ingredients, for better and worse.

Serves 4

Equipment
Pasta machine + Baking sheets + Straight wheel cutter (optional)
Garganelli comb or gnocchi board + Dowel + Blender

Store-bought option
Dried penne or ziti

Garganelli
1 recipe Standard Egg Dough (page 6)

Pea Puree
5 ounces English peas (130 grams)
½ cup pea shoots (55 grams)
1 tablespoon whole milk
About ¼ cup water
Kosher salt

To Finish
2 tablespoons pure olive oil
3 ounces diced prosciutto (85 grams)
1 tablespoon minced green garlic, or 1½ teaspoons minced garlic
1½ ounces spring onions, diced into ⅛-inch pieces
1½ cups chicken stock (355 milliliters; page 169 or store-bought)
5½ ounces shelled English peas (156 grams)
4 tablespoons butter, chilled (57 grams)
3 cups baby arugula (50 grams)
Juice of ½ lemon
Kosher salt
Freshly ground black pepper
Freshly grated Parmigiano-Reggiano, for finishing
20 arugula flowers, stemmed, for garnish (optional)

Dust 2 baking sheets with semolina flour and set aside.

To make the pasta, follow the instructions for the Egg Dough (page 6).

Using a pasta machine, roll out the dough to $\frac{1}{16}$ inch thick. Cut a 2-foot section of the pasta sheet and cover the rest of the dough with plastic wrap. With a sharp knife or straight wheel cutter, cut the pasta dough into 2-inch squares. Place one square on the garganelli comb, positioned diagonally, so two corners are at the top and bottom.

Place the dowel on the bottom of the comb. Using your fingers if necessary, curl up the corner so it curls up around the dowel to help get the tube started. In one smooth but firm motion, roll the dowel away from you from the bottom corner to the top corner, forming the tube-like garganelli.

Place the garganelli on the prepared baking sheet, uncovered, to air dry at room temperature until ready to cook. Repeat with the remaining dough.

Have ready a bowl of ice water.

To make the puree, cook the peas and shoots in boiling salted water until tender, about 2 minutes. Transfer to the ice bath and cool completely, about 2 minutes. Remove the peas from the water and store, refrigerated, until ready to use.

Put the peas and shoots in the jar of a blender. Add the milk and begin to puree. Add just enough water, roughly ¼ cup, to achieve a smooth puree. Season with salt. You should have about 2 cups (475 milliliters).

To finish, bring a large pot of seasoned water to a boil (see page 18).

Heat a 12-inch sauté pan over medium heat until hot but not smoking. Add the olive oil and heat until it gently ripples on the surface of the pan. Add the prosciutto. It should sizzle the moment it hits the pan. You want to brown it a bit without making it crispy, about 1 minute. This step will infuse the oil with the prosciutto flavor, which will permeate the entire dish.

Add the green garlic and spring onions and cook, stirring occasionally, until the vegetables are translucent, about 5 minutes. You want to keep stirring to prevent the garlic from burning.

Add the chicken stock, bring to a boil over medium heat, and allow the stock to begin to reduce. If using homemade garganelli, you want the stock to begin boiling in the pan before you drop the pasta in the water.

If using store-bought dried penne you should add the pasta to the water when you begin cooking the proscuitto.

Increase the heat under the sauté pan to medium-high and bring the liquid to a boil. Cook about 1 minute. Add the peas to warm through. Once the pasta is cooked 80 percent through, until almost al dente, about 2 to 3 minutes if using homemade gargamelli, add it to the pan. Cook in the pan for about 2 minutes. Add the butter and the pea puree and vigorously swirl the pan to create an emulsion. We want to keep reducing until the sauce coats the noodle.

Turn off the heat and gently fold in the arugula. Toss the pasta to incorporate the arugula. Add the lemon juice and season with salt and freshly ground black pepper.

To serve, divide the pasta and sauce between four plates. Garnish with grated Parmigiano-Reggiano, sprinkle with arugula flowers, if using, and serve immediately.

Hen Raviolini with Fennel Pollen and Olive Oil–Braised Radish

One rule of thumb for me when making pasta dishes is that the vegetables or other parts of the dish should not compete in texture with the pasta. The actual pasta should always be the most textured thing in the dish, crunchy garnishes aside; if the other components are too hard, the pasta seems overcooked by comparison. For example, radishes, which are often served raw with butter or sliced in salads, here are braised until they are very smooth and creamy but still hold their shape.

The radishes get paired with hen raviolini, probably the closest thing you'll see to a roast chicken at Flour + Water. Chicken thighs, seared and then roasted on the bone, are a guilty pleasure of mine; I found a way to get them on the menu somehow.

For this shape, we use a ravioli stamp that has a diameter of 1½ inches. If yours is a different size, you should adjust the space between the dollops of filling. If you don't have a ravioli stamp handy, feel free to get creative with something that can mimic it, like a circle cutter or small water glass; or spend the few dollars for one.

Serves 4

Equipment
Pasta machine + Rolling pin + Baking sheets
Straight wheel cutter (optional) + Spray bottle
Ravioli stamp + 1½-inch ring mold or cookie cutter

Store-bought option
Any fresh, meat-based ravioli

Filling
4 skin-on, bone-in chicken thighs (585 grams)
Kosher salt
Freshly ground black pepper
1 teaspoon fennel pollen (see Sources, page 250)
2 tablespoons pure olive oil
2 stalks celery, diced (136 grams)
½ fennel bulb, diced (60 grams)
½ yellow onion, diced (128 grams)
2 bay leaves
¾ ounce minced green garlic

Raviolini
1 recipe Rav Dough (page 6)

Braised Radish
1 8-ounce bunch radishes (230 grams)
2 teaspoons kosher salt
1¼ cups pure olive oil (295 milliliters)

To Finish
1 tablespoon pure olive oil
1 fennel bulb, diced (120 grams)
¼ cup prosecco (59 milliliters)
2 cups chicken stock (475 milliliters; page 169 or store-bought)
Radish tops
Juice of 1 Meyer lemon
Freshly grated Parmigiano-Reggiano cheese, for finishing
Fennel pollen, for finishing, optional (see Sources, page 250)

To make the filling, season both sides of the chicken thighs with salt, pepper, and fennel pollen, preferably 24 hours in advance but at least 2 hours before cooking. Cover and refrigerate.

Preheat the oven to 325°F.

Heat a Dutch oven over medium heat. Add the oil and lay the chicken in the pan, skin side down. You want to render as much fat as possible, so you may need to decrease the heat to medium-low to prevent burning. Cook to a deep golden brown, about 12 minutes. Turn the thighs over, increase the heat to medium-high. and cook the other side until golden brown, about 4 minutes. Remove the chicken thighs to a plate and set aside.

Pour off all but 2 tablespoons of the fat in the pan and add the celery, fennel, onion, and bay leaves. Season with a generous pinch of salt and sweat until the vegetables are tender but still crisp, about 4 minutes. Add the green garlic and cook 2 minutes more. Return the chicken thighs to the pan, nestling them in the onions. Place the pan in the oven and roast until the meat is fork-tender, about 45 minutes.

Once the chicken is cool enough to handle, remove it from the pot, reserving the vegetables. Pick the meat and skin from the bones and discard the bay leaves and chicken bones. Coarsely chop the chicken thighs and skin together. Add the chicken meat and skin and the reserved vegetables and juices to the bowl of a stand mixer fitted with a paddle attachment and mix until you achieve a coarse ball that is barely bound together. Refrigerate until completely cool.

To make the pasta, using a pasta machine, roll out the dough until the sheet is just translucent (see page 10). Cut a 2-foot section of the dough sheet and cover the rest of the dough with plastic wrap.

Dust 2 baking sheets with semolina flour and set aside.

Using a straight wheel cutter or a knife and a ruler, cut the pasta sheets lengthwise into 4-inch wide strips. Separate the strips into foot long segments, putting the rest under plastic wrap. Take the first strip and using a piping bag or a spoon, place dollops of the filling, about 2 teaspoons each, an inch

apart from each other and in a row about a half inch from the top of the sheet, leaving space on the bottom. When ready to fold, use a spritz of water from a spray bottle to help seal if necessary. Fold the sheet over gently but don't seal it, bringing the two edges together. Leave a ½ inch of "fold room" on the bottom crease, so the filling is in the middle of the folded strip. Using the blunt side of a 1½-inch ring mold, gently press around the mound of filling to firm up the shape. With your fingertips gently press around the filling to remove as much air as possible, creating a vacuum, working around the filling lumps. Then come back with a ravioli stamp and cut out the shapes. Place the raviolini on the prepared baking sheet until ready to cook, making sure they are evenly spaced.

Repeat until you run out of dough or filling. You should have about 50 pieces.

To braise the radishes, scrub, trim, and quarter the radishes, leaving about ¼ inch of the green stems on top. Reserve the radish leaves. Put the radishes in 1-quart saucepan, add the salt, and cover with olive oil. Over medium heat, bring to a simmer, or just until you see a few bubbles rising, then turn off the heat and allow to sit until cool, about 20 minutes.

To finish, bring a large pot of seasoned water to a boil (see page 18).

To finish, in a 12-inch sauté pan, heat the olive oil over medium-low heat. Add the fennel and cook gently until tender but not browned, about 20 minutes. Add the prosecco and reduce until the pan is almost dry. Then, add the chicken stock, increase the heat to high, and bring to a simmer.

Drop the pasta in the boiling water. Once the pasta is cooked 80 percent through, until almost al dente, about 2 to 3 minutes, add it to the pan until the sauce coats the back of a spoon, about 3 minutes. Add the radishes and radish tops just to warm through, then remove from the heat.

To serve, divide the pasta and sauce between four plates. Finish with 3 tablespoons of the reserved radish confit oil, freshly grated Parmigiano-Reggiano, and a few pinches of fennel pollen, if using.

Red Hawk Mezzalune with Morels and Watercress

The Mission District—and San Francisco as a whole—has a small-town feeling, especially within the restaurant industry. Over the years we have developed relationships not only with farmers and purveyors, but food artisans from all walks of life. A great example is the legion of local foragers that bring us waves of mushrooms from all over the Bay Area. For those foragers, it's a semi professional hobby, since most are paid in trade. For us, it's a way to get unique ingredients that reflect our Northern California setting.

Depending on the season, we have at least five foraging friends cycling through to bring mushrooms to the restaurant. Black trumpets, hedgehogs, and chanterelles all find their way through the back door, but for me, the springtime haul of porcini mushrooms and morels is the most prized.

Morels in particular lend themselves especially nicely to fat, umami, and richness. Here, they're paired with a funky cheese, a ragu of morels, and a garnish of peppery watercress.

If you can't find Red Hawk, any triple cream cheese or soft fresh cheese is fine, but the thing that really plays well with the morels is Red Hawk's distinct funk factor—and that comes with the cheese's washed rinds. Cowgirl Creamery is one of our favorite local cheesemakers, and its Red Hawk cheese is its triple cream, made with wild bacteria from Point Reyes in West Marin; in other words, Cowgirl Creamery could not make this cheese anywhere except for the Bay Area.

Serves 4

Equipment
Food processor + Pasta machine + Rolling pin
Piping bag (optional) + Baking sheets
2½-inch ring mold or cookie cutter + Spray bottle

Store-bought option
Any fresh, cheese-stuffed pasta

Red Hawk Filling
1 wheel of Red Hawk cheese (340 grams)
½ cup heavy cream (57 milliliters)

Mezzalune
1 recipe Rav Dough (page 6)

To Finish
6 ounces morel, chantarelle, or other wild mushrooms (170 grams)
½ cup unsalted butter (113 grams)
1¾ ounces finely diced spring onion (50 grams)
2 tablespoons finely minced green garlic,
    or 3 cloves regular garlic, minced
1 teaspoon kosher salt
1 tablespoon chopped fresh thyme
1 tablespoon chopped fresh Italian parsley
2 teaspoons sherry vinegar
Freshly grated Parmigiano-Reggiano, for finishing
Young watercress leaves, for garnish

To make the filling, chop the cheese into 5 or 6 large chunks and add to the work bowl of a food processor fitted with the steel blade. Turn on the motor and slowly drizzle in the cream until you achieve a thick, creamy puree. Transfer to an airtight container and refrigerate until ready to use. You should have about 1⅔ cups filling.

Using a pasta machine, roll out the dough until the sheet is just translucent (see page 10). Cut a 2-foot section of the dough sheet and cover the rest of the dough with plastic wrap.

Using a 2½-inch-diameter ring mold or round cookie cutter, cut out rounds of dough.

Dust 2 baking sheets with semolina flour and set aside.

Using a piping bag or a spoon, place a teaspoon of filling in the middle of the dough round, leaving ¼ inch of dough bare around the edge. Fold the circle in half to create a half-moon shape. Use a spritz of water from a spray bottle to help seal if necessary. Start the seal at the top of the half-moon (12 o'clock) and gently but firmly seal the dough and remove the air pocket by moving your fingers down the edges on both sides simultaneously, caressing the filling to create an airless, tight pillow.

Put the mezzalune on a flat surface and crimp the edges with a fork. Working quickly, place the mezzalune on the prepared baking sheets, slightly apart. Don't let the mezzalune touch each other or they may stick together. You should have about 45 to 50 pieces.

To finish, clean the mushrooms, then tear (or cut) them into ½-inch pieces. The smaller mushrooms may not need to be cut or torn. The goal is to get the mushrooms the same size so they cook evenly.

Bring a large pot of seasoned water to a boil (see page 18).

Heat a 12-inch sauté pan over high heat. Add 2 tablespoons of the butter and heat until sizzling. Add the mushrooms to the pan. Immediately add the green garlic and spring onions. Add 1 teaspoon kosher salt. The salt will help the mushrooms and onions to sweat without browning.

Continue to cook, stirring constantly, until the liquid has evaporated and the mushrooms begin to brown and caramelize, about 4 minutes. The more and more "vocal" the pan becomes the dryer the contents, which means that the moisture has evaporated and the ingredients are frying.

Drop the pasta in the boiling water.

Add 1 cup of pasta water and the remaining butter to the pan and swirl vigorously to create an emulsion. Once the pasta is cooked 80 percent through, until almost al dente, 2 to 3 minutes, add it to the pan. Add the thyme and the parsley and continue swirling to maintain the emulsion. When the sauce is properly coating the pasta, and the sauce coats the back of a spoon, 1 to 2 more minutes, remove from heat, add the sherry vinegar, and stir to combine.

To serve, divide the pasta and sauce between four plates. Finish with Parmigiano-Reggiano and garnish with the watercress leaves.

Whole Wheat Spaghetti with Anchovies, Spring Onions, and Green Garlic

Bay Area anchovy season begins in April and lasts through the summer. We are constantly using anchovies in the restaurant during the spring, even though they rarely actually appear on the printed menu. This is because anchovies, for us, often function as a seasoning agent (see the recipe for braised goat, page 190). When used properly, they don't impart a fishy flavor, but rather, a hard-to-place punch of salinity and umami.

As soon as we get a delivery of fresh anchovies, we eviscerate them and then quickly pack them in salt for twenty-four hours. A day later, they have completely transformed into something magical, with an entirely different flavor and texture. We pull them out of the salt, rinse them in water, and pack them in olive oil, where they can stay indefinitely in the fridge.

Stewed onions and anchovies is a classic Venetian dish, and a delicious one at that. It's made by cooking down onions and garlic in butter, tossing in the anchovy fillets, and then simmering with chicken stock until the pasta is ready.

At Flour + Water, we take that Old World base and give it a springtime Northern California twist, which in all honesty isn't that far off from the original. Onions and garlic are replaced by spring onions and green garlic, and to cap it off with a San Francisco Bay Area essential, a generous splash of Meyer lemon juice is added at the end to brighten up the sauce.

We usually use whole wheat bigoli in the restaurant, but any thick, long whole wheat noodle works well.

Serves 4

Equipment
Extruder (optional) + Blender

Store-bought option
Whole wheat spaghetti

Whole Wheat Spaghetti
Whole Wheat Spaghetti Dough, made like normal extruded dough, but converting 25 percent of the flour weight to whole wheat flour. See extruded pasta recipe, page 16

Stewed Onions
20 ounces julienned spring onions (580 grams)
3¼ ounces minced green garlic (92 grams)
14 anchovy fillets (398 grams)
½ cup pure olive oil (118 milliliters)
½ cup white wine (118 milliliters)
2 cups chicken stock (473 milliliters; page 169 or store-bought)

Green Garlic Puree
1 cup chopped green garlic tops or scallions, green parts only
1 cup spinach loosely packed
1 tablespoon whole milk
1 tablespoon unsalted butter, at room temperature

To Finish
Whole wheat spaghetti (340 grams)
Juice of 1½ Meyer lemons
¼ cup plus 1 tablespoon Green Garlic Puree (74 milliliters)
4 tablespoons extra-virgin olive oil (59 milliliters)
¼ cup minced fresh Italian parsley
Freshly grated Parmigiano-Reggiano cheese, for finishing

To prepare the onions, combine the spring onions, green garlic, anchovies, and olive oil in a Dutch oven and stew, uncovered, over medium-low heat, stirring every 5 minutes, for 45 minutes. Add the white wine and cook until completely evaporated. Add the chicken stock and bring to a simmer over medium-low heat. If you aren't finishing the dish immediately, refrigerate the onions until ready to use. You can make this up to 3 days in advance.

Have ready a bowl of ice water.

To make the green garlic puree, blanch the green garlic tops and spinach in boiling salted water until tender, about 1 minute. Drain and transfer to an ice water bath. Once cool, drain off the excess water. Add the green garlic, spinach, milk, and butter to the jar of a blender and puree until smooth.

To finish, bring a large pot of seasoned water to a boil (see page 18).

Drop the pasta in the boiling water.

In 12-inch sauté pan, bring the stewed onions to a simmer over medium heat and add the lemon juice. Once the pasta is cooked 80 percent through, 2 to 3 minutes, add it to the pan, stirring to combine. Continue cooking until you achieve a thick, sauce-like consistency, about 3 minutes. Fold in the green garlic puree and olive oil.

To serve, divide the pasta and sauce between four plates. Finish with parsley and freshly grated Parmigiano-Reggiano.

IT TAKES A VILLAGE

While chefs are held up as a face of the country's thriving food movement, it's no secret that a restaurant is a highly collaborative and orchestrated dance, timed to the second. We have dozens of hard-working staff members at Flour + Water, from waiters to sous chefs.

And you know what? In just about every restaurant, the cooks on the line probably directly affect individual dishes more than the chef. A chef has to help create, invent, and then implement systems of technique and production but it is the cooks that transform a great idea into an amazing actuality every single night. Many thankless, hard hours have been put into a restaurant's busy line. In addition, at Flour + Water, every cook shares the responsibility for the ideas that go into our menu. But that's just the tip of the iceberg. The prep cooks and dishwashers are the motor that runs the restaurant. In the dining room, the front of the house staff are the ones that interact with diners directly. Local artists' work adorns the walls.

Our one-woman-pasta-machine, Reyna, makes most of the stuffed pasta in the restaurant, but you don't read about her in the media. Both she and her husband, Alejandro, have been integral parts of the restaurant since it opened; today, Ale handles much of the butchery in the restaurant. They have truly become a part of the restaurant family, and of my family.

The village mentality goes even deeper. Designers, contractors and investors helped build the restaurant. We work closely with dozens of farmers, ranchers and fishermen. Every ingredient comes from a real person—and often many real persons.

The support of the local restaurant industry is paramount, and in San Francisco—the Mission District in particular—chefs find ourselves working together, learning together, and yes, drinking together. This is not a cheap or easy city in which to conduct business, but if I have a quick question about health codes or kitchen equipment, or need a place to hang 500 pounds of cured meat, there's always someone ready to help out. Early interactions like that changed my mentality that this shouldn't be a competitive or secretive industry; we're all in this together. Nowadays, we have an open door policy when comes to sharing our business plan, giving infrastructure advice, or cluing a chef friend in on a hidden wild mushroom location. It's a community in the truest sense of the word.

Whether it's the first person that turns the key to open the door at 7 a.m., the office admin that plugs all the numbers or the dishwasher that works two jobs, every single person contributes to the dance. And when one person goes out of sync, everyone goes out of sync. Dozens of people work together in order for that one simple, delicious plate of food to be served in a restaurant.

SOURCES

Most of the seasonal ingredients in this book can be found at specialty markets, local butcher shops, or local farmers' market; that's where we find our ingredients in the restaurant, after all. But if you can't find certain goods, there is always the internet.

When it comes to pasta-making equipment, a little more creativity is needed. Italian cooking shops are always a good place to start looking for specialty equipment, but even though pasta-making tools are increasingly common in American culinary stores, the best bet might still be Amazon.

Dried Goods
Baia Pasta: baiapasta.com
dried pasta

Far West Funghi: farwestfungi.com
Dried mushrooms, morels

Pacific Gourmet: pacgourmet.com
Balsamic vinegar, agrumato, specialty flours

Le Sanctuaire: le-sanctuaire.com
Rare herbs and spices

Pasta Shop (Bay Area only): rockridgemarkethall.com/pasta-shop
Fresh pasta, wholesale

Amazon: amazon.com
Specialty flours, salt cod, specialty spices

Meat and Cheese
Cowgirl Creamery: cowgirlcreamery.com
Red Hawk cheese, ricotta

Bellwether Farms: bellwetherfarms.com
Crescenza cheese

Fatted Calf: fattedcalf.com
Cured meats, butchery, sausages

4505 Meats: 4505meats.com
Cured meats, butchery, sausages

Black Pig Meat Company: blackpigmeatco.com
Cured meats

Olympic Provisions: olympicprovisions.com
Cured meats, mortadella, sausages

D'Artagnan: dartagnan.com
Duck parts, wild boar, mushrooms, truffles

Pastamaking Equipment
Emilio Miti (page 180): pastabiz.com, emiliomiti.com
Pasta machines, meat slicers, extruders

Fatto in America: artisanalpastatools.com
Garganelli combs, corzetti stamps, mattarello rolling pins

Williams-Sonoma: williams-sonoma.com
Pasta machines, wheel cutters, raviolo stamps

Amazon: amazon.com

Ebay: ebay.com

And if you're ever in Bologna…
Aguzzeria del Cavallo: aguzzeriadelcavallo.it
New and vintage pasta-making equipment, knives, corzetti stamps, and more.

Bruno e Franco la Salumeria: la-salumeria.it
Meats, cheeses, olives, fresh pasta, and many good stories.

Marcello Tori: bluone.com
Perhaps the best source we had for this book, Marcello and his wife Raffaella live in Bologna. They know every single thing about the traditions and history of Bolognese cuisine, and they have parlayed that knowledge into culinary tour business.

ACKNOWLEDGMENTS

Tom

There are a lot of people that have supported me along the path of my career. Although they may not even realize it, they all have contributed to this book in one way or another.

Noble and Dotty McNaughton, my father and mother, have taught me through example countless lessons in life. My father's undeniable drive, work ethic, and dedication to his family have made me aspire to be the best person I can be. My mother's limitless warmth, care, and love is the foundation of who I am. And it was her cooking that made me want to want to be a chef; after years of research, chocolate chicken is not a classic dish nor should it be repeated, as the rest of my family can attest.

My partners David Steele and David White have supported every decision I have ever made, including the bad ones! Through good times and bad we have only become closer. I consider them family and know that their continued support is what makes me such a confident chef and business owner.

There are so many amazing people that have come through my kitchens that have aspired me to be the best chef that I can be:

Mathew Sigler started day one at flour+water as a young line cook with a terrible bandana. He left years later as the Chef de Cuisine. He played a major roll in shaping what the restaurant is today.

Ryan Pollnow stepped into Mathew's role and has taken this restaurant group by storm. His unwavering dedication and drive have inspired me and every cook that has picked up a knife next to him.

The many names that deserve more than just a simple thank you and played an intricate roll in developing the pasta program at flour+water are: Freedom Rains, Jimmy Hall, Evan Allumbaugh, Alejandro Hernandez and Reyna Hermenegildo.

I was surprised, delighted and honored with how much faith Ten Speed Press had in this book. Really allowing us to do what we wanted with a guiding hand is one of the biggest reasons this book is so special. Jenny, thank you for all of you help and forgiveness on all the missed deadlines!

The Cookbook team, Paolo, Travis Rea, Eric Wolfinger and Elizabeth Subauste, THANK YOU. It is fascinating to watch people excel at what they do and it was nothing short of amazing watching this team come together. I had nothing but faith in Paolo and Eric who brought so much of themselves into this book. Travis Rea was a meticulous recipe tester and was a pain in my ass documenting and making me re- and re- and re- measure.

Elizabeth is my partner in this book and without her pushing me, organizing my life, and cleaning up all my messes (literally and figuratively) this book would not be here. Thank you, Elizabeth.

Paolo

Vorrei ringraziare dal profondo del cuore tutti Bolognesi che mi hanno sostenuto e incoraggiato a scrivere questo libro. Non finerò mai di ringraziarti Franco. Spero di avere raccontato e narrato bene le sue storie. A Rafa e Marcello, grazie mille per avermi tramandato la tradizione della cucina Bolognese. Ma sopratutto, un abbraccio speciale alle meravigliose sfogline del laboratorio Bruno e Franco: Maria Grazia Foschini, Mara Aldrovandi, Monica Baccolini, Maria Colosimo, Angela Moncada, Irene Mengoli, Paola Mazzetti e Adriana Parma.

And a huge thank you to Danielle Chock. Without your incredible generosity, we couldn't have done this. Thanks for bringing us behind the scenes.

Thanks to Eric Wolfinger for the beautiful photography, for the advice, for the inspiration, for the maxim that there's always room for another Aperol Spritz, and for the reminder that pigeons can fly.

Thank you to everyone who put so much love and time into this book. Thanks to Travis Rea, for tirelessly generating and testing the recipes; Liz Subauste, for all the wrangling and organization; Jenny Wapner for guiding us through this process so seamlessly, and everyone else at Ten Speed, including Aaron Wehner.

Special thanks to Mr. Harold McGee for taking the time to muse about the wonder that is pasta.

Sincere thanks to everyone in the community who has inspired me both directly and indirectly: Greg Lopez, Daniel Patterson, Brock Keeling, Anthony Myint, Kate Krader, Chris Ying, Cecilia Chiang, Gayle Pirie, Josh Harris, Scott Baird, Alice Waters, Shannon Waters, Anthony Mangieri, Jeremiah Tower, Mark Pastore, Dana Cowin, Amaryll Schwertner, Chris Cosentino, the Rebbes, David Prior, Giovanni Costabile, David Kinch, Mourad Lahlou, Andrew Knowlton, Jeannette Etheredge, Ben Leventhal, Lockhart Steele, and pretty much everyone else I've encountered in professional settings.

Thanks to all my family and friends for your endless love: Special thanks to Brigid, for putting up with all the late nights and early mornings of writing and also all the pasta eating.

Thanks to Kitty Cowles for all the advice and guidance. Thanks to Jake Godby and Sean Vahey of Humphry Slocombe. I wouldn't be here without your trust.

Many thanks to everyone at the *San Francisco Chronicle*, especially Michael and Miriam, for the endless support. Thanks to Kona for never biting me, and sincere thanks to the whole Flour + Water family, particularly David Steele and David White. I hope this turned out OK.

And most of all, thanks to Tom for bringing me along for the ride. It's been inspiring, educational and thoroughly enjoyable to explore your brilliant, crazy world. I hope you get your goat farm one day.

INDEX

All rights reserved.

Published in the United States by Ten Speed Press, an imprint of
the Crown Publishing Group, a division of Random House LLC,
New York, a Penguin Random House Company.

www.crownpublishing.com

www.tenspeed.com

Ten Speed Press and the Ten Speed Press colophon are registered
trademarks of Random House LLC.

Library of Congress Cataloging-in-Publication Data

CIP data on file with publisher

Hardcover ISBN: 978-1-60774-470-2

eBook ISBN: 978-1-60774-471-9

Printed in China

Design by Sarah Adelman

10 9 8 7 6 5 4 3 2 1

First Edition